Introductory Accounting

Introductory Accounting

Marvin Rauch

Larsen & Keller
www.larsen-keller.com

Introductory Accounting
Marvin Rauch
ISBN: 978-1-64172-619-1 (Hardback)

Larsen & Keller
Published by Larsen and Keller Education,
5 Penn Plaza,
19th Floor,
New York, NY 10001, USA

Cataloging-in-Publication Data

Introductory accounting / Marvin Rauch.
p. cm.
Includes bibliographical references and index.
ISBN 978-1-64172-619-1
1. Accounting. 2. Bookkeeping. 3. Financial statements. I. Rauch, Marvin.
HF5636 .I58 2022
657--dc23

For more information regarding Larsen and Keller Education and its products, please visit the publisher's website www.larsen-keller.com

Table of Contents

Preface

The measurement, processing and communication of non-financial and financial information about economic organizations takes place within accounting. It is used to measure the economic activities undertaken by an organization and provide this information to different users such as creditors, regulators and investors. Accounting is classified into various categories such as financial accounting, management accounting, tax accounting, cost accounting and external auditing. Financial accounting involves the preparation of financial statements and reporting information related to an organization's finance for external users. Management accounting is used to measure, analyze and report information for decision-making. This textbook provides comprehensive insights into the field of accounting. It provides significant information of this discipline to help develop a good understanding of this subject and related fields. This book, with its detailed analyses and data, will prove immensely beneficial to professionals and students involved in this area at various levels.

A foreword of all chapters of the book is provided below:

Chapter 1 - The process of recording financial transactions related to a business is known as accounting. Some of the key aspects which are dealt with in accounting are assets, liabilities, profit and expenses. The topics elaborated in this chapter will help in gaining a better perspective about these concepts of accounting.; **Chapter 2** - The branch of accounting which deals with the summary, analysis and reporting of financial transactions pertaining to a business is known as financial accounting. This chapter closely examines the key concepts of financial accounting such as trial balance, financial capital and capital expenditure to provide an extensive understanding of the subject.; **Chapter 3** - The set of procedures which are used to record and report measurements of the cost of producing goods and services in detail is known as cost accounting. Some of the different types of costs which are studied within this field are direct cost, indirect cost, fixed cost and variable cost. The topics elaborated in this chapter will help in gaining a better perspective about cost accounting and cost accounting systems.; **Chapter 4** - The process of systematically and independently examining the books, accounts and documents of an organization to determine the accuracy of the financial statements and non-financial disclosures is known as auditing. Some of the different types of audits are financial audit, cost audit and internal audit. This chapter has been carefully written to provide an easy understanding of these varied types of auditing.; **Chapter 5** - The reports which are prepared by the management of a company to show the financial performance and position at any given time are known as financial statements. Some of the major components of financial statements are income statement, balance sheet and cash flow statement. All these diverse components of financial statements have been carefully analyzed in this chapter.

At the end, I would like to thank all the people associated with this book devoting their precious time and providing their valuable contributions to this book. I would also like to express my gratitude to my fellow colleagues who encouraged me throughout the process.

Marvin Rauch

1

Understanding Accounting

The process of recording financial transactions related to a business is known as accounting. Some of the key aspects which are dealt with in accounting are assets, liabilities, profit and expenses. The topics elaborated in this chapter will help in gaining a better perspective about these concepts of accounting.

Accounting has rightly been termed as the language of the business. The basic function of a language is to serve as a means of communication Accounting also serves this function. It communicates the results of business operations to various parties who have some stake in the business viz., the proprietor, creditors, investors, Government and other agencies. Though accounting is generally associated with business but it is not only business which makes use of accounting. Persons like housewives, Government and other individuals also make use of a accounting. For example, a housewife has to keep a record of the money received and spent by her during a particular period. She can record her receipts of money on one page of her "household diary" while payments for different items such as milk, food, clothing, house, education etc. on some other page or pages of her diary in a chronological order. Such a record will help her in knowing about:

1. The sources from which she received cash and the purposes for which it was utilised.
2. Whether her receipts are more than her payments or vice-versa.
3. The balance of cash in hand or deficit, if any at the end of a period.

In case the housewife records her transactions regularly, she can collect valuable information about the nature of her receipts and payments. For example, she can find out the total amount spent by her during a period (say a year) on different items say milk, food, education, entertainment, etc. Similarly she can find the sources of her receipts such as salary of her husband, rent from property, cash gifts from her relatives, etc. Thus, at the end of a period (say a year) she can see for herself about her financial position i.e., what she owns and what she owes. This will help her in planning her future income and expenses (or making out a budget) to a great extent.

The need for accounting is all the more great for a person who is running a business. He must know: (i) What he owns? (ii) What he owes? (iii) Whether he has earn a profit or suffered a loss on account of running a business? (iv) What is his financial position i.e. whether he will be in a position to meet all his commitments in the near future or he is in the process of becoming a bankrupt.

The main purpose of accounting is to ascertain profit or loss during a specified period, to show financial condition of the business on a particular date and to have control over the firm's property. Such accounting records are required to be maintained to measure the income of the business and communicate the information so that it may be used by managers, owners and other interested parties. Accounting is a discipline which records, classifies, summarises and interprets financial information about the activities of a concern so that intelligent decisions can be made about the concern. The American Institute of Certified Public Accountants has defined the Financial Accounting as "the art of recording, classifying and summarising in as significant manner and in terms of money transactions and events which in part, at least of a financial character, and interpreting the results thereof". American Accounting Association defines accounting as "the process of identifying, measuring, and communicating economic information to permit informed judgements and decisions by users of the information.

From the above the following attributes of accounting emerge:

1. Recording: It is concerned with the recording of financial transactions in an orderly manner, soon after their occurrence In the proper books of accounts.

2. Classifying: It Is concerned with the systematic analysis of the recorded data so as to accumulate the transactions of similar type at one place. This function is performed by maintaining the ledger in which different accounts are opened to which related transactions are posted.

3. Summarising: It is concerned with the preparation and presentation of the classified data in a manner useful to the users. This function involves the preparation of financial statements such as Income Statement, Balance Sheet, Statement of Changes in Financial Position, Statement of Cash Flow, and Statement of Value Added.

4. Interpreting: Nowadays, the aforesaid three functions are performed by electronic data processing devices and the accountant has to concentrate mainly on the interpretation aspects of accounting. The accountants should interpret the statements in a manner useful to action. The accountant should explain not only what has happened but also (a) why it happened, and (b) what is likely to happen under specified conditions.

Distinction between Book-keeping and Accounting

Book-keeping is a part of accounting and is concerned with the recording of transactions which is often routine and clerical in nature, whereas accounting performs other functions as well, viz., measurement and communication, besides recording. An accountant is required to have a much higher level of knowledge, conceptual understanding and analytical skill than is required of the book-keeper.

An accountant designs the accounting system, supervises and checks the work of the book-keeper, prepares the reports based on the recorded data and interprets the reports. Nowadays, he is required to take part in matters of management, control and planning of economic resources.

Distinction between Accounting and Accountancy

Although in practice Accountancy and Accounting are used interchangeably yet there is a thin line of demarcation between them. The word Accountancy is used for the profession of accountants - who do the work of accounting and are knowledgeable persons. Accounting is concerned with recording all business transactions systematically and then arranging in the form of various accounts and financial statements. And it is a distinct discipline like economics, physics, astronomy etc. The word accounting tries to explain the nature of the work of the accountants (professionals) and the word Accountancy refers to the profession these people adopt.

Nature of Accounting

The various definitions and explanations of accounting has been propounded by different accounting experts from time to time and the following aspects comprise the nature of accounting:

Accounting as a Service Activity

Accounting is a service activity. Its function is to provide quantitative information, primarily financial in nature, about economic entities that is intended to be useful in making economic decisions, in making reasoned choices among alternative courses of action. It means that accounting collects financial information for the various users for taking decisions and tackling business issues. Accounting in itself cannot create wealth though, if it produces information which is useful to others, it may assist in wealth creation and maintenance.

Accounting as a Profession

Accounting is very much a profession. A profession is a career that involve the acquiring of a specialised formal education before rendering any service. Accounting is a systematized body of knowledge developed with the development of trade and business over the past century. The accounting education is being imparted to the examinees by national and international recognised the bodies of India (ICAI), New Delhi in India and American Institute of Certified Public Accountants (AICPA) in USA etc. The candidate must pass a vigorous examination in Accounting Theory, Accounting Practice, Auditing and Business Law. The members of the professional bodies usually have their own associations or organisations, where in they are required to be enrolled compulsorily as Associate member of the Institute of Chartered Accountants (A.C.A.) and fellow of the Institute of Chartered Accountants (F.C.A.). In a way, accountancy as a profession has attained the stature comparable.

Accounting as a Social Force

In early days, accounting was only to serve the interest of the owners. Under the changing business environment the discipline of accounting and the accountant both have to watch and protect the interests of other people who are directly or indirectly linked with the operation of modern business. The society is composed of people as customer, shareholders, creditors and investors. The accounting information/data is to be used to solve the problems of the public at large such as determination and controlling of prices. Therefore, safeguarding of public interest can better be facilitated with the help of proper, adequate and reliable accounting information and as a result of it the society at large is benefited.

Accounting as a Language

Accounting is rightly referred the "language of business". It is one means of reporting and communicating information about a business. As one has to learn a new language to converse and communicate, so also accounting is to be learned and practised to communicate business events.

A language and accounting have common features as regards rules and symbols. Both are based and propounded on fundamental rules and symbols. In language these are known as grammatical rules and in accounting, these are termed as accounting rules. The expression, exhibition and presentation of accounting data such as a numerals and words and debits and credit are accepted as symbols which are unique to the discipline of accounting.

Accounting as Science or Art

Science is a systematised body of knowledge. It establishes a relationship of cause and effect in the various related phenomenon. It is also based on some fundamental principles. Accounting has its own principles e.g. the double entry system, which explains that every transaction has two fold aspect i.e. debit and credit. It also lays down rules of journalising. So we can say that accounting is a science.

Art requires a perfect knowledge, interest and experience to do a work efficiently. Art also teaches us how to do a work in the best possible way by making the best use of the available resources. Accounting is an art as it also requires knowledge, interest and experience to maintain the books of accounts in a systematic manner. Everybody cannot become a good accountant. It can be concluded from the above discussion that accounting is an art as well as a science.

Accounting as an Information System

Accounting discipline will be the most useful one in the acquisition of all the business knowledge in the near future. You will realise that people will be constantly exposed to accounting information in their everyday life. Accounting information serves both profit-seeking business and non-profit organisations. The accounting system of a profit-seeking organisation is an information system designed to provide relevant financial information on the resources of a business and the effect of their use. Information is relevant and valuable if the decision makers can use it to evaluate the financial consequences of various alternatives.

Accounting generally does not generate the basic information (raw financial data), rather the raw financial data result from the day to day transactions of the business. As an information system, accounting links an information source or transmitter (generally the accountant), a channel of communication (generally the financial statements) and a set of receivers (external users).

Objectives of Accounting

The following are the main objectives of accounting:

1. To keep systematic records: Accounting is done to keep a systematic record of financial transactions. In the absence of accounting there would have been terrific burden on human memory which in most cases would have been impossible to bear.
2. To protect business properties: Accounting provides protection to business properties from unjustified and unwarranted use. This is possible on account of accounting supplying the following information to the manager or the proprietor:
    - The amount of the proprietor's funds invested in the business.
    - How much the business have to pay to others?
    - How much the business has to recover from others?

- How much the business has in the form of (a) fixed assets, (b) cash in hand, (c) cash at bank, (d) stock of raw materials, work-in-progress and finished goods?

  Information about the above matters helps the proprietor in assuring that the funds of the business are not necessarily kept idle or underutilised.

3. To ascertain the operational profit or loss: Accounting helps in ascertaining the net profit earned or loss suffered on account of carrying the business. This is done by keeping a proper record of revenues and expense of a particular period. The Profit and Loss Account is prepared at the end of a period and if the amount of revenue for the period is more than the expenditure incurred in earning that revenue, there is said to be a profit. In case the expenditure exceeds the revenue, there is said to be a loss.

   Profit and Loss Account will help the management, investors, creditors, etc. in knowing whether the business has proved to be remunerative or not. In case it has not proved to be remunerative or profitable, the cause of such a state of affairs will be investigated and necessary remedial steps will be taken.

4. To ascertain the financial position of the business: The Profit and Loss Account gives the amount of profit or loss made by the business during a particular period. However, it is not enough. The businessman must know about his financial position i.e. where he stands?, what he owes and what he owns? This objective is served by the Balance Sheet or Position Statement. The Balance Sheet is a statement of assets and liabilities of the business on a particular date. It serves as barometer for ascertaining the financial health of the business.

5. To facilitate rational decision making: Accounting these days has taken upon itself the task of collection, analysis and reporting of information at the required points of time to the required levels of authority in order to facilitate rational decision-making. The American Accounting Association has also stressed this point while defining the term accounting when it says that accounting is the process of identifying, measuring and communicating economic information to permit informed judgements and decisions by users of the information. Of course, this is by no means an easy task. However, the accounting bodies all over the world and particularly the International Accounting Standards Committee, have been trying to grapple with this problem and have achieved success in laying down some basic postulates on the basis of which the accounting statements have to be prepared.

6. Information System: Accounting functions as an information system for collecting and communicating economic information about the business enterprise. This information helps the management in taking appropriate decisions. This function, as stated, is gaining tremendous importance these days.

Users of Accounting Information

The basic objective of accounting is to provide information which is useful for persons inside the organisation and for persons or groups outside the organisation. Accounting is the discipline that provides information on which external and internal users of the information may base decisions that result in the allocation of economic resources in society.

External users of Accounting Information

External users are those groups or persons who are outside the organisation for whom accounting function is performed. Following can be the various external users of accounting information:

1. Investors: Those who are interested in investing money in an organisation are interested in knowing the financial health of the organisation of know how safe the investment already made is and how safe their proposed investment will be. To know the financial health, they need accounting information which will help them in evaluating the past performance and future prospects of the organisation. Thus, investors for their investment decisions are dependent upon accounting information included in the financial statements. They can know the profitability and the financial position of the organisation in which they are interested to make that investment by making a study of the accounting information given in the financial statements of the organisation.

2. Creditors: Creditors (i.e. supplier of goods and services on credit, bankers and other lenders of money) want to know the financial position of a concern before giving loans or granting credit. They want to be sure that the concern will not experience difficulty in making their payment in time i.e. liquid position of the concern is satisfactory. To know the liquid position, they need accounting information relating to current assets, quick assets and current liabilities which is available in the financial statements.

3. Members of Non-profit Organisations: Members of non-profit organisations such as schools, colleges, hospitals, clubs, charitable institutions etc. need accounting information to know how their contributed funds are being utilised and to ascertain if the organisation deserves continued support or support should be withdrawn keeping in view the bad performance depicted by the accounting information and diverted to another organisation. In knowing the performance of such organisations, criterion will not be the profit made but the main criterion will be the service provided to the society.

4. Government: Central and State Governments are interested in the accounting information because they want to know earnings or sales for a particular period for purposes of taxation. Income tax returns are examples of financial reports which are prepared with information taken directly from accounting records. Governments also needs accounting information for compiling statistics concerning business which, in turn helps in compiling national accounts.

5. Consumers: Consumers need accounting information for establishing good accounting control so that cost of production may be reduced with the resultant reduction of the prices of goods they buy. Sometimes, prices for some goods are fixed by the Government, so it needs accounting information to fix reasonable prices so that consumers and manufacturers are not exploited. Prices are fixed keeping in view fair return to manufacturers on their investments shown in the accounting records.

6. Research Scholars: Accounting information, being a mirror of the financial performance of a business organisation, is of immense value to the research scholars who wants to make a study to the financial operations of a particular firm. To make a study into the financial operations of a particular firm, the research scholar needs detailed accounting information relating to purchases, sales, expenses, cost of materials used, current assets, current

liabilities, fixed assets, long term liabilities and shareholders' funds which is available in the accounting records maintained by the firm.

Internal users of Accounting Information

Internal users of accounting information are those persons or groups which are within the organisation. Following are such internal users:

1. Owners: The owners provide funds for the operations of a business and they want to know whether their funds are being properly used or not. They need accounting information to know the profitability and the financial position of the concern in which they have invested their funds. The financial statements prepared from time to time from accounting records depicts them the profitability and the financial position.

2. Management: Management is the art of getting work done through others, the management should ensure that the subordinates are doing work properly. Accounting information is an aid in this respect because it helps a manager in appraising the performance of the subordinates. Actual performance of the employees can be compared with the budgeted performance they were expected to achieve and remedial action can be taken if the actual performance is not upto the mark. Thus, accounting information provides "the eyes and ears to management".

   The most important functions of management are planning and controlling. Preparation of various budgets, such as sales budget, production budget, cash budget, capital expenditure budget etc., is an important part of planning function and the starting point for the preparation of the budgets is the accounting information for the previous year. Controlling is the function of seeing that programmes laid down in various budgets are being actually achieved i.e. actual performance ascertained from accounting is compared with the budgeted performance, enabling the manager to exercise controlling case of weak performance. Accounting information is also helpful to the management in fixing reasonable selling prices. In a competitive economy, a price should be based on cost plus a reasonable rate of return. If a firm quotes a price which exceeds cost plus a reasonable rate of return, it probably will not get the order. On the other hand, if the firm quotes a price which is less than its cost, it will be given the order but will incur a loss on account of price being lower than the cost. So, selling prices should always be fixed on the basis of accounting data to get the reasonable margin of profit on sales.

3. Employees: Employees are interested in the financial position of a concern they serve particularly when payment of bonus depends upon the size of the profits earned. They seek accounting information to know that the bonus being paid to them is correct.

Branches of Accounting

To meet the ever increasing demands made on accounting by different interested parties such as owners, management, creditors, taxation authorities etc., the various branches have come into existence. There are as follows:

1. Financial accounting: The object of financial accounting is to ascertain the results (profit or loss) of business operations during the particular period and to state the financial position (balance sheet) as on a date at the end of the period.

2. Cost accounting: The object of cost accounting is to find out the cost of goods produced or services rendered by a business. It also helps the business in controlling the costs by indicating avoidable losses and wastes.

3. Management accounting: The object of management accounting is to supply relevant information at appropriate time to the management to enable it to take decisions and effect control.

Financial accounting is the oldest and other branches have developed from it. The objects of financial accounting, as stated above, can be achieved only by recording the financial transactions in a systematic manner according to a set of principles. The art of recording financial transactions and events in a systematic manner in the books of account is known as book-keeping. However, mere record of transactions is not enough. The recorded information has to be classified, analysed and presented in a manner in which business results and financial position can be ascertained.

Role of Accounting

Accounting plays an important and useful role by developing the information for providing answers to many questions faced by the users of accounting information:

- How good or bad is the financial condition of the business?
- Has the business activity resulted in a profit or loss?
- How well the different departments of the business have performed in the past?
- Which activities or products have been profitable?
- Out of the existing products which should be discontinued and the production of which commodities should be increased?
- Whether to buy a component from the market or to manufacture the same?
- Whether the cost of production is reasonable or excessive?
- What has been the impact of existing policies on the profitability of the business?
- What are the likely results of new policy decisions on future earning capacity of the business?
- In the light of past performance of the business how should it plan for future to ensure desired results?

Above mentioned are few examples of the types of questions faced by the users of accounting information. These can be satisfactorily answered with the help of suitable and necessary information provided by accounting. Besides, accounting is also useful in the following respects:

- Increased volume of business results in large number of transactions and no businessman can remember everything. Accounting records obviate the necessity of remembering various transactions.

- Accounting records, prepared on the basis of uniform practices, will enable a business to compare results of one period with another period.
- Taxation authorities (both income tax and sales tax) are likely to believe the facts contained in the set of accounting books if maintained according to generally accepted accounting principles.
- Accounting records, backed up by proper and authenticated vouchers, are good evidence in a court of law.
- If a business is to be sold as a going concern, then the values of different assets as shown by the balance sheet helps in bargaining proper price for the business.

Limitations of Financial Accounting

Following are the limitations:

Financial Accounting Permits Alternative Treatments

No doubt accounting is based on concepts and it follows "generally accepted accounting principles", but there exist more than one principle for the treatment of any one item. This permits alternative treatments within the framework of generally accepted accounting principles. For example, the closing stock of a business may be valued by any one of the following methods: FIFO (First-in-first-out); LIFO (Last-in-first-out); Average price, Standard price etc., Application of different methods will give different results but the methods are generally accepted. So, the results are not comparable.

Financial Accounting is Influenced by Personal Judgements

Inspite of the fact that convention of objectivity is respected in accounting but to record certain events estimates have to be made which requires personal judgement. It is very difficult to expect accuracy in future estimates and objectivity suffers. For example, in order to determine the amount of depreciation to be charged every year for the use of fixed asset it is required to estimate (a) future life of the asset, and (b) scrap value of the asset. Thus in accounting we do not determine but measure the income. In other words, the income disclosed by accounting is not authoritative but approximation.

Financial Accounting Ignores Important Non-monetary Information

Financial accounting takes into consideration only those transactions and events which can be described in money. The transactions and events, however important, if non-monetary in nature are ignored i.e., not recorded. For example, extent of competition faced by the business, technical innovations possessed by the business, loyalty and efficiency of the employees etc. are the important matters in which management of the business is highly interested but accounting is not tailored to take note of such matters. Thus any user of financial information is, naturally, deprived of vital information which is of non-monetary character.

Financial Accounting does not Provide Timely Information

Financial accounting is designed to supply information in the form of statements (Balance Sheet and Profit and Loss Account) for a period, normally, one year. So the information is, at best, of historical interest and only postmortem analysis of the past can be conducted. The business requires timely information at frequent intervals to enable the management to plan and take corrective action. For example, if a business has budgeted that during the current year sales should be Rs. 12,00,000 then it requires information – whether the sales in the first month of the year amounted to Rs. 1,00,000 or less or more? Traditionally, financial accounting is not supposed to supply information at shorter intervals than one year.

Financial Accounting does not Provide Detailed Analysis

The information supplied by the financial accounting is in reality aggregate of the financial transactions during the course of the year. Of course, it enables to study the overall results of the business activity during the accounting period. For proper running of the business the information is required regarding the cost, revenue and profit of each product but financial accounting does not provide such detailed information product-wise. For example, if a business has earned a total profit of, say, Rs. 5,00,000 during the accounting year and it sells three products namely petrol, diesel and mobile oil and wants to know profit earned by each product. Financial accounting is not likely to help him.

Financial Accounting does not Disclose the Present Value of the Business

In financial accounting the position of the business as on a particular date is shown by a statement known as balance sheet. In balance sheet the assets are shown on the basis of going concern concept. Thus it is presumed that business has relatively longer life and will continue to exist indefinitely, hence the asset values are going concern values. The realised value of each asset if sold today can't be known by studying the balance sheet.

Systems of Accounting

The following are the main systems of recording business transactions:

- Cash System: Under this system, actual cash receipts and actual cash payments are recorded. Credit transactions are not recorded at all until the cash in actually received or paid. The Receipts and Payments Account prepared in case of non-trading concerns such as a charitable institution, a club, a school, a college, etc. and professional men like a lawyer, a doctor, a chartered accountant etc. can be cited as the best example of cash system. This system does not make a complete record of financial transactions of a trading period as it does not record outstanding transactions like outstanding expenses and outstanding incomes. The system being based on a record of actual cash receipts and actual cash payments will not be able to disclose correct profit or loss for a particular period and will not exhibit true financial position of the business on a particular day.

- Mercantile (Accrual) system: Under this system all transactions relating to a period are recorded in the books of account i.e., in addition to actual receipts and payments of cash income receivable and expenses payable are also recorded. This system gives a complete picture of the financial transactions of the business as it makes a record of all transactions relating to a period. The system being based on a complete record of the financial transactions discloses correct profit or loss for a particular period and also exhibits true financial position of the business on a particular day.

Assets

An asset is a resource owned or controlled by an individual, corporation, or government with the expectation that it will generate future cash flows. Common types of assets include: current, non-current, physical, intangible, operating, and non-operating. Correctly identifying and classifying the types of assets is critical to the survival of a company, specifically its solvency and associated risks.

The International Financial Reporting Standards (IFRS) Framework defines an asset as follows: "An asset is a resource controlled by the enterprise as a result of past events and from which future economic benefits are expected to flow to the enterprise."

Examples of assets include:

- Cash and cash equivalents
- Inventory
- Investments
- PPE (Property, Plant, and Equipment)
- Land
- Buildings
- Vehicles
- Furniture
- Patents
- Stock
- Equipment

Properties of an Asset

There are three key properties of an asset:

- Ownership: Assets represent ownership that can be eventually turned into cash and cash equivalents.
- Economic Value: Assets have economic value and can be exchanged or sold.
- Resource: Assets are resources that can be used to generate future economic benefits.

Classification of Assets

Assets are generally classified in three ways:

- Convertibility: Classifying assets based on how easy it is to convert them into cash.

- Physical Existence: Classifying assets based on their physical existence.
- Usage: Classifying assets based on their business operation usage.

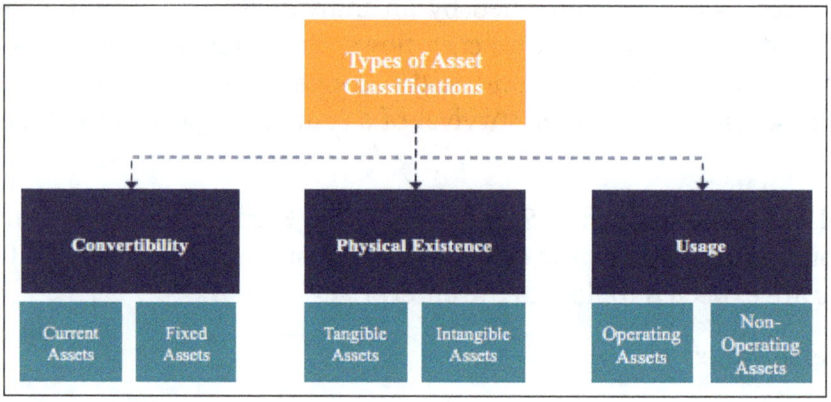

Classification of Assets: Convertibility

If assets are classified based on their convertibility into cash, assets are classified as either current assets or fixed assets:

Current Assets

Current assets are assets that can be easily converted into cash and cash equivalents (typically within a year). Current assets are also termed liquid assets and examples of such are:

- Cash
- Cash equivalents
- Short-term deposits
- Stock
- Marketable securities
- Office supplies

Fixed or Non-Current Assets

Non-current assets are assets that cannot be easily and readily converted into cash and cash equivalents. Non-current assets are also termed fixed assets, long-term assets, or hard assets. Examples of non-current or fixed assets include:

- Land
- Building
- Machinery
- Equipment

- Patents
- Trademarks

Classification of Assets: Physical Existence

If assets are classified based on their physical existence, assets are classified as either tangible assets or intangible assets:

Tangible Assets

Tangible assets are assets that have a physical existence (we can touch, feel, and see). Examples of tangible assets include:

- Land
- Building
- Machinery
- Equipment
- Cash
- Office supplies
- Stock
- Marketable securities

Intangible Assets

Intangible assets are assets that do not have a physical existence. Examples of intangible assets include:

- Goodwill
- Patents
- Brand
- Copyrights
- Trademarks
- Trade secrets
- Permits
- Corporate intellectual property

Classification of Assets: Usage

If assets are classified based on their operational usage, assets are classified as either operating assets or non-operating assets.

Operating Assets

Operating assets are assets that are required in the daily operation of a business. In other words, operating assets are used to generate revenue. Examples of operating assets include:

- Cash
- Stock
- Building
- Machinery
- Equipment
- Patents
- Copyrights
- Goodwill

Non-operating Assets

Non-operating assets are assets that are not required for daily business operations but can still generate revenue. Examples of non-operating assets include:

- Short-term investments
- Marketable securities
- Vacant land
- Interest income from a fixed deposit

Importance of Asset Classification

Classifying assets is important to a business. For example, understanding which assets are current assets and which are fixed assets is important in understanding the net working capital of a company. In the scenario of a company in a high-risk industry, understanding which assets are tangible and intangible will help it determine its solvency and risk. Determining which assets are operating assets and which assets are non-operating assets is important to understanding the contribution of revenue from each asset. Therefore, knowing how to classify assets is integral to business success.

Liabilities

A liability, in general, is an obligation to, or something that you owe somebody else. Liabilities are defined as a company's legal financial debts or obligations that arise during the course of business operations. Liabilities are settled over time through the transfer of economic benefits including money, goods, or services. Recorded on the right side of the balance sheet, liabilities include loans, accounts payable, mortgages, deferred revenues, and accrued expenses.

In general, a liability is an obligation between one party and another not yet completed or paid for. In the world of accounting, a financial liability is also an obligation but is more defined by previous business transactions, events, sales, exchange of assets or services, or anything that would provide economic benefit at a later date. Liabilities are usually considered short term (expected to be concluded in 12 months or less) or long term (12 months or greater).

Liabilities are also known as current or non-current depending on the context. They can include a future service owed to others; short- or long-term borrowing from banks, individuals, or other entities; or a previous transaction that has created an unsettled obligation. The most common liabilities are usually the largest like accounts payable and bonds payable. Most companies will have these two line items on their balance sheet, as they are part of ongoing current and long-term operations.

Liabilities are a vital aspect of a company because they are used to finance operations and pay for large expansions. They can also make transactions between businesses more efficient. For example, in most cases, if a wine supplier sells a case of wine to a restaurant, it does not demand payment when it delivers the goods. Rather, it invoices the restaurant for the purchase to streamline the dropoff and make paying easier for the restaurant.

The outstanding money that the restaurant owes to its wine supplier is considered a liability. In contrast, the wine supplier considers the money it is owed to be an asset.

Other Definitions of Liability

Generally, liability refers to the state of being responsible for something, and this term can refer to any money or service owed to another party. Tax liability, for example, can refer to the property taxes that a homeowner owes to the municipal government or the income tax he owes to the federal government.

Liability may also refer to the legal liability of a business or individual. For example, many businesses take out liability insurance in case a customer or employee sues them for negligence.

Current versus Long-term Liabilities

Businesses sort their liabilities into two categories: current and long-term. Current liabilities are debts payable within one year, while long-term liabilities are debts payable over a longer period. For example, if a business takes out a mortgage payable over a 15-year period, that is a long-term liability. However, the mortgage payments that are due during the current year are considered the current portion of long-term debt and are recorded in the short-term liabilities section of the balance sheet.

Ideally, analysts want to see that a company can pay current liabilities, which are due within a year, with cash. Some examples of short-term liabilities include payroll expenses and accounts payable, which includes money owed to vendors, monthly utilities, and similar expenses. In contrast, analysts want to see that long-term liabilities can be paid with assets derived from future earnings or financing transactions. Debt is not the only long-term liability companies incur. Items like rent, deferred taxes, payroll, and pension obligations can also be listed under long-term liabilities.

The Relationship between Liabilities and Assets

Assets are the things a company owns—or things owed to the company—and they include tangible items such as buildings, machinery, and equipment as well as intangible items such as accounts receivable, interest owed, patents or intellectual property.

If a business subtracts its liabilities from its assets, the difference is its owner's or stockholders' equity. This relationship can be expressed as follows:

$$\text{Assets} - \text{Liabilities} = \text{Owner's Equity}$$

However, in most cases, this accounting equation is commonly presented as such:

$$\text{Liabilities} + \text{Equity} = \text{Assets}$$

Current Liabilities

Using the AT&T (NYSE:T) balance sheet as of Dec. 31, 2012, current/short-term liabilities are segregated from long-term/non-current liabilities on the balance sheet. AT&T clearly defines its bank debt maturing in less than one year. For a company this size, this is often used as operating capital for day-to-day operations rather than funding larger items, which would be better suited using long-term debt.

Like most assets, liabilities are carried at cost, not market value, and under GAAP rules can be listed in order of preference as long as they are categorized. The AT&T example has a relatively high debt level under current liabilities. With smaller companies, other line items like accounts payable (AP) and various future liabilities like payroll, taxes, and ongoing expenses for an active company carry a higher proportion.

AP typically carries the largest balances, as they encompass the day-to-day operations. AP can include services, raw materials, office supplies, or any other categories of products and services where no promissory note is issued. Since most companies do not pay for goods and services as they are acquired, AP is equivalent to a stack of bills waiting to be paid.

Examples of Common Current Liabilities

- Wages Payable: The total amount of accrued income employees have earned but not yet received. Since most companies pay their employees every two weeks, this liability changes often.
- Interest Payable: Companies, just like individuals, often use credit to purchase goods and services to finance over short time periods. This represents the interest on those short-term credit purchases to be paid.
- Dividends Payable: For companies that have issued stock to investors and pay a dividend, this represents the amount owed to shareholders after the dividend was declared. This

period is around two weeks, so this liability usually pops up four times per year, until the dividend is paid.

Less Common Current Liabilities

- Unearned Revenues: This is a company's liability to deliver goods and/or services at a future date after being paid in advance. This amount will be reduced in the future with an offsetting entry once the product or service is delivered.
- Liabilities of Discontinued Operations: This is a unique liability that most people glance over but should scrutinize more closely. Companies are required to account for the financial impact of an operation, division, or entity that is currently being held for sale or has been recently sold. This also includes the financial impact of a product line that is or has recently been shut down.

Since most companies do not report line items for individual entities or products, this entry points out the implications in aggregate. As there are estimates used in some of the calculations, this can carry significant weight.

A good example is a large technology company that has released what it considered to be a world-changing product line, only to see it flop when it hit the market. All the R&D, marketing and product release costs need to be accounted for under this section.

Non-current Liabilities

Considering the name, it's quite obvious that any liability that is not current falls under non-current liabilities expected to be paid in 12 months or more. Referring again to the AT&T example, there are more items than your garden variety company that may list one or two items. Long-term debt, also known as bonds payable, is usually the largest liability and at the top of the list.

Companies of all sizes finance part of their ongoing long-term operations by issuing bonds that are essentially loans to each party that purchases the bonds. This line item is in constant flux as bonds are issued, mature, or called back by the issuer.

Examples of Common Non-current Liabilities

- Warranty Liability: Some liabilities are not as exact as AP and have to be estimated. It's the estimated amount of time and money that may be spent repairing products upon the agreement of a warranty. This is a common liability in the automotive industry, as most cars have long-term warranties that can be costly.
- Lawsuit Payable: This is another liability that is estimated and requires more scrutiny. If a lawsuit is considered probable and predictable, an estimated cost of all court, attorney and settled fees will be recorded. These are common line items for pharmaceutical and medical manufacturers.

Less Common Non-current Liabilities

- Deferred Credits: This is a broad category that may be recorded as current or non-current depending on the specifics of the transactions. These credits are basically revenue collected prior to it being earned and recorded on the income statement. It may include customer advances, deferred revenue, or a transaction where credits are owed but not yet considered revenue. Once the revenue is no longer deferred, this item is reduced by the amount earned and becomes part of the company's revenue stream.

- Post-Employment Benefits: These are benefits an employee or family members may receive upon his/her retirement, which are carried as a long-term liability as it accrues. In the AT&T example, this constitutes one-half of the total non-current total second only to long-term debt. With rapidly rising health care and deferred compensation, this liability is not to be overlooked.
- Unamortized Investment Tax Credits (UITC): This represents the net between an asset's historical cost and the amount that has already been depreciated. The unamortized portion is a liability, but it is only a rough estimate of the asset's fair market value. For an analyst, this provides some details of how aggressive or conservative a company is with its depreciation methods.

Expenses

An expense is defined as an outflow of money or assets to another individual or company as payment for an item or service. An expense is the costs experienced by a company, paid out to suppliers or for products or services from other sources. Within a business context, only expenses that relate the the cost of business operations should be included in the company's records.

As one of the main aspects of running a business, managing expenses is a crucial part of keeping tabs of your company's financial health. Expenses ultimately mean money that is spent in order to continue and grow the operations of a business.

An expense is an event where an asset is used up or a liability is incurred. With regards to the accounting equation, expenses effectively reduce owner's equity.

Recording an Expense

Expenses are recorded on the debit side of an expense account (which is an income statement account) and a credit is recorded to either a liability or an asset account in accordance with double-entry bookkeeping.

When the expense is recorded on the profit & loss report is dependent upon the accounting method chosen by a business. Under the accrual method of accounting, an expense is recorded when it is incurred by a business (which might differ from when cash actually changes hand).

For example: A business pays for internet service in their offices monthly but receives and pays the bill the following month. However, they will record the rent for the month the cost was incurred even though payment was made the following month under accrual accounting.

Registering an expense under the cash accounting method, on the other hand, means that each expense is recorded only when money actually changes hands.

For example: A business pays for electricity quarterly, and receives the bill at the end of each quarter. Although the period covers several months, the amount is only entered into the record at the end of each quarter when the bill is paid.

Operating Expense

Operating Expense is the cost that is incurred in the normal course of business and does not include expenses such as the cost of goods sold which are directly related to product manufacturing or service delivery. They are easily available in the income statement along with other costs which are subtracted from the operating income to determine net profit.

List of Operating Expenses

Operating expenses are the expenses which are incurred by the business in the normal course of its operations. Operating Expense includes cost related to the production of goods, however, finance cost such as the interest expenses is always excluded from the operating expenses as they are not related to the day to day operations of the business.

Other costs that are excluded from the operating cost include auditor fees, debt replacement cost, bank fees etc.

Every company always tries to reduce the burden of operating expenses as much as possible because this is one of the deciding factors of the firm's ability to compete with its competitors.

The list of Operating Expenses is sub-divided into two parts – Selling, General and Admin Expense (SG&A) and Costs of Goods Sold.

List of Operating Expense under SG&A Expenses

These costs are part of operating expenses because they are incurred due to the main business activities. These expenses include telephone expense, traveling expense, utility expense, sales expense, Rent, repair & maintenance, bank charges, legal expenses, office supplies, insurance, salaries and wages of administrative staff, Research expenses etc.

Below is the list of 13 Operating expenses that come under Selling, General and Admin costs:

1. Telephone Expenses: These are the cost incurred on landline or mobile phones. Generally, monthly bills are payable for them. Many Companies also reimburse their employees for their telephone expenses. Depending upon the company policy telephone expenses are charged to Profit and loss account.

2. Travelling Expenses: These are the expenses which are paid by the company for their staff during their official visit. The staff can travel to meet customers, for some supplies or any other event. In such a case either company pays staff expense directly or reimburses the staff after their visit. These expenses are charged in the P&L as traveling expense.

3. Office Equipment and Supplies: These are the expenses which are incurred for the purpose of purchasing office supplies used on a day to day basis in the office. For example, pen, papers, clippers etc.

4. Utility Expenses: The expenses which are related to payment of utility bills of the company like expenses of water and electricity that generally are used for the daily operating activities are the utility expenses and are charged to the profit and loss account of the company.
5. Property Tax: The property tax paid by the company on its properties forms the part of the operating expenses of the company.
6. Legal Expenses: These operating expenses which are incurred for using the legal services by the company. These are charged in the profit and Loss account of the company under the head legal expenses.
7. Bank Charges: The fees charged by the banks for the general transactions going in the business are known as the bank charges. For example transaction charges for cheque fees etc.
8. Repair and Maintenance Expenses: The Repair and maintenance operating expense on the asset used for production like repairing requirements of machines, or the vehicles in the company.
9. Insurance Expenses: The expenses which are incurred for taking insurance of health care, general insurance of staff and fire insurance are to be charged to the profit and loss account under the head insurance expenses.
10. Advertising Expenses: This operating expense related to the promotion and advertising forms part of the operating expenses of the company as they are done for increasing the sales. The same however does not include the trade discount which the company gives to its customers.
11. Research Expenses: This type of operating expenses which are incurred for research of the new products are treated as revenue expenses and should not be capitalized. These are charged to Profit and Loss account
12. Entertainment Expenses: The entertainment expenses incurred for the sales and related support activities forms the part of the operating expenses of the company.
13. Sales Expenses: This operating expense that are incurred for the purpose of increasing sales are part of the sales expenses. For example, a discount on sales and the sales commission expenses etc.

List of Operating Expense under COGS

Cost of the Goods Sold is the Costs which are incurred for the Goods or products sold by the organization during a specific time period. The cost which is considered while calculating the cost of goods sold refers to the cost which is directly attributable to goods or products sold by the company. This includes cost related to direct labor, direct overheads, and direct material. The cost should be matched with corresponding revenues which the entity has recognized in the income statement.

Below is the list of 6 Operating expenses that come under Cost of Goods Sold:

1. Freight in Cost: Freight-in is the shipping cost which buyer has to pay for purchasing the merchandise when terms are the FOB shipping point. The expense related to freight-in is

considered as part of the cost of merchandise and in case if the merchandise is not yet sold then the same should be considered in the inventory.

2. Freight out Cost: Freight out is the cost of transportation which is associated with the delivery of the goods from the place of the supplier to customers and the same should be included within cost of the goods sold classification in the income statement.
3. Product Cost: These are the costs which are incurred to make the product in the condition to sell it to customers. The product costincludes cost related to direct labor, direct overheads and direct material
4. Rental Cost: Rental Cost which is paid for the properties used for providing the support related to the production. The Salaries, wages, and other benefits are given to the staff related to the production of goods.
5. Depreciation Expenses: The reduction in the value of the asset due to wear and tear while using at the time of production is the depreciation expense and forms the part of the cost of goods sold.
6. Others Costs: These are incurred which is directly attributable to production form part of the cost of goods sold.

Non-operating Expense

A non-operating expense is a business expense unrelated to the core operations. The most common types of non-operating expenses are interest charges and losses on the disposition of assets. Accountants sometimes remove non-operating expenses and non-operating revenues to examine the performance of the business, ignoring effects of financing and other irrelevant issues.

Non-operating expense, like its name implies, is an accounting term used to describe expenses that occur outside of a company's day-to-day activities. These types of expenses include monthly charges like interest payments on debt but can also include one-off or unusual costs. For example, a company may categorize any costs incurred from restructuring, reorganizing, costs from currency exchange, or charges on obsolete inventory as non-operating expenses.

Non-operating expenses are recorded at the bottom of a company's income statement. The purpose is to allow financial statement users to assess the direct business activities that appear at the top of the income statement alone. It is important for a business' future outlook that its core business operations generate a profit.

Examples of Non-operating Expense

Most public companies finance their growth with a combination of debt and equity. Regardless of the allocation, any business that has corporate debt also has monthly interest payments on the amount borrowed. This monthly interest payment is considered a non-operating expense because it does not arise due to a company's core operations.

If a company sells a building, and it is not in the business of buying and selling real estate, the sale of the building is a non-operating activity. If the building sold at a loss, the loss is considered a non-operating expense.

Recording Non-operating Expense

When looking at a company's income statement from top to bottom, operating expenses are the first costs displayed just below revenue. The company starts the preparation of its income statement with top-line revenue. The firm's cost of goods sold (COGS) is then subtracted from its revenue to arrive at its gross income. After gross income is calculated, all operating costs are then subtracted to get the company's operating profit, or earnings before interest, tax, depreciation, and amortization (EBITDA). Then, after operating profit has been derived, all non-operating expenses are recorded on the financial statement. Non-operating expenses are subtracted from the company's operating profit to arrive at its earnings before taxes (EBT). Taxes are then assessed to derive the company's net income.

Revenue

Revenue is the value of all sales of goods and services recognized by a company in a period. Revenue (also revered to as Sales, Turnover, or Income) forms the beginning of a company's Income Statement and often considered the "Top Line" of a business. Expenses are deducted from a company's revenue to arrive at its Profit or Net Income.

Revenue Example

Below is an example of Amazon's 2017 income statement. Let's take a closer look to understand how revenue works for a very large public company.

Amazon refers to its revenue as "sales," which is equally as common as a term. It reports sales in two categories, product and service, which then combine to form total net sales.

AMAZON.COM,
CONSOLIDATED STATEMENTS OF OPERATIONS
(In millions, except per share data)

	Year ended December 31.		
	2015	2016	2017
Net product sale	$ 79.268	$ 94.665	$ 118.573
Net service sale	27.738	41.322	59.293
Total net sales	107,006	135.987	177.866
Operating expenses:			
Cost of sales	71,651	88.265	111,934
Fulfilment	13,410	17,619	25,249
Marketing	5,254	7,233	10,069
Technology and content	12,540	16.085	22,620

General and administrative	1,747	2,432	3,674
Other operating expense .net	171	167	214
Total operating expenses	104,773	131.801	173,760
Operating income	2,233	4,186	4,106
Interest income	50	100	202
Interest expense	(459)	(484)	(848)
Other income (expense) .net	(256)	90	346
Total non-operating income (expenses)	665	(294)	(300)
Income before income taxes	1,568	3,892	3,806
Provision for income taxes	(950)	(14,425)	(769)
Equity –method investment activity. Net of tax	(22)	(96)	(4)
Net income	$ 596	$ 2,371	$ 3,033

In 2017, Amazon recorded $118.6 billion of product sales and $59.3 billion of service sales, for a grand total of $178.9 billion. The figure forms the top line of the income statement.

Beneath that are all operating expenses, which are deducted to arrive at Operating Income, also sometimes referred to as Earnings Before Interest and Taxes (EBIT).

Finally, interest and taxes are deducted to reach the bottom line of the income statement, $3.0 billion of net income.

Revenue Formula

The revenue formula may be simple or complicated, depending on the business. For product sales, it is calculated by taking the average price at which goods are sold and multiplying it by the total number of products sold. For service companies, it is calculated as the value of all service contracts, or by the number of customers multiplied by the average price of services.

Revenue = No. of Units Sold x Average Price

Or

Revenue = No. of Customers x Average Price of Services

The formulas above can be significantly expanded to include more detail. For example, many companies will model their revenue forecast all the way down to the individual product level or individual customer level.

Revenue Forecast

Below is an example of a company's forecast based on many drivers, including:

- Website traffic
- Conversion rates
- Product prices
- Volume of different product

- Discounts
- Return and refunds

A B C D	E	F	G	H	I	J	K
	Start-up year 2016	2017	2018	2019	2020	2021	Terminal Year 2022
Balance sheet check	OK	OK	OK	OK	OK	OK	OK
Order placed							
E-mail	0	3,600	7,200	21,600	36,000	36,000	43,200
Orginic search	2,400	12,000	24,000	37,200	40,800	40.800	43,200
Paid search	7.920	5,280	2,640	2,640	2,640	2,640	2,640
Affiliates	9,600	4,800	2,400	2,400	2,400	2,400	2,400
Total order placed	19,920	25,680	36,240	50,640	63,840	81,840	91,440
Order details							
Average item value (gross)	250	250	250	250	250	250	250
#of items per order	1.1	1.2	1.3	1.4	1.5	1.6	1.7
Average markdown	10%	10%	10%	10%	10%	10%	10%
Average promotion/discount	20%	18%	15%	12%	10%	8%	8%
Cost of goods sold (gross product marine)	50%	50%	50%	50%	50%	50%	50%
Average gross order value	275	300	325	350	375	400	425
Average net order value	193	216	244	273	300	328	349
Customers							
Churn Rate	25%	25%	25%	25%	25%	25%	25%
Opening active customers base	0	17,940	27,765	42,604	59,133	76,030	91,402
Plus new customers	19,920	22,080	29,040	36,240	42,240	45,840	48,240
Subtotal	19,920	37,020	56,805	78,844	101,373	121,870	139,642
Less churned customers	4,980	9,255	14,201	19,711	25,343	30,467	34,911
Closing customers base	14,940	27,765	42,604	59,133	76,030	91,402	104,732

As you can see in the example above, there is much more that can be included in a forecast other than just No. of Units x Average Price.

CFI's e-Commerce Financial Modeling Course provides a detailed breakdown of how to build this type of model, which is extremely important for forecasting and business valuation.

Revenue on the Income Statement and other Financials

Sales are the lifeblood of a company, as it's what allows it to pay its employees, purchase inventory, pay suppliers, invest in research and development, build new property, plant, and equipment (PP&E), and be self-sustaining.

If a company doesn't have sufficient revenue to cover the above items, it will need to use an existing cash balance on its balance sheet. The cash can come from financing, meaning that the company borrowed the money (in the case of debt), or raised it (in the case of equity).

In order to perform a comprehensive analysis of a business, it's important to know how the 3 financial statements are linked and see how a company either uses its sales to fund to the business or must turn to financing alternatives to fund the business.

Revenue in Different Sectors

Below, we will explore what the concept of revenue means in different sectors. As you will see, it can be composed of many different things and varies widely in terms of what the most common examples are, by sector.

Personal finance:

- Salaries
- Bonuses
- Hourly wages
- Dividends
- Interest
- Rental income

Public finance:

- Income tax
- Corporate tax
- Sales tax
- Duties and tariffs

Corporate finance:

- Sale of goods
- Sales of services
- Dividends
- Interest

Non-profits:

- Membership Dues
- Fundraising
- Sponsorships
- Product/service sales

The three main areas that typically make up the finance industry are public finance, personal finance, and corporate finance. And we demonstrated above, the various sources of income in each type can be quite different.

Profit

Profit is the revenue remaining after all costs are paid. These costs include labor, materials, interest on debt, and taxes. Profit is usually used when describing business activity. But everyone with an income has profit. It's what's left over after paying the bills.

Profit is the reward to business owners for investing. In small companies, it's paid directly as income. In corporations, it's often paid in the form of dividends to shareholders.

When expenses are higher than revenue, that's called a loss. If a company suffers losses for too long, it goes bankrupt.

Profit Formula

Profit is calculated by the following formula:

$\pi = R - C$

- Where π (the symbol for pi) = profit
- Revenue = Price (x)
- C = Fixed cost, such as cost for a building +Variable cost, such as the cost to produce each product (x)
- x = number of units

For example, the profit for a kid selling lemonade might be:

$\pi = \$20.00 - \$15.00 = \$5.00$

- R = $0.10 (Price for each cup) (200 cups) = $20.00
- C = $5.00 (for wood to build lemonade stand) + $.05 (for the cost of sugar and lemons per cup) (200 cups sold) = $5.00 + $10.00 = $15.00

Importance of Profit

Profit is one of the most important measurements in determining the health and success of a business. However, the measurement of profit can vary and should be considered with other factors.

For example, profit varies greatly from company to company and from industry to industry. Because companies vary in size, it is often more appropriate to consider profit as a percentage of sales (profit margin) when comparing one company to another. As well, varying accounting methods can greatly influence profit, and these changes may have little to do with a company's actual operations.

Changes in profit are the subject of much analysis. In general, high or rising profits are indicative of a successful business while low profits could suggest a myriad of problems, including inadequacies in customer or expense management.

Gross Profit

Gross profit is net sales minus the cost of goods sold. It reveals the amount that a business earns from the sale of its goods and services before the application of additional selling and administrative expenses. Gross profit is typically stated partway down the income statement, prior to a listing of selling, general, and administrative expenses. The gross profit formula is:

Revenue - (Direct materials + Direct labor + Factory overhead)

How to Calculate Gross Profit

The calculation of gross profit is a multi-step process, as outlined below:

1. Aggregate gross sales information and all deductions from sales to arrive at net sales. The deductions from sales should include sales discounts and allowances.
2. Aggregate direct cost of goods sold information. Be consistent in drawing this information from the same expense accounts from period to period, in order to report a consistent gross profit figure.
3. Shift factory overhead costs into one or more cost pools.
4. Collect allocation information for the period. Again, be careful to use the same basis of information from period to period, to create consistent results.
5. Allocate the factory overhead cost pool(s) to cost objects (i.e., produced goods).
6. Charge sold units to the cost of goods sold.
7. Subtract the direct cost of goods sold and the factory overhead charged to the cost of goods sold from net sales. The result is the gross profit for the period.

Gross Profit Example

ABC International has revenues of $1,000,000, direct materials expense of $320,000, direct labor expense of $100,000, and factory overhead of $250,000. Therefore, its gross profit is $330,000.

Gross Profit Analysis

From an analysis perspective, gross profit can be a flawed calculation, depending on the level at which it is used. For example:

- Product level: Overhead should not be applied at the individual product level, so contribution margin (which excludes overhead) is a better analysis tool. Another option is to use just throughput, which is essentially revenue minus direct materials expense.
- Product line level: Some overhead related to a product line can be applied at this level, so a portion of factory overhead can be included in the calculation.

- Business unit level: Probably all of the factory overhead costs listed in the gross profit on a company's financial statements can be included in this calculation.

Thus, the gross profit calculation is less relevant at the unit level, and more relevant at the business unit level.

Gross profit is more useful when tracked as a percentage of sales on a trend line. You can then drill down on those periods where the percentage is lower than average to see what caused the reduction. Examples of reasons for a gross profit change are:

- The presence or absence of sales allowances.
- A change in the mix of products sold.
- Changes in product prices.
- Differences in the material content of different products.
- Differences in the amount of labor needed to manufacture different products.
- Changes in the purchased cost of materials.
- Changes in the cost of labor per hour.
- Changes in the amount of overtime paid.
- Changes in the cost of overhead.
- Changes in the method used to allocate overhead.
- Changes in the amount of outsourced manufacturing used.

Net Profit

Net profit represents the number of sales dollars remaining after all operating expenses, interest, taxes and preferred stock dividends (but not common stock dividends) have been deducted from a company's total revenue.

Example:

Net profit is also referred to as the bottom line, net income, or net earnings. The formula for net profit is as follows:

Total Revenue -Total Expenses = Net Profit

Net profit is found on the last line of the income statement, which is why it's often referred to as the bottom line. Let's look at a hypothetical income statement for Company XYZ:

Income Statement for Company XYZ, Inc. for the year ended December 31, 2008	
Total Revenue	$100,000
Cost of Goods Sold	($ 20,000)
Gross Profit	$ 80,000

Operating Expenses	
Salaries Rent Utilities Depreciation	$10,000 $10,000 $ 5,000 $ 5,000
Total Operating Expenses	($ 30,000)
Interest Expense	($ 10,000)
Taxes	($ 10,000)
Net Profit	$ 30,000

By using the formula we can see that Net Profit = $100,000 - $20,000 - $30,000, - $10,000 - $10,000 = $30,000.

Importance of Net Profit

Net profit is one of the most closely followed numbers in finance, and it plays a large role in ratio analysis and financial statement analysis. Shareholders look at net profit closely because it is the source of compensation to shareholders of the company, and if a company cannot generate enough profit to compensate owners, the value of shares will plummet. Conversely, if a company is healthy and growing, higher stockprices will reflect the increased availability of profits.

One of the most important concepts to understand is that net profit is not a measure of how much cash a company earned during a given period. This is because the income statementincludes a lot of non-cash expenses such as depreciation and amortization.

Changes in net profit are endlessly scrutinized. In general, when a company's net profit is low or negative, a myriad of problems could be to blame, ranging from decreasing sales to poor customer experience to inadequate expense management.

Net profit varies greatly from company to company and from industry to industry. Because net profit is measured in dollars and companies vary in size, it is often more appropriate to consider net profit as a percentage of sales, known as "profit margin." Another common ratio is the price-to-earnings ratio(P/E), which tells investors how much they are paying (the stock's price) for each dollar of net profit the company is able to generate.

Loss

Losses are a one-time removal or decrease in a business resource or asset. Losses are unrecoverable and unanticipated. The most common types of loss refer to the amount that an asset decreases in value over the course of its useful life for your business. All fixed (long-term) assets suffer from depreciation over time, and the differences in these value is what is referred to as loss. These assets do not include any inventory sold.

Another common type of loss can also mean that the total expenses encountered by a company is greater than the income for a particular period. This is more specifically known as 'net operating loss' or simply 'net loss'.

While the more well-known situations wherein losses are experienced are mentioned above, there are a variety of other circumstances in which a company can face losses. In accounting, losses occur in any of the following situations:

- Costs that produce no benefit.
- Decrease in value of resources.
- Excess of expenditure over income.
- Excess of cost over net proceeds from a transaction.
- Contingent losses as a result of lawsuit or unexpected events.

Recording Losses for Financial Statements

It is important to keep thorough financial records for your business, and while losses aren't necessarily a pleasant element to include, they are nevertheless crucial for maintaining balanced and legal accounts.

Losses are recorded and displayed in one of two reports, depending on the type of loss:

- Losses that result from events that are not related to the primary operations of a business are recorded in the profit and loss statement.
- Losses that do result from events that are directly related to the operations of the business are recognized in the balance sheet.

Impact of Losses

While losses are not a positive addition to a company's finance, there is no reason that a loss should spell the demise of the business. However, repeated net operating loss over an extended period of time can result in insolvency, which may require eventual liquidation.

Many businesses can bounce back from a net operating loss using previous revenue or relying on loans such as a small business loan, for example. But these companies will need to develop a long-term plan to try to turn things around.

Losses due to asset depreciation, even to capital assets such as real estate, mean that these assets are worth less than their original purchase price. This can be due to poor market performance, or a weak economy and must be taken into account in the financial reporting of a business.

Integrated Accounting System

Integrated accounting system refers to the interlocking of the financial and cost accounting systems to ensure all relevant expenditure is absorbed into the cost accounts. Under this accounting system transactions are classified both according to their function and nature.

Under integrated accounting system, both Financial and Cost Accounting records are maintained in one set of books to meet the requirements of Financial Accounting and Cost Accounting purposes. In other words, we can say, that Cost Accounting is integrated into the Financial Accounting System.

Integrated accounting records provide the necessary information for ascertainment of cost of each unit, batch or job or any other cost unit and simultaneously financial statements viz., Profit and Loss Account and Balance Sheet can be prepared without any distortion of the Financial Accounting information.

In this system transactions are recorded based on double entry bookkeeping and costs are classified on the basis of function which enables the firm in ascertainment of product cost with necessary classification.

For example, the purchase of raw material is analyzed by its nature and instead of posting it to the Purchases Account as in Financial Accounts, directly posted into Stores Ledger Control Account, Work-in-progress Ledger Control Account or Overhead Account. Similarly the payment of direct wages instead of posting into Direct Wages Account, posting is directly made into Wages Control Account or Overheads Control Account.

Benefits of Integrated Accounting System

The important benefits of maintaining records on Integrated Accounting System are as follows:

- In this system only one set of accounts are maintained and there will be single profit figure. The necessity of preparation of reconciliation statement does not arise.
- The maintenance of one set of accounts avoids the duplication of efforts and substantial time and expense is saved.
- There will not be any delay in getting information from the accounting records for financial and costing purposes.
- This system can be more advantageous only if operated in computerised environment and mechanized accounting.
- With the integration of cost and financial accounts, centralization of accounting and information is possible and it saves both time and expense.
- The simplification of accounting procedures helps in better control of the operations.
- Costing information is generated from the books of original entry. It avoids delay in obtaining information.
- It furnish all information regarding cost of each product, job or operation and variances will also be highlighted for effective control purpose.
- It provides all information about the profit or loss of the whole organization and financial position of the concern and help the management in better control over the operations.
- This accounting system ensures the ascertainment of marginal cost, variances, abnormal loss and gains.

Prerequisites for Integration of Accounts

The important prerequisites for integration of Cost and Financial Accounts are as follows:

- The top management must be convinced of the advantages of maintenance of records under Integrated Accounting System and should decide upon the degree of integration is necessitated for the concern. Some firms may prefer to full integration and certain firms may prefer to integrate upto a certain stage of process i.e., prime cost, factory cost, cost of production etc.
- The next step is that convenient coding system should be adopted to identify the accounts for the purpose of Cost Accounting and Financial Accounting.
- Accounting staff should be properly trained in dealing with the accounting records for recording of transactions and generation of information for financial and costing purposes.
- Close coordination is required between staff dealing with the financial information and costing information.
- The formats are to be developed for increase of speed in accounting and generation of information for financial and costing purpose.
- The adjustment entries for prepaid expenses and outstanding expenses should made routine for ascertainment of cost and profit.

1. Administrative overheads may be treated as cost of manufacture. In that case administrative overheads are absorbed to Work-in-progress A/c instead of finished goods A/c.
2. Administrative overheads may be treated as cost of sales. In that case administrative overheads are transferred to Cost of sales A/c instead of finished goods A/c.

The simple illustrations explaining the entries that are passed in integrated and non-integrated accounting is given below:

Materials

The raw material purchased during the month Rs. 4,25,000 and its standard cost is Rs. 4,00,000.

Particulars		Debit (Rs.) credit (Rs.)	
(a) Financial Books:			
Purchase A/c	Dr.	4,25,000	
To Creditors A/c			4,25,000
(b) Cost Books			
Stores ledger control A/c	Dr.	4,00,000	
Material price variance A/c	Dr.	25,000	
To Cost ledger control A/c			4,25,000
(c) Integral Accounts			

Stores ledger control A/c	Dr.	4,00,000	
Material price variance A/c	Dr.	25,000	
To Creditors A/c			4,25,000

Wages

The wages paid to the direct labour during the month amounts to Rs. 2,65,000 and its standard cost is Rs. 2,50,000:

Particulars		Debit (Rs.) credit (Rs.)	
(a) Financial Books:			
Wagas A/c Dr.	Dr.	2,65,000	
To Bank A/c			2,65,000
(b) Cost Books			
Wagas control A/c	Dr.	2,50,000	
Labour rate variance A/c	Dr.	15,000	
To cost ledger control A/			265,000
(c) Integral Accounts			
Wagas control A/c	Dr.	2,50,000	
Labour rate variance A/c	Dr.	15,000	
To Bank A/c			265,000

Overheads

Factory expenses incurred during the month is Rs. 1,40,000 compared with standard cost of Rs. 1,20,000:

Particulars		Debit (Rs.) credit (Rs.)	
(a) Financial Books:			
Production expenses A/c	Dr.	1,40,000	
To Bank A/c			1,40,000
(b) Cost Books			
Production overhead A/c	Dr.	1,20,000	
Production overhead expenditure variance A/c	Dr.	20,000	
To cost ledger control A/c			1,40,000
(c) Integral Accounts			
Production overhead A/c	Dr.	1,20,000	
Production overhead expenditure variance A/c	Dr.	20,000	
To bank A/c			1,40,000

Sales during the month is Rs. 9,80,000 compared with the budgeted sales of Rs. 9,50,000:

Particulars	Debit (Rs.) credit (Rs.)		
(a) Financial Books:			
Debtors A/c	Dr.	9,80,000	
To Sales A/c			9,80,000
(b) Cost Books			
Cost ledger control A/c	Dr.	9,80,000	
To Budgeted sales A/c	Dr.		9,50,000
To Sales price variance A/c			30,000
(c) Integral Accounts			
Debtors A/c	Dr.	9,80,000	
To Budgeted sales A/c	Dr.		9,50,000
To Sales price variance A/c			30,000

Advantages of Integrated Accounting

A business management system with integrated accounting makes accounting as easy as processing orders.

Rather than manually re-keying information from order management into a standalone accounting system, which costs time and errors, an integrated accounting system automatically receives a constant flow of data from order management.

Since the information flows automatically, the financials are always up to date. And even sophisticated accounting operations like job costing and commission calculation are performed automatically just by processing the orders.

Here are 4 advantages of a business management system with integrated accounting:

1. Integrated Accounting Eliminates Re-keying:

   Re-keying creates two major problems. One is that it costs time and labor that could otherwise be devoted to more productive activities. The other is that that it invites errors and omissions that either go uncorrected or require more time and labor to find and fix.

   A business management system or ERP with integrated accounting eliminates re-keying, which frees up staff to focus on sales and opportunities. Re-keying information from an order management system into a standalone accounting system is not an efficient use of time, and will inevitably lead to mistakes that no one wants on their books.

2. Integrated Accounting Provides Real-Time Information:

   Standalone accounting is always behind as it waits for someone to manually take information from the ordering system and re-enter it in the accounting system. That means never having the up-to-date financial information that's required for the best decision making possible. Since data re-entry also invites human error, standalone accounting also stands a greater chance of leading to decisions based on faulty information.

Integrated accounting provides a complete real-time picture of the business at any time since information automatically flows into the accounting system as orders are processed. A web-based business management system with integrated accounting even lets you take complete, accurate financials with you wherever you go.

3. Integrated Accounting Can Automatically Perform Job Costing:

   With integrated accounting, even sophisticated accounting processes like job costing can be performed automatically -- effectively as a side-effect of processing orders. Postings are automatically made to Accounts Receivable, Accounts Payable, and the General Ledger so that the accounting system automatically has the information it needs to calculate job costs and to perform other accounting processes.

   Standalone accounting systems that do perform some form of job costing often run into problems. Standalone accounting doesn't "talk to" the order management system like an integrated accounting system would and so it doesn't inherently know which costs go with which jobs. Attributing certain costs and information to certain jobs and orders might become a new manual process in itself.

4. Integrated Accounting Results in Accurate Commission:

   Similar to the way that an integrated accounting system can automatically perform job costing, an integrated accounting system can automatically calculate sales commission including split commissions. Once again as orders are processed the integrated accounting system receives the information it needs to calculate commission.

5. Integrated accounting systems are especially useful for companies that make job costs part of commission formulas. By automatically performing the job costing, the integrated accounting system automates one of the major factors to calculating accurate commission.

References

- Types-of-assets, accounting, knowledge: corporatefinanceinstitute.com, Retrieved 2 May, 2019
- Liability: investopedia.com, Retrieved 10 January, 2019
- Expense: debitoor.com, Retrieved 14 August, 2019
- Operating-expense-opex: wallstreetmojo.com, Retrieved 8 March, 2019
- List-of-operating-expenses: wallstreetmojo.com, Retrieved 15 January, 2019
- Non-operating-expense: investopedia.com, Retrieved 5 June, 2019
- Revenue, accounting, knowledge: corporatefinanceinstitute.com, Retrieved 25 April, 2019
- What-is-profit-and-how-does-it-work-3305878: thebalance.com, Retrieved 4 February, 2019

- Profit: investinganswers.com, Retrieved 28 May, 2019
- Net-profit: investinganswers.com, Retrieved 8 March, 2019
- Losses: debitoor.com, Retrieved 13 July, 2019
- Integrated-accounting-system-cost-accounting, cost-accounting: accountingnotes.net, Retrieved 9 February, 2019
- 4-Advantages-of-Integrated-Accounting: essent.com, Retrieved 28 April, 2019

2

Financial Accounting

The branch of accounting which deals with the summary, analysis and reporting of financial transactions pertaining to a business is known as financial accounting. This chapter closely examines the key concepts of financial accounting such as trial balance, financial capital and capital expenditure to provide an extensive understanding of the subject.

Financial accounting is a specialized branch of accounting that keeps track of a company's financial transactions. Using standardized guidelines, the transactions are recorded, summarized, and presented in a financial report or financial statement such as an income statement or a balance sheet.

Companies issue financial statements on a routine schedule. The statements are considered external because they are given to people outside of the company, with the primary recipients being owners/stockholders, as well as certain lenders. If a corporation's stock is publicly traded, however, its financial statements (and other financial reportings) tend to be widely circulated, and information will likely reach secondary recipients such as competitors, customers, employees, labor organizations, and investment analysts.

It's important to point out that the purpose of financial accounting is not to report the value of a company. Rather, its purpose is to provide enough information for others to assess the value of a company for themselves.

Important Concepts in Financial Accounting

The end product of the financial accounting process are the financial statements that communicate useful information to decision-makers. The financial statements reflect a combination of recorded facts, accounting conventions and personal judgments of the preparers.

There are three primary financial statements for a profit making entity ,the Income Statement (statement of revenues, expenses and profit), and the Balance Sheet (statement of assets, liabilities and owner's equity) and cash flow statement. The accounting information generated by financial accounting is quantitative, formal, structured, numerical and past-oriented material.

Accounting System

The accounting system includes the various techniques and procedures used by the accountant (preparer) in measuring, describing and communicating financial data to users. Journals, ledgers and other accounting techniques used in processing financial accounting information depend upon the concept of the double-entry system. This technique includes generally accepted accounting principles (GAAP). The standard of generally accepted accounting principles includes not only broad guidelines of general application but also detailed practices and procedures.

Measurement Unit

Financial accounting is primarily concerned with measurement of economic resources and obligations and changes in them. Financial accounting measures in terms of monetary units of a society in which it operates. For example, the common denominator or yardstick used for accounting measurement is the rupee in India and dollar in the U.S.A. The assumption is that the rupee or the dollar is a useful measuring unit.

Users of Financial Accounting Information

Financial accounting information is intended primarily to serve external users. Some users have direct interest in reported information. Examples of such users are owners, creditors, potential owners, suppliers, management, tax authorities, employees, customers. Some users need financial accounting information to help those who have direct interest in a business enterprise.

Examples of such users are financial analysts and advisers, stock exchanges, financial press and reporting agencies, trade associations, labour unions. These user groups having direct/indirect interest have different objectives and diverse informational needs. The emphasis in financial accounting has been on generals-purpose information which, obviously, is not intended to satisfy any specialised needs of individual users or specific user groups.

Limitations of Financial Accounting

Financial accounting is significant for management as it helps them to direct and control the firm activities. It also helps business managements in determining appropriate managerial policies in different areas, such as production, sales, administration and finance.

Following are the limitations of financial accounting:

- Financial accounting does not provide detailed cost information for different departments, processes, products, jobs in the production divisions. Management may need information about different products, sales territories and sales activities which are also not available in financial accounting.
- Financial accounting does not set up a proper system of controlling materials and supplies. Undoubtedly, if material and supplies are not controlled in a manufacturing concern, they will lead to losses on account of misappropriation, misutilisation, scrap, defectives, etc.
- The recording and accounting for wages and labour is not done for different jobs, processes, products, departments. This creates problems in analysing the costs associated with different activities.
- It is difficult to know the behaviour of costs in financial accounting as expenses are not classified into direct and indirect and therefore cannot be classified as controllable and uncontrollable. Cost management which is the most important objective of all business enterprises, cannot be achieved with the aid of financial accounting alone.
- Financial accounting does not possess an adequate system of standards to evaluate the performance of departments and employees working in departments. Standards need to be

developed for materials, labour and overheads so that a firm can compare the work of workers, supervisors and executives with what should have been done in an allotted period of time.

- Financial accounting contains historical cost information which is accumulated at the end of the accounting period. The historical cost is not a reliable basis for predicting future earnings, solvency, or overall managerial effectiveness. Historical cost information is relevant but not adequate for all purposes.
- Financial accounting does not provide information to analyse the losses due to various factors, such as idle plant and equipment, seasonal fluctuations in volume of business, etc. It does not help management in taking important decisions about expansion of business, dropping of a product, alternative methods of production, improvement in product, etc.
- Financial accounting does not provide necessary cost data to determine the price of the product being manufactured or the service being rendered to the consumers.

In spite of the above limitations, financial accounting has utility and is an important and conceptually rich area. Because of growing business complexities and advances in knowledge of human behaviour and decision processes, the scope and methods of financial accounting are changing. Financial accounting theory and practice will probably be broadened and improved considerably in the future.

Trial Balance

A trial balance is a bookkeeping or accounting report that lists the balances in each of an organization's general ledger accounts. The report is primarily used to ensure that the total of all debits equals the total of all credits, which means that there are no unbalanced journal entries in the accounting system that would make it impossible to generate accurate financial statements. The year-end trial balance is typically asked for by auditors when they begin an audit, so that they can transfer the account balances on the report into their auditing software; they may ask for an electronic version, which they can more easily copy into their software.

Even when the debit and credit totals stated on the trial balance equal each other, it does not mean that there are no errors in the accounts listed in the trial balance. For example, a debit could have been entered in the wrong account, which means that the debit total is correct, though one underlying account balance is too low and another balance is too high. For example, an accounts payable clerk records a $100 supplier invoice with a debit to supplies expense and a $100 credit to the accounts payable liability account. The debit should have been to the utilities expense account, but the trial balance will still show that the total amount of debits equals the total number of credits.

The trial balance can also be used to manually compile financial statements, though with the predominant use of computerized accounting systems that create the statements automatically, the report is rarely used for this purpose. In effect, there is no longer a need to use the trial balance report in accounting operations.

When the trial balance is first printed, it is called the unadjusted trial balance. Then, when the accounting team corrects any errors found and makes adjustments to bring the financial statements into compliance with an accounting framework (such as GAAP or IFRS), the report is called the adjusted trial balance. The adjusted trial balance is typically printed and stored in the year-end book, which is then archived. Finally, after the period has been closed, the report is called the post-closing trial balance.

The trial balance is strictly a report that is compiled from the accounting records. However, since adjusting entries may be made as a result of reviewing the report, it could be said that trial balance accounting encompasses the adjustment process that converts an unadjusted trial balance into an adjusted trial balance.

If there are subsidiaries in an organization that report their results to a parent company, the parent may request an ending trial balance from each subsidiary, which it uses to prepare consolidated results for the entire company.

The general ledger is the report preferred by internal accountants, since it also shows the detailed transactions that comprise the ending balance, or at least points toward the relevant subledger that contains this information. This additional level of detail reveals the activity in an account during an accounting period, which makes it easier to conduct research and spot possible errors.

Trial Balance Format

The initial trial balance report contains the following columns:

- Account number
- Account name
- Ending debit balance (if any)
- Ending credit balance (if any)

Each line item only contains the ending balance in an account. All accounts having an ending balance are listed in the trial balance; usually, the accounting software automatically blocks all accounts having a zero balance from appearing in the report.

The adjusted version of a trial balance may combine the debit and credit columns into a single combined column, and add columns to show adjusting entries and a revised ending balance (as is the case in the following example).

Example of a Trial Balance

The following trial balance example combines the debit and credit totals into the second column, so that the summary balance for the total is (and should be) zero. Adjusting entries are added in the next column, yielding an adjusted trial balance in the far right column.

ABC International Trial Balance August 31, 20XX			
	Unadjusted Trial Balance	Adjusting Entries	Adjusted Trial Balance
Cash	$60,000		$60,000
Accounts receivable	180,000	50,000	230,000

Inventory	300,000		300,000
Fixed assets (net)	210,000		210,000
Accounts payable	(90,000)		(90,000)
Accrued liabilities	(50,000)	$(25,000)	(75,000)
Notes payable	(420,000)		(420,000)
Equity	(350,000)		(350,000)
Revenue	(400,000)	(50,000)	(450,000)
Cost of goods sold	290,000		290,000
Salaries	200,000	25,000	225,000
Payroll taxes	20,000		20,000
Rent	35,000		35,000<
Other expenses	15,000		15,000
Total	$0	$0	$0

Possible Errors in Trial Balance

A trial balance can trace the mathematical inaccuracy of the general ledger. However, there is a number of errors that could not be detected by this report:

- Error of omission: The transaction was not entered into the system.
- Error of original entry: The double-entry transaction includes the wrong amounts on both sides.
- Error of reversal: When a double-entry transaction was entered with the correct amounts, but the account to be debited is credited and the account to be credited is debited.
- Principle error: The entered transaction violates the fundamental principles of accounting. For example, the amount entered was correct and the appropriate side was chosen, but the type of an account was wrong (e.g., expense account instead of liability account).
- Commission error: The transaction amount is correct, but the account debited or credited is wrong.

Uses of Trial Balance

- Ease of posting adjustments: A tallied Trial Balance offers significant comfort regarding accuracy and hence post TB adjustments can be affected.
- Aids in Audit: Trial Balance gives a list of all ledgers with balances. For the purpose of audit the trial balance is analyzed. For example if the nature of an account is debit, but it holds a credit balance, then the entire ledger will be scrutinized. So trial balance is also an important tool for auditors.
- Defines credibility: Trial Balance is also used by Banks and lending agencies to understand the borrowing capacity of the business and credibility.

  Despite the numerous benefits of a Trial balance, it is imperative to understand that a tallied Trial Balance does not ensure zero errors. If there are offsetting errors, the Trial Balance will tally despite the error.

Advantages of Trial Balance

- Arithmetical accuracy: Given the nature of double entry system, every transaction will result in two entries of equal and opposite nature. Hence at any point in time all debit ledger totals will match to credit ledger totals. Since Trial Balance lists all the accounts as on a particular date, the debit total of a trial balance must match to the credit total.

  With softwares being used for accounting, the above advantage of the trial balance is not very relevant. As data entry systems does not allow entries to be posted if there is a difference in the debit and credit amount hence leaving no room for error.

- Bird's-eye view: A trial balance is a summary sheet listing all ledges and balances. Hence it provides a bird eye view of the accounting transactions of an organization.

- Prerequisite for preparation of Financial statements: An organization needs to know profit or loss and financial position at year end. And thus to prepare financial statements, Trial Balance is prerequisite. All stakeholders also need this information. It is the first step towards closure of accounts for a particular period.

Limitations of a Trial Balance

Trial Balance only confirms that the total of all debit balances match the total of all credit balances. Trial balance totals may agree in spite of errors. An example would be an incorrect debit entry being offset by an equal credit entry. Likewise, a trial balance gives no proof that certain transactions have not been recorded at all because in such case, both debit and credit sides of a transaction would be omitted causing the trial balance totals to still agree.

Financial Capital

Financial capital is the money, credit, and other forms of funding that build wealth. Individuals use financial capital to invest, by making a down payment on a home or creating a portfolio for retirement.

Capital in Business

In business accounting, capital is how companies invest in their businesses. They use financial capital to buy more equipment, buildings, or materials. Managers can't use the money to give themselves raises, increase dividends, or lower prices. They must use it to produce greater future gains. A business uses this investment capital to transform itself into something more profitable.

Types of Business Capital

There are three types of financial capital in the business world. The first is debt. Companies receive capital now that they pay back with interest. At first, many entrepreneurs borrow from family members or their credit cards. Once they have a track record, they can get bank loans and federal government assistance from the Small Business Administration.

As these businesses continue to grow, they become large enough to issue individual bonds to investors. The advantage of debt is that owners don't have to share the profits. The disadvantage is that they must repay the loan even if the business fails.

The second type of capital is equity. The business receives cash now from investors for a share of the profits later. Most entrepreneurs use their own cash to get started. They put their own equity into the business in hopes of receiving 100 percent of the return later. If the company is profitable, they forgo spending some of the cash flow now and instead invest it in the business.

A larger firm gets equity from partners, venture capitalists, or angel investors. It must give up some control and ownership of the business in exchange for the cash. Once a company becomes really large and successful, it can get additional capital from issuing stocks. This is called an initial public offering. It means any investor can purchase the company's stock.

The third type of capital is specialty capital. It's extra cash flow that comes from managing the company's operations better. Vendor financing is when the company's suppliers are willing to accept delayed payment for their goods or services.

A popular form of specialty capital is supply chain financing. It's like a pay-day loanfor businesses. Banks lend the company the amount of an invoice, minus a fee. They receive payment for the loan when the invoice is paid. Company finance managers also create extra capital through investing wisely. In a bull market, some companies make more money from their investments than from their operations.

Capital Structure

How a company creates and manages its capital is known as its capital structure. Most public companies use a combination of debt, through bonds, and equity, through various types of stock. Many analysts use a simple formula, the debt-to-equity ratio, to determine how solid a company is. Companies with a ratio of 50 percent or more have more debt than equity. Analysts consider them to be highly leveraged and therefore riskier.

Another component of the capital structure is working capital. It's the cash on hand needed to run the company's operations. The formula is current assets minus current liabilities. The working capital ratio is current assets divided by current liabilities. A working capital ratio of 2:1 means the company has enough liquidity to meet its immediate needs. If the ratio is higher, it means the company is not putting its money to use to build future profits.

Capital Markets

Easy access to capital has been one of the most important drivers of U.S. economic success. America has the world's most sophisticated capital markets. The transparency of the U.S. stock market allows investors to gain up-to-date information about every aspect of companies in which they might invest.

The U.S. bond market is serviced by the best investment banks in the world. They have the experience to walk the company through the bond process. They have the financial clout to underwrite the bonds and guarantee their success. And they have the contacts among investors to sell the bonds for the best price.

Financial Capital versus Capital in Economics

Financial capital should not be confused with the economics term capital. It's one of the four factors of production that drive supply. That includes capital goods, such as machinery, equipment, and tools.

The other three factors are:

- Natural resources, which are the raw materials.
- Entrepreneurship or the drive to profit from innovation.
- Labor, which refers to the number of employees. Labor includes human capital, which is the skills and abilities of people. Social capital is the value of a network of people.

A market economy automatically provides these components of supply to meet demand from consumers.

Sometimes financial capital is called the fifth factor of production, although that's not exactly accurate. It facilitates production by providing income to the owners of production, but it is not itself a factor of production.

Debt Financing

Debt financing is when a company raises money by taking out a loan and then repays that loan over time with interest. This is also known as borrowing on credit.

Debt financing is when a company raises money by taking out a loan and then repays that loan over time with interest. This is also known as borrowing on credit. It can come from selling bonds, bills, or notes to lending institutions, or from private investors who are not looking to receive equity in your business.

It's good to be aware of the fact that banks often shy away from small businesses that are experiencing rapid sales growth, a temporary decline or a seasonal slump. They are not completely stable.

Sources of Debt Financing

Small businesses can get debt financing from several different sources:

Private Sources

A lot of startups borrow money from friends and family. People that are close to you are much more likely to give flexible terms of repayment. They are also more willing to invest their money into a business that may not be fully developed yet.

A disadvantage is that friends and family may want to be more involved in the management or decision-making than a bank or investor may be. If you want to avoid these sort of situations, it may be best to make formal arrangements with your family before any money changes hands.

Banks are also a private source of debt financing. Large commercial banks will often have more experience in making business loans than small savings banks. Credit unions can also be a good source for business loans. Credit unions are there to assist members of a group, like employees of a company or members of a labor union. They will usually give more favorable terms than banks.

Finance companies will charge higher interest rates than banks and credit unions. They also usually want you to put assets up as collateral in addition to paying interest on the loan. This is the best option for people with poor credit ratings.

Trade credit is another type of debt financing. Trade credit is when a supplier lets a small business delay their payment on some of the products or services it buys from the supplier. Payment terms will differ between the suppliers.

Another type of debt financing is when a factoring company helps small businesses to free up cash. They do this by purchasing that company's accounts receivable. Once the small business is paid their invoices, they can then repay the factoring company.

Similarly, leasing companies can also help small businesses to free up cash. They small business can rent different types of equipment instead of having to make a huge capital expenditure to purchase it. The payments are usually only small monthly installments, and they allow the small business to upgrade the equipment quickly and easily.

Public Sources

The state and federal governments sponsor a large number of programs that give funding to help with the formation and growth of small businesses.

Small Business Investment Companies (SBICs) are another source for public debt financing. They are government-backed companies that give direct loans or equity investments to small businesses. They are usually less risk-averse than banks, so funds are more available to startup companies. They also often are able to give technical assistance to small business borrowers.

Debt Financing Repayment Terms

There are three main types of repayment terms for debt financing, long-term, intermediate, and short-term:

- Long-term debt financing is usually for purchasing assets for the company like equipment, buildings, land, or machinery. The repayment of these loans and the usefulness of the asset that you've purchased will last for more than five years.
- Intermediate debt financing loans are for medium-sized purchases and may help the company grow. They are to be paid back within three years.
- Short-term debt financing is usually for day-to-day spending. You might use a short-term loan for buying inventory, paying wages, or purchasing supplies. These loans are short-term because the repayment will take less than a year. A popular form of short-term debt financing is a credit card.

Interest Rates on Debt Financing

The interest rate you will receive on your debt financing will depend on current rates as well as your credit score. The more of a risk that the bank thinks you are, the higher the interest rate will be.

Advantages of using Debt Financing

- Keeping control of your business: When you take out a loan for your business, the person lending the money has no say in the running of your company. You remain the decision maker and simply pay back your debt.
- Gaining tax benefits: The amount of money you pay in interest is tax deductible, therefore reducing the amount paid overall.

Disadvantages of using Debt Financing

- You use your business as collateral: If you default on the repayment of your loan, you put your business in direct danger of being lost: You may also be asked to put your personal finances and assets up as collateral for your business, which is a very big risk.
- It can make it difficult to grow: Being locked into a loan repayment means that you have a priority to make payments every single month. This means that you may not have the money left over to grow and expand your business.
- It affects your credit rating: If your business relies too heavily on debt financing, it could negatively affect your credit and the ability to get additional loans in the future.

Secured versus Unsecured Loans

Most loans you receive will need to be secured. Meaning, you will need to put up some type of collateral in case you cannot repay the loan. If you default on the loan, the lender will take your collateral as repayment.

There are several ways you can secure a loan:

- Guarantors: You can have someone else with a better credit rating or more assets sign an agreement stating they will pay the loan in case you cannot.
- Endorsers: Similar to guarantors, endorsers promise to pay the loan, but they also post some form of collateral.
- Accounts receivable: You promise to give the bank 65 to 80 percent of the receivables' value of the products that you sell as soon as they ship or are purchased from your store.
- Equipment: Any equipment you have can provide 60 to 65 percent of its value as collateral.

Securities: If you are a publicly held company, you can offer stocks and bonds as collateral for re-paying the loan.

- Real estate: Any property, either commercial or private, that is owned by the company can be counted on for up to 90 percent of its assessed value and used as collateral on the loan.

- Savings accounts or certificate of deposit: Any business or personal accounts can also be used as collateral for the loan.
- Chattel mortgage: If you use any equipment that you own as collateral, the lender makes a loan based on something less than the equipment's present value and holds a mortgage on it until the loan is repaid.
- Insurance policies: Any personal or business insurance policies can be considered collateral for up to 95 percent of the policy's cash value.
- Warehouse inventory: If you hold inventory then this can usually secure up to only 50 percent of the loan.
- Display merchandise: Any additional display merchandise or equipment that you have such as furniture, cars, or home electronics can be used to secure loans through what's known as "floor planning."

Equity Financing

Equity can mean a variety of things, but it generally means how much of something you own after you have paid off any money that you owe to others (debt). In accounting terms, equity is represented with the equation:

Equity = Assets – Liabilities

However, in the startup world, equity usually refers to two specific things:

- Venture Capital Financing – Giving a company a piece of your company in exchange for getting money from them today.
- Equity compensation – To get better workers, a startup may offer stock options as a source of additional income. These options may be used at a later date and the worker gets cash.

Importance of Equity

Equity is important because it has value. Think about equity like a pizza. If you have a pizza you own 100 percent of that pizza. If someone else has something you want, you can swap a piece, a quarter or a half of that pizza for that item. This is a simple way of explaining what happens with equity financing or when you use equity as a form of pay. In effect, you give away stock options in exchange for something else you value. That means you no longer have 100 percent of the equity in your company.

Value of Equity Financing

The good news is you can take a piece of your pizza and get something you want. With equity financing, you can exchange a piece of your company in return for cash. While you now own less of your company, you gained cash that you do not have a legal obligation to pay back to your investors (debt).

The value of this money can be significant. If you are trying to grow your company, you need money. Money buys new equipment, allows you to hire new staff and allows investment in whatever you think will make your company better.

Getting cash in exchange for equity also has other benefits. Venture capital firms have a percentage of ownership in your business which means they may give you opinions on different issues that can be very helpful to your business.

Equity Financing Pitfalls

Giving an employee a stock option does change your equity. However, that doesn't mean your employee can tell you how to run the business. This isn't always true with venture capital money. The company may want to have a say in how your business runs. The person who provides you with cash may also want some of the money you make from your business.

Difference between Equity Financing and Debt Financing

Some businesses believe a bank loan is better than equity financing. Debt financing may be an option but has certain hidden traps. What you owe is more and therefore your equity is worth less. What happens is you owe more money. Since you now have additional debt, your equity has less value:

(Assets) $60,000 - $8,000 (Liabilities) = $52,000 (100 percent equity)

With $20,000 debt financing it will look like this:

(Assets) $60,000 - $28,000 (Liabilities) = $32,000 (100 percent equity)

Here's how debt and equity financing compare:

Debt Financing	Equity Financing
• You borrow money from a bank or private lender.	• A company provides cash in return for equity in your business.
• You can use the money any way you want.	• Often the money comes with strings attached.
• You keep the equity in your company but you owe the money you borrowed. The payments may be difficult if you have any cash flow issues.	• The money you get is paid back over a long term. The terms of your agreement determine if you get any of your equity back when you're done making payments.
• The bank only cares they get their payments on time.	• The money you get also helps with your business.

Convertible Debt Financin

There is another option that is not often discussed. This is an option where you get money today and at a later date, the investor gets equity. This is also known as a convertible loan. This option may be offered by investors if they believe your company will have a higher value in the future. The way this works is simple: the investor gives you cash and you agree to exchange that cash for equity at a date decided ahead of time. You should always discuss this option carefully with a lawyer before agreeing to this type of financing.

When should you Consider Equity Financing?

If you need money to grow your business, you can think about equity financing. There are times when it is helpful and necessary; for example:

- You don't have a good credit record – any marks against your credit can stop you from getting a loan.
- When you need outside help – if you need help that you can't afford to hire, an equity investor is usually a better idea than taking on debt.
- Concerns about payments – bank loans have to be paid back monthly. Failing to do so could put your company out of business. Equity partners are looking for long-term not short-term gains.

What happens when you use Equity Financing?

Simply put, you get money and the company gets equity. Going back to the pizza, you give up a few slices of pizza for the cash you need. You have less equity but now you have cash and that means the total equity is more. Think about the equation we used above.

Let's say it starts out like this:

> (Assets) $60,000 - $8,000 (Liabilities) = $52,000 (100 percent equity)
>
> With $20,000 equity financing it will look like this:
>
> (Assets) $80,000 – $8,000 (Liabilities) = $72,000 (100 percent equity)
>
> With $20,000 debt financing it will look like this:
>
> (Assets) $60,000 - $28,000 (Liabilities) = $32,000 (100 percent equity)

Assuming you have given away 25 percent equity in return for the money you got, your equity would be $54,000 (75 percent of $72,000). This is more equity than you had at the start and nearly half of what you would have if you took out a loan.

Avoiding Common Equity Financing Mistakes

When you need money to grow your business you can make mistakes. You can avoid equity financing mistakes by making sure of the following:

- You keep great records – Your business records should be current and accurate. An equity investor will want to make sure your company has value before they give you money.
- You understand the time it takes – You have to be aware that equity financing can take a while. This is important because it impacts your business. In general, it's a good idea to start at least three to six months before you need money.
- You don't expect something for nothing – Your time has value but if a venture capital firm does not see that you've spent money to keep your business going, they may not wish to invest in your business. Going back to the pizza story, if someone gave you a pizza, you own it. However, if you bought the pizza, you have the same pizza but you have given something in return.

- Find the right investor – Venture capital companies often restrict where they invest. You wouldn't ask someone who invested in high-tech companies to give cash to a company that does construction.
- Don't try to do it yourself – If you're not a lawyer and an accountant, don't try to negotiate with a venture capital firm on your own.

Before you get involved in equity financing, work with an attorney. Find an attorney who understands small business and equity financing. A lawyer can help you from the beginning of the process until the end.

Cost of Capital

Cost of capital refers to the weighted average cost of various capital components, i.e. sources of finance, employed by the firm such as equity, preference or debt. In finer terms, it is the rate of return that must be received by the firm on its investment projects, to attract investors for investing capital in the firm and to maintain its market value.

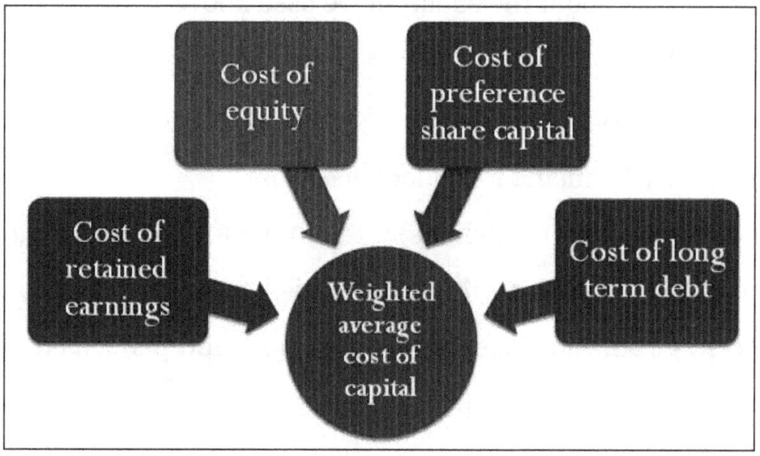

The factors which determine the cost of capital are:

- Source of finance
- Corresponding payment for using finance.

On raising funds from the market, from various sources, the firm has to pay some additional amount, apart from the principal itself. The additional amount is nothing but the cost of using the capital, i.e. cost of capital which is either paid in lump sum or at periodic intervals.

Classification of Cost of Capital

1. Explicit cost of capital: It is the cost of capital in which firm's cash outflow is oriented towards utilisation of capital which is evident, such as payment of dividend to the shareholders, interest to the debenture holders, etc.
2. Implicit cost of capital: It does not involve any cash outflow, but it denotes the opportunity foregone while opting for another alternative opportunity.

To cover the cost of raising funds from the market, cost of capital must be obtained. It helps in assessing firm's new projects because it is the minimum return expected by the shareholders, lenders and debtholders for supplying capital to the business, as a consideration for their share in the total capital. Hence, it establishes a benchmark, which must be met out by the project.

However, if a firm is incapable of reaping the expected rate of return, the value of shares in the market will tend to decline, which will lead to the reduction in the wealth of the shareholders as a whole.

Importance of Cost Capital

- It helps in evaluating the investment options, by converting the future cash flows of the investment avenues into present value by discounting it.
- It is helpful in capital budgeting decisions regarding the sources of finance used by the company.
- It is vital in designing the optimal capital structure of the firm, wherein the firm's value is maximum, and the cost of capital is minimum.
- It can also be used to appraise the performance of specific projects by comparing the performance against the cost of capital.
- It is useful in framing optimum credit policy, i.e. at the time of deciding credit period to be allowed to the customers or debtors, it should be compared with the cost of allowing credit period.

Cost of capital is also termed as cut-off rate, the minimum rate of return, or hurdle rate.

Capital Surplus

A capital surplus is the additional paid-in capital in excess of par value that an investor pays when buying shares from an issuing entity. This amount represents the difference between the market value of shares and their par value. The term is is no longer commonly used; instead, the concept is now called additional paid-in capital in the accounting literature.

Par value was originally the price at which a company's shares were initially offered for sale, so that prospective investors could be assured that the company would not issue shares at a price below the par value. However, par value is no longer required by some states; in other states, companies are allowed to set the par value at a minimal amount, such as $0.01 per share. The result is that nearly all of the price paid for a share of stock is recorded as additional paid-in capital (or capital surplus, to use the older term). If a company issues shares that have no stated par value at all, then there is no capital surplus; instead, the funds are recorded in the common stock account.

For example, if ABC Company were to sell 100 shares of its $1 par value common stock for $9 per share, it would record $100 of the $900 in total proceeds in the Common Stock account and $800 in the Additional Paid-in Capital account. In earlier days, the $800 entry to the Additional Paid-In Capital account would instead have been made to the Capital Surplus account.

Thus, if the capital surplus term were still used, a company would acquire a capital surplus by selling its stock to investors at a price above the designated par value of the stock, with the incremental amount above the par value being identified as capital surplus.

Capital Expenditure

A capital expenditure is the use of funds or assumption of a liability in order to obtain or upgrade physical assets. The intent is for these assets to be used for productive purposes for at least one year. This type of expenditure is made in order to expand the productive or competitive posture of a business. Examples of capital expenditures are funds paid out for buildings, computer equipment, machinery, office equipment, vehicles, and software. An example of an asset upgrade is adding a garage onto a house, since it increases the value of the property, whereas repairing a dishwasher merely keeps the machine in operation. Capital expenditures tend to be quite substantial in certain industries, such as utilities and manufacturing.

A capital expenditure is recorded as an asset, rather than charging it immediately to expense. It is classified as a fixed asset, which is then charged to expense over the useful life of the asset, using depreciation. For example, if you acquire a $25,000 asset and expect it to have a useful life of five years, then charge $5,000 to depreciation expense in each of the next five years. The asset is initially recorded in the balance sheet, while the periodic depreciation charges against it appear in the income statement.

Since there is a record keeping cost associated with capital expenditures, these items are generally charged to expense if they cost less than a certain predetermined limit, which is known as the capitalization limit. For example, if a company's capitalization limit is $2,000, then a computer costing $1,999 would be charged to expense in the period incurred, whereas it would be recorded as a fixed asset if it cost $2,001.

The reverse of a capital expenditure is an operational expenditure, where the cost is incurred strictly for current operations. Always charge operational expenditures to expense when incurred. Since they are charged to expense in the period incurred, they are also known as period costs.

From a financial analysis perspective, a business should at least maintain its historical level of capital expenditures. Otherwise, it will be suspected that management is not adequately reinvesting in the organization, which will eventually lead to a decline in the business.

Inventory

Inventory, often called merchandise, refers to goods and materials that a business holds for sale to customers in the near future.

In other words, these goods and materials serve no other purpose in the business except to be sold to customers for a profit. They are not used in the produce things or promote the business. The sole purpose of these current assets is to sell them to customers for a profit, but just because an asset is for sale doesn't mean that it's considered inventory. We need to look at three main characteristics of inventory to determine whether an asset should be accounted for as merchandise.

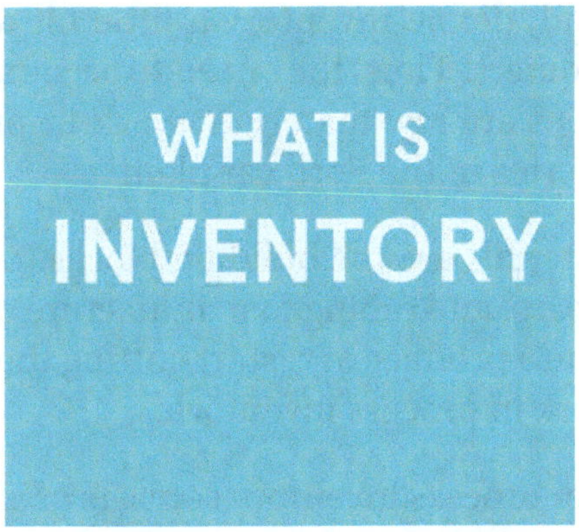

First, the assets must be part of the company's primary business. For instance, a sandwich shop's delivery truck is not considered inventory because it has nothing to do with the primary business of making and selling sandwiches. This is considered a fixed asset for the sandwich shop. To a car dealership, on the other hand, this truck would be considered inventory because they are in the business of selling vehicles.

Second, the assets must be available for sale or will soon be ready to sell. If some business assets could be sold but are never actually made available for sale, they aren't inventory. These are just assets or investments of the company.

Third, the purpose of owning the assets must be to sell them to customers. Going back to our sandwich shop example, the truck was never meant to be sold to a customer. It was purchased to deliver sandwiches and was sold when it couldn't perform that job. The car dealership, on the other hand, purchases vehicles for the sole purpose of reselling them. Thus, the truck is considered inventory to them.

These characteristics can be applied to all businesses in all industries, so if you ever unsure what should be included or not just remember this inventory template.

Types of Inventory

According to our inventory definition, there are many different types of inventory and each is accounted for slightly differently. Retailers are the easiest to account for because they typically only have one kind of goods called merchandise. They purchase it from wholesalers or manufacturers as finished products to sell to their customers.

Manufacturers, on the other hand, define inventory a little bit differently because they produce their own products to sell to customers. Thus, they need to account for the inventory at every stage of production. The three categories are raw materials, work-in-process, and finished goods. Let's take a look at each of these categories in the Ford car plant:

- Raw materials – Raw materials are the building blocks to make finished goods. Ford purchases sheet metal, steel bars, and tubing to manufacture car frames and other parts. When they put these materials into produce and start cutting the bars and shaping the metal, the raw materials become work in process inventories.
- Work in process – Work in process inventory consists of all partially finished products that a manufacturer produces. As the unfinished cars make their way down the assembly line, they are considered a work-in-progress until they are finished.
- Finished goods – Finished goods are exactly what they sound like. These are the finished products that can be sold to wholesalers, retailers, or even the end users. In Ford's case, they are finished cars that are ready to be sent to dealers.

Each of these different categories is important and managing them is key to any business' survival. Inventory control is one of the most important concepts for any business especially retailers. Since they purchase goods from manufacturers and resell them to consumers at small margins, they have to manage their purchasing and control the amount of cash that is tied up in merchandise.

Recording Inventory in Accounting

There are many different methods that can be used to record the cost of inventory, but first let's take a look at what each business attributes to the cost.

When retailers purchase goods from wholesalers or manufacturers, they record the price that they paid for the goods. This includes sales tax, delivery fees, and any other fees associated with receiving the goods.

Manufacturers, however, must include all the of the production costs and any other cost like packaging that is necessary to make the inventory ready for sale.

Businesses typically use one of two different accounting systems to keep track of their goods: periodic and perpetual.

The periodic inventory system is simple and only requires an inventory spreadsheet to keep track of sales and goods remaining in stock. Basically, a count is performed periodically throughout the year to see what was sold and what was left. Although this is a very simple way to keep track of merchandise, it has many downsides.

The perpetual inventory system is a highly sophisticated system that keeps tracks of goods as they are purchased and sold in real time using a bar code scanner and computer system. This is far more accurate than a period system and far more costly.

Financial Statement Presentation Example

Inventory is reported on the balance sheet as a current asset. It's typically presented right after cash and accounts receivable. Retailers typically only list one type of merchandise on their balance sheet whereas manufacturers tend to list the three different categories of inventory separately.

Using the FIFO, LIFO, or the weighted average costing method, cost is assigned to the inventory that was sold during the year and is reported as cost of goods sold on the income statement.

Inventory Management Example

Good inventory management is what sets successful retailers apart from unsuccessful ones. Controlling purchasing and evaluating turns helps management understand what they need to stock and what they need to get rid of. It also helps them become more profitable.

Management uses the inventory turnover and the margin ratios to measure the earnings from each piece of merchandise and stock items that will produce more profits for the company. Investors and creditors also look at these ratios as a health indicator of the company.

For instance, a retailer with low turns and high margins is a normal. A retailer with low turns and low margins might indicate the company isn't doing well.

Bill of Exchange

A bill of exchange is a written and unconditional order issued by the drawer (the seller of goods/services) and addressed to the drawee (the buyer) to pay a certain sum, either immediately (a sight bill) or on a fixed date (a term bill) to a specified person (usually the drawer himself) or to the bearer of the bill.

A bill of exchange can be payable to bearer or payable to order:

- Payable to bearer means payable to the holder or presenter. When a bill of exchange is payable to bearer, it means whoever holds the bill can receive the payment due on it.
- Payable to order (or payable to the order of) means the drawee is agreeing after signature that he will repay the money to the drawer or the person the drawer designates to receive the payments. With this mention, the drawer can later request the drawee to make the payment to another person / company that the drawer owes money to. A bill of exchange payable to order gives the drawer or bearer flexibility in designating who will receive the funds.

Unlike promissory notes, Bills of exchange are used almost exclusively in trade. If a bill is issued by a bank, it is referred to as a bank draft. If it is issued by an individual, it is usually referred to as trade draft.

Contents of a Bill of Exchange

- Drawer of the bill of exchange: This is the individual or entity (company) that issues the bill and gives order to pay the sum of money. Name and address must be mentioned.
- Drawee / Payor of the bill of exchange: This is the person upon whom the bill of exchange is drawn and who accepts and pays the bill. Name and address are generally requested.
- Payee of the bill of exchange: This is the person to whom the payment is made. Name and address are generally requested. The Drawer and the Payee is usually the same person.
- Creation date and place of the bill of exchange: The date and place where the bill of exchange is created.
- Amount of the bill of exchange: The sum of money that the payee will receive must be clearly featured on the document. The amount is usually given both in figures and words.
- Term of the bill of exchange: Also called tenure or maturity of the bill, it is the date on which the bill is to be paid. It should be specified in the body of the bill. In certain countries, a grace period of few days is given after the expiry of the term. If the exact due date is not explicitly indicated on the bill, information should be available allowing to calculate the term. If a bill of exchange is payable after two months, then it means 60 days after it was issued.
- For Value Received: In certain countries, this aspect is crucial in the sense that law does not consider those agreements which have been made without consideration. Consideration refers to the context in which the bill of exchange was issued. It means the bill is drawn in exchange of some benefit that has already been received.
- Drawer's signature: The drawer must to sign or stamp his signature after the drafting or drawing of the bill of exchange. A bill of exchange that does not have an authentic signature is considered null and is not eligible for the payment. The signature (handwritten or electronic) is the binding force of the bill of exchange.

A bill of exchange that is not correctly completed might cause problems. Among others, the delay of payment or the impossibility to discount. A correctly completed bill of exchange is essential and it is recommended to use forms that banks provide for that purpose.

Below is an example of a simple specimen of a bill of exchange.

<table>
<tr><td>Place of issue</td><td>Date of issue</td></tr>
<tr><td>Pay against this Bill of Exchange</td><td>Maturity date</td></tr>
<tr><td>To the order of Payee's Name</td><td>Currency and Amount in figures</td></tr>
<tr><td colspan="2">Currency and Amount in words</td></tr>
<tr><td>Drawee's name and address</td><td>Drawer's name, address and signature</td></tr>
<tr><td>Accepted</td><td>Date of acceptance</td></tr>
</table>

Example of a simple Bill of exchange.

Additional elements might be added if relevant for the situation, but the drawer must ensure that all mandatory information is featured on the note.

Parties Involved in a Bill of Exchange

Bills of exchange are negotiable instruments that involve three main parties: the drawer, the drawee and the payee. But depending on how it used, other parties listed below might be involved too. In this paragraph, we will see when the different parties come in and which role they play:

- Drawer: The person who makes the bill and gives the order to pay a certain sum of money.
- Drawee: The person who is directed to pay a certain sum.
- Payee: The person receiving payment is called the payee. It is the drawer himself in the vast majority of the cases, but can be a designated person too.
- Acceptor: The person who accepts the bill. The drawee is normally the acceptor but a third person can accept a bill on behalf of the drawee.
- Bearer: The person who is in possession of a bill of exchange. He is also called the holder. The bearer and the payee is usually the same person.
- Endorser: The person who endorses a bill of exchange.
- Endorsee: The person in whose favor the bill of exchange is endorsed and who receives it after endorsement. He becomes the new bearer and payee after endorsement.

Now let us consider the different parties and when they step in from the time the bill of exchange is written and issued. We begin with the drawer, the drawee and the payee.

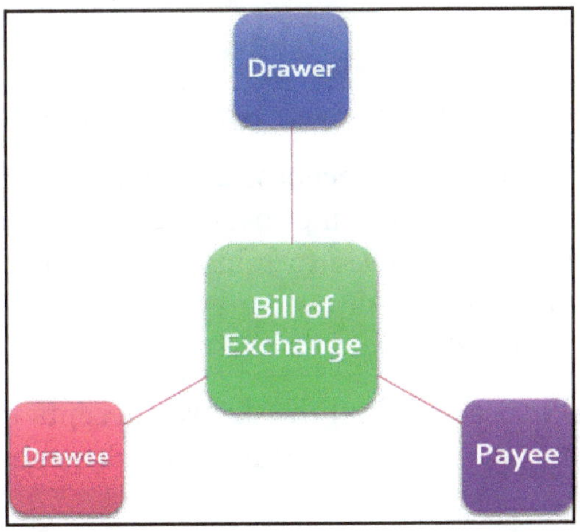

Three main parties involved in a bill of exchange

- Drawer: It is the person who makes the bill and orders the drawee to pay a certain sum of money to the payee. The drawer generally issues the bill as part of a domestic or international commercial transaction to receive payment for value delivered.
- Drawee: The drawee is the other main party involved in the bill of exchange. He is directed to pay for goods or services received from the drawer.

- Payee: The creditor of the bill of exchange is called the payee. Since the drawer is the one who delivers value to the payee, he is also the one who is entitled to receive the money. This explains why the drawer and the payee are the same unless the drawer requests the payee to pay to another party.

The bill of exchange is therefore an order to pay and requires acceptance to be valid. By acceptance, the drawee engages himself to pay the amount from the bill of exchange to the person who will bear or hold it on the due term.

Acceptance of a Bill of Exchange

After drawing the bill of exchange, the first thing the drawer does, is to present it to the drawee for acceptance. Unless it is accepted, the bill is not valid.

The drawee (or someone representing him) accepts the drawer's bill of exchange by writing a date and signing under the words 'accepted' on face of the bill. If the bill of exchange does not contain the phrase "accepted on", the drawee can write it himself if necessary (For example for bills payable after certain events). The signature is enough for acceptance. If there is no acceptance date, the bill is supposed to have been accepted on the day of issue.

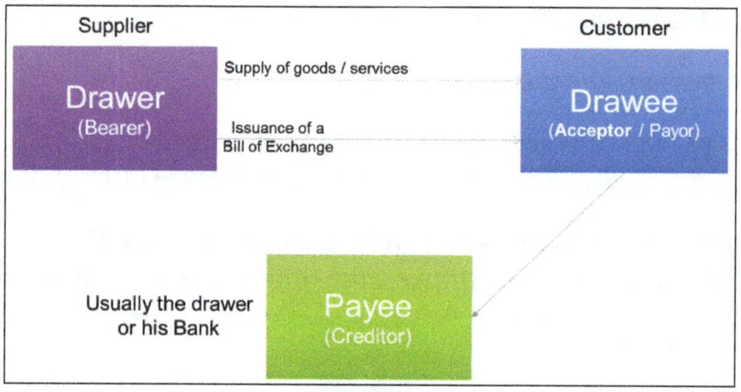

The acceptor of the bill of exchange is most of the time the drawee.

After acceptance, the drawee becomes the acceptor and engages himself to unconditionally pay the bill on or before its maturity date. The bill of exchange becomes a legal document only after acceptance. This document binds the drawee to honour the bill on due date. An acceptance is unconditional, but in certain countries the drawee may restrict it to part of the sum payable. The acceptance may be general or qualified:

- General Acceptance: This occurs when the drawee accepts the liability on the instrument without any condition and limitation on the amount. So general acceptance is unconditional and unqualified.
- Qualified Acceptance: When the acceptor puts some condition while accepting the instrument, the acceptance is said to be qualified. The acceptor can put only conditions that are legally allowed.

Once the bill of exchange is accepted, the drawee returns it to the drawer and bearer. And the bearer now has many options to choose between the following:

1. Wait until maturity and present the bill of exchange for payment.

2. Negotiate the bill of exchange to another person.
3. Receive a short term finance by performing a discounting of the bill of exchange.
4. Receive a short term finance by performing a factoring of the bill of exchange.

Endorsement of a Bill of Exchange

The second option consists for the drawer to endorse the bill of exchange and deliver it to another party. Endorsement requires to sign the bill and optionally to put words qualifying that act on it. The drawer, who then uses the bill as a financial instrument, becomes the endorser and the party receiving the bill is the endorsee, the new holder of the bill of exchange. He is also called the holder in due course. Below is a figure showing what happens. We assume in this and the following pictures that the drawer and the payee are the same.

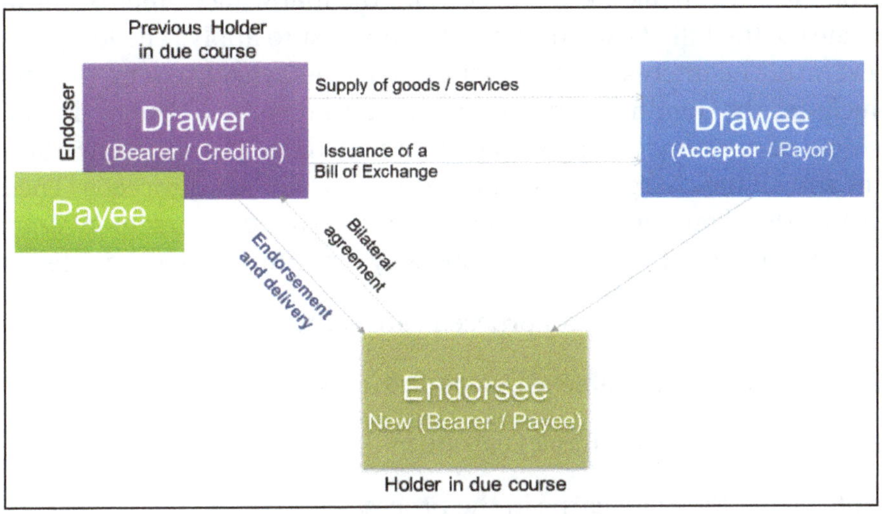

Endorsement of a bill of exchange.

There are several reasons for the drawer (first holder) to negotiate the bill of exchange to another party. He may have a debt with that party that he wants to resolve. He may agree with the next party to negotiate the note in exchange of a sum of money. The negotiation is done to fix a financial problem. Otherwise, it is of no interest.

The negotiation process can happen as many time as needed. There is no limit to the number of endorsements that may be made on a bill of exchange. The endorser is not obliged to inform the initial drawer or any previous party that the bill has been negotiated. At maturity, the holder in due course presents the bill of exchange to the drawee for payment.

Discounting of a Bill of Exchange

As third option, the drawer or any subsequent endorsees can choose to discount the bill of exchange. Discounting is the arrangement in which a bank grants a short term credit on the basis of a bill of exchange to his holder, for less than the value shown on it before it is due to be paid. The holder, after providing evidence that he is in possession of a bill of exchange, receives the bill of exchange amount less administrative charges, fees and interest. The holder uses the bill in this context as a credit instrument.

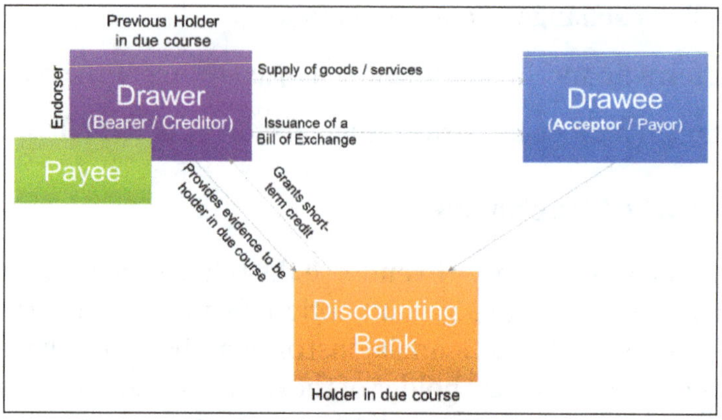

Discounting of a bill of exchange.

To compute the total fees, the bank takes into account the following elements: the amount and maturity date (due date) of the bill of exchange and the interest to apply. The longer the maturity, the higher the interest rate. The interest rate is referred to as the bank discount, or simply the discount rate. It usually includes the nominal interest rate and other charges. The period of discount is the period from the date of discount to the term or maturity date. The difference between the bill of exchange amount and all the charges, fees and interest is called the proceeds. The bank expects to receive the face value (total amount of the bill of exchange) as reimbursement amount at maturity date, generally in 30, 60 or 90 days. This explains why discounting is a short-term credit.

In general this is how Bank Discount and proceeds are computed:

- Bank Discount = Maturity Value × Discount Rate × Period of Discount.
- Proceeds = Maturity Value – Bank Discount.

The bank discount is what the bank earns in the process.

Note that unless agree otherwise with the discounting bank, the drawer (or any subsequent holder) remains responsible for collecting the bill of exchange amount after this arrangement. And in case the bill of exchange is dishonoured, the holder may get into big trouble, because he must pay back the credit to the bank anyway.

Factoring of a Bill of Exchange

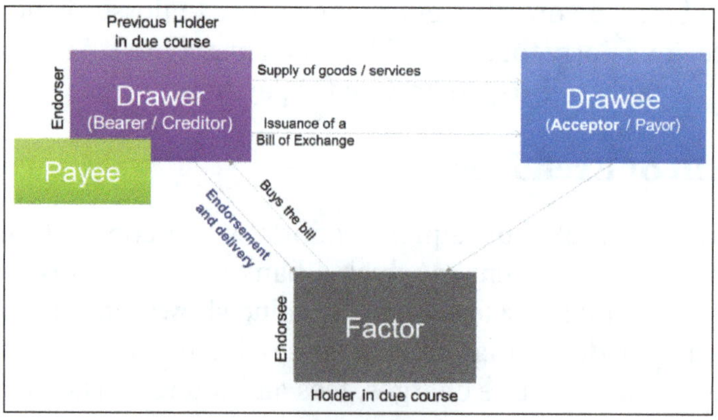

Factoring of a bill of exchange.

The last option listed above is the factoring agreement. Factoring means an arrangement between a factor and his client where the factor buys a debt from its client. In Factoring, accounts receivable are highly discounted in order to allow the buyer, the factor, to make a profit when the debt is settled later. Discount rate are much higher in factoring than in normal discounting. Factoring transfers the ownership of accounts receivable to the factor that then chases up the debt.

In factoring the drawer (or any subsequent holder) negotiates the bill of exchange to the factor. He is not responsible for collecting the bill of exchange amount anymore and therefore does not care that much if the bill of exchange is later dishonoured. The risk of non-payment (at maturity date) is completely transferred on the factor. That is why rates applied by factors are generally much higher than for those applied by discounting banks. And furthermore, the factor sometimes pays in two installments to limit own risks: one advance payment after the negotiation of the bill of exchange and a final payment when the face value is collected.

Dishonour of a Bill of Exchange

The bill of exchange, like any negotiable instruments, gives the holder a legal right of recourse against the endorsers and the drawer in case the bill is dishonoured. But the holder must undertake specific actions.

A bill of exchange is dishonoured by non-acceptance when the drawee refuses to accept and sign it. Unless there is something wrong with the content of the bill, acceptance is never a problem since the drawee does not have to pay immediately but only in one or many months. And even if the drawee has financial problems, he expects to fix them in the period between the acceptance date and the term. So he will sign the bill so that the other party does not become aware of his financial problems before the maturity of the bill.

If the bill is not accepted because the content is not right, the drawee will request the drawer to fix the content and then will sign the bill when he agrees with the content. A bill presented for acceptance when the drawee has been declared insolvent will be refused since the drawer is anyway unable to pay because of insolvency. If the drawee is dead, he obviously cannot accept the bill of exchange. A bill of exchange is dishonoured by non-payment when the drawee makes default in payment of the sum partially or totally.

When the bill is violated, the holder must give a sign or notice of dishonour to all the earlier parties to make them accountable. A notice of dishonor is simply a notice given by the holder of the bill of exchange to previous endorsers and to the drawee to inform them that bill has been dishonoured. Only after giving due notice of dishonour, the holder can sue the liable parties for the recovery of amount due on the instrument.

To provide a notice of dishonour, the holder takes the bill to a notary public who presents it again for acceptance or payment. In case the drawee refuses again, the notary public records the refusal on the bill. Thus 'noting' means recording the fact of dishonour on the dishonoured instrument or on a paper attached thereto for that purpose. It is recommended not to wait too long before doing noting. It should be done in the next 24 to 48 hours. Noting should specify the following on the instrument:

- Identification (Initials) of the notary;

- A minute indicating that the instrument has been dishonoured and why; if the instrument has not been expressly dishonoured, the reason, why it is being treated as dishonoured;
- The date of dishonour;
- The noting charges;
- The noting reference to the notary's register.

In certain cases, noting may not be suitable to sue the previous endorser(s) and the drawee. The holder can then request the Notary public to draw a certificate of protest or certificate of dishonor.

When a bill gets dishonored and a formal certificate of dishonor is issued by the Notary Public, the bill can still be accepted for honour. The *acceptor for honour* is a person who voluntarily becomes a party to a bill as acceptor, in the event of the refusal by original drawee, and accepts to pay the bill if requested by the notary. The acceptor *for* honor offers to accepts the bill with a view to safeguard the honor of the original drawer or any subsequent endorser.

Types of Bill of Exchange

Documentary Bill

Documentary commercial bills of exchange drawn upon firms or banks where documents are for payment cannot be discounted upon the market, as in the case of such bills where documents are for acceptance, for the reason that banks abroad to which bills are sent for collection will not undertake to discount commercial bills unless they are what is called "clean" bills - that is, those having no documents or those which permit the documents to be delivered when the draft is accepted by the drawee.

A documentary or commercial bill of exchange, accompanied by instructions from the exporter or drawer, to deliver documents (bill of lading, etc.) only upon payment of the draft by the importer or drawee, which are drawn upon a firm, are subject to a discount rate of 1 per cent. below the Bank of England official minimum discount rate. If the instructions are to deliver documents upon acceptance of the draft, the same rate of discount by the holder (bank) at 1/4 of 1 Percent. above the private discount rate of the day.

Documentary Acceptance and Documentary Payment Bills

When drafts are deliverable only upon acceptance, the draft is known as a documentary acceptance bill; when deliverable only upon payment, the draft is called a documentary payment bill. The major portion of English international banking business is to take up documentary drafts, either for acceptance on a commission basis or for collection.

Clean and Secured Bills of Exchange

Drafts known as clean bills, that is, those without documents attached, are issued usually against credit balances abroad. Such a bill, for example, is the bank's own draft drawn on any one of its foreign correspondents. Then there are so-called secured bills, drawn in connection with the sale of stocks and bonds, which may be shipped along- with the draft or forwarded under separate cover.

The last method is adopted, however, only when the credit standing of the drawee, the purchaser and the securities is best known.

Finance Bills

Frequently interest rates are lower in Europe than they are in the United States, and our international bankers are quick to take advantage of the opportunity for profit, which may be gained by borrowing funds there to be loaned out here. Suppose the rate for money in New York is quoted at five per cent. In London at that time bills of exchange may be discounted at three per cent. Under such circumstances, the New York banker will draw a bill of exchange for so many pounds sterling, the maturity of which bill is, say, sixty or ninety days, upon his London correspondent who agrees to accept the bill upon presentation. This is known as a "finance bill." The New York banker is enabled to discount this bill drawn on his London correspondent, in New York. The purchaser of the bill in New York would invariably have it discounted in London. For the funds to reach London before maturity, the New York bank would have to remit to his London "accepting" correspondent, a demand draft in payment of the finance bill.

Finance bills are used by banks very frequently, and they make up a large amount of the commercial paper offered on the London market. They are a means of profit to the banks, which can secure money by the discount of such paper, loaning out the funds so acquired at a higher rate than that at which finance bills discount.

Commercial Letters of Credit

Similar to the methods used, though more in the financing of American trade than that of England, is the "commercial letter of credit," which is an authorization to the shipper to draw on the bank, up to a stipulated amount, upon terms and conditions clearly expressed in such letter of credit, and which drafts so drawn the bank binds itself to either accept or to pay upon presentation. Here too, the bank is provided in advance with funds to take up the draft at maturity. For this service, the bank charges a round commission.

Advances on Consignments

English banks, as we have seen, make purchases of drafts or make partial or total advances. They also make advances on consignments of merchandise. Here, the signature of the drawer of the draft forms one part of the security and the goods form the other. The bank may turn over the goods to the firm, retaining a lien on such goods until the draft is paid, such lien being acknowledged in a "letter of hypothecation" given to the bank by the acceptors of the draft, stating that "such goods in the meantime, and the proceeds thereof, to be held by the firm in trust, on behalf of the bank, for the payment of said sum." Clauses as to insurance, sale, etc., are also continued in letters of hypothecation used in making advances on consignments.

The English banks, further, protect themselves from loss in the event the transaction results in unprofitableness to the parties concerned. A letter "of lien" or "of trust" provides that the firm "shall hold the said goods in trust on behalf of the bank, and have them duly stored, insured against fire, and remit the proceeds to the bank as and when sold. In such cases, when advancements on consignments are made by English banks, they may protect themselves in whatever way and by whatever means they think best, if this forms a part of the agreement with, and is acceptable by the firm.

Usance Bills

Usance bills are the bills payable by the drawee at a specified period 'after date' or 'after sight 'of the bill. The term 'after date' means the due date will be calculated from the date of the bill. The term 'after sight' means the due date will be calculated from the date of presentation of a bill for the acceptance of the drawee. A Usance bill shall be adequately stamped at the time when it is drawn as it attracts stamp duty which varies according to the value of the bill and usance period.

Advantages of Usance Bills

As a business strategy, the suppliers of goods like traders or manufacturing company may offer to sell their products to their clients on credit basis. The supplier of goods raises a bill of exchange expressed to be payable (i.e. 30/45/60/90/120 days etc.) after sight/ date of bills. The client on acceptance of such bills binds himself liable to make the payment of the bills at a fixed future date. The supplier of goods may present the accepted bills to his banker and request the bank to discount such bills so that he gets immediate money for the goods sold by him. The banks discount such bills if they hold reports on both supplier and client that both are of good financial standing. In the case of discounted bills, the drawer's liability is changed to that of a surety and acceptor of the bill is a principal debtor.

Accomodation Bill

Accommodation Bills are drawn and accepted with no consideration passed or received. The Bill, which is drawn just to oblige a friend, who is in need of money, of course without any trading activities, with sole intention of raising funds required for ready cash is known as Accommodation Bill.

The accommodating party, i.e., the drawee accepts the Bill drawn by the accommodated party (drawer). That is the Drawer of the accommodation bill can be called accommodated party and drawee can be called accommodating party. After the Bill is accepted, the drawer discounts it with a bank and obtains the cash.

Before the due date of the Bill, Drawer provides funds to the Acceptor, who honours the Bill. Since the acceptance is given without consideration and to help the accommodated party to raise the funds, the accommodated party has to discharge the Bill by himself or provide funds to accommodating party.

Thus, there is always a mutual understanding between the parties and hence, these bills are called Accommodation Bills. The language of an Accommodation Bill is the same as that of an ordinary Trade Bill. The modes of drawing, accepting, discounting, honoring etc. are similar to that of any Trade Bills. A banker cannot make distinction between a genuine Trade Bill and Accommodation bill. These Bills are also called "Kites" or "Finance Bills".

However, there is following distinction between the two:

Trade Bill	Accommodation bill
1. It is a real bill.	1. It is an imaginary bill.
2. Rightly used for financing.	2. Misused for raising a loan.
3. Drawer is a creditor.	3. Drawer is pretended creditor (really creditor is the real debtor).

4.	Drawer is a debtor.	4.	Drawer is a pretended debtor.(really a creditor).
5.	Valuable consideration is there by backing real transection.	5.	No valuable consideration is there because there is no backing of real transection.
6.	Bankers are wiling to buy such documents.	6.	Bankers are reluctant or unwilling to buy accommodation bills.
7.	Documents of title to goods are attached to the bill.	7.	No documents are attached because of no transection existed.

From accounting point of view, there is no difference between the Trade Bill and Accommodation Bill. Therefore, the rules and procedure of Accommodation Bill is the same as for a Trade Bill, except the reimbursement to the accommodating party by the accommodated party as their relation is that of lender and borrower.

Methods of Dealing with Accommodation Bill

There are three common methods of dealing with accommodation Bills and they are:

When one Party Accepts a Bill to Accommodate the Drawer Only

When a party, who is in urgent need of cash, approaches a business friend to raise funds through a bill of exchange. In such situation, the party, who needs cash, draws a Bill which is accepted by his friend, without any valuable consideration. The drawer can discount the Bill with a bank and the proceeds are used by him alone. At the time of maturity, the drawer pays the amount to the Acceptor, who honours the Bill.

Illustration:

Mr. A accepted a bill for $ 20,000 drawn by B to enable the latter to raise funds at three months on 1st October 2004. The bill was duly discounted by B at their Bank at 6% per annum. On the due date B remitted the amount to the acceptor and the Bill was duly met. Pass journal entries in the books of both the parties.

	B's journal			A's journal		
		$	$		$	$
2004 Oct.1	Bills receivable account Dr. To A Account (Being Bill drawn on A for 3 month)	20,000	 20,000	B Account Dr. To bills payable account (Being acceptance of Bill drawn by B)	20,000	 20,000
Oct 2	Cash Account Dr. Discount on bills account Dr. To Bills Receivable (Being Bill discounted) at 6% p.a)	19,700 300	 20,000	NO ENTRY		
2005 Jan 4	A Account Dr. To cash Account (Being amount paid to A to meet the bill on the due date)	20,000	 20,000	Cash Account Dr. To B Account (Being cash received from B to honour the Bill)	20,000	 20,000
Jan 4	NO ENTRY			Bills Payable Account To Cash Account (Being bill honoured on maturity)	20,000	 20,000

Discount: 20,000 x 6/100 x 3/12 = $ 300.

Where a Bill is Drawn for Mutual Benefit of Both the Parties

Sometimes an accommodation Bill is drawn and accepted for mutual benefit of the Drawer and Drawee. The Drawer draws a Bill and Drawee accepts it. The same Bill is discounted by the Drawer and an agreed portion of the proceeds is remitted to the Acceptor.

The discounting charge is also shared by both the parties in the same proportion in which the collection proceeds of the Bill were shared. Before the due date, the Drawer pays his share to the Acceptor, who meets the Bill by adding his share of money.

Illustration:

Mr. Ram draws a Bill for $ 15,000 on Mr. Gopal on 1st January payable three months after the date at Canada Bank, Ernakulum. The Bill after acceptance is discounted by Ram at 6% p.a. and he remits 1/3 of the proceeds to Gopal. On the due date, Ram sends the necessary amount to Gopal who meets the Bill.

Record these transactions in the journal of both the parties.

Solution:

	Ram's Journal		$	$	Gopal' Journal		$	$
Jan 1	Bills Receivable Account To Gopal Account (Being acceptance received from Gopal)	Dr.	15,000	15,000	Ram Account To Bills Payable Account (Being RAM'S bill accepted)	Dr.	15,000	15,000
	Cash Account Discount on Bills Account To bills Receivable Account (Being Bill discounted at 6% p.a)	Dr. Dr.	14,775 225	15,000	NO ENTRY			
	Gopal Account To Discount on Bills Account To Cash Account (Being 1/3 of proceeds and 1/3 of discount charges transferred)	Dr.	5,000	75 4,925	Cash Account Discount on bills account To Ram Account (Being 1/3 of proceeds and1/3 of discount Charge transferred)	Dr. Dr.	4,925 75	5,000
April 4	Gopal Account To Cash Account (2/3 of the bill sent to Gopal who met the Bill)	Dr.	10,000	10,000	Cash Account To ram Account (Being 2/3 contribution received from Ram)	Dr.	10,000	15,000
	NO ENTRY				Bills payable account To Cash Account (Being Bill paid on maturity)	Dr.	15,000	15,000

Where the two Parties, each Drawing a Bill

There are two parties to a Bill-the Drawer and the Drawee. Both these parties draw each a Bill of equal amount or different amount on the other. Both the parties are in need of money. For instance, Mr. A draws a Bill on Mr. B for $ 1,000 and Mr. B draws a Bill on Mr. A for $ 1,000. Both

A and B discount their Bills with a Bank to meet their financial needs. They bear charges of their respective Bills. Both the parties honour their acceptances on the due date.

Illustration (Two Bills of Equal Value)

Mr. A drew a Bill on B on November 1st, 2004 for an amount $ 4,000 payable three months after that date. On the very same date Mr. A accepted a Bill for $ 4,000 drawn by B for a period of three months. Both the parties discounted their Bills at 12% p.a. On the due date both the Bills were honoured. Make journal entries in the books of both the parties.

A's Journal				B's Journal		
		$	$	$	$	$
2004 Nov 1	Bill Receivable A/c Dr. To B A/c (Being acceptance of B received)	4,000	 4,000	A A/c Dr. To Bills payable A/c (Being acceptance given to A)	4,000	 4,000
	B A/c Dr. To Bills Payable A/c (Being acceptance given to B)	4,000	 4,000	Bill Receivable A/c Dr. To A A/c (Being acceptance received from A)	4,000	 4,000
	Cash A/C Dr. Discount on Bills A/c To Bills Receivable A/c (Being discounting of Bill at 12% p.a)	3,880 120	 4,00	NO ENTRY		 4,000
	NO ENTRY			Cash A/C Dr. Discount on Bills A/c To Bills Receivable A/c (Being discounting of Bill at 12% 9 a)	3,880 120	 4,000
Feb 4	Bill Payable A/c Dr. To cash A/c (Being the Bill is met)	4,000	 4,00	NO ENTRY		
	NO ENTRY			Bills Payable A/c Dr. To Cash A/c (Being the bill is met)	4,000	 4,000

Fictitious Bill

When the name of the drawer or payee or both are fictitious, the bill is called a fictitious bill . The word 'fictitious' means (i) a non-existing person and (ii) a pretended person, i.e., a person other than the actual person intended by the parties. Where a bill is drawn in the name of a fictitious person and payable to the drawer's order, the acceptor is liable to pay to the order of the person who signed it as drawer.

Therefore, the endorsee can recover the amount as against the acceptor provided he is in a position to show that the signature of the supposed drawer of the bill and the first endorsement on it are in the handwriting of the same person. In case of fictitious instruments, only a holder in due course can recover the money as against the acceptor.

Hundis

A hundi, though a negotiable instrument, is not necessarily a bill of exchange as defined in the Act per se. For example, contrary to the Act, if the custom or usage in a particular area or part of the country allows interest on hundis drawn and payable for as many days after sight, it would be recognized as lawful.

Forms or Types of Hundis

The following are some of the popular forms of hundis:

- Darshani hundi
- Shahjog hundi
- Dhanijog hundi
- Jawabee hundi
- Firmanjog hundi
- Miadi hundi
- Namjog hundi
- Jokhmi hundi
- Zikri hundi.

1. Darshani hundi: A hundi payable at sight is called darshani hundi. It is negotiable and is like a demand bill. It may be sold at par or at premium or at discount. A darshani hundi should be presented for payment within a reasonable time of its receipt by the holder. If the drawer suffers a loss due to delay in presentment, holder shall be responsible for it.

2. Miadi hundi: Also known as muddati hundi, miadi hundi is one which is payable after a specified period of time like a 'time bill'. Banks usually provide loans against the security of such hundis.

3. Shahjog hundi: This is a hundi made payable only to a Shah (a respectable person of financial worth and substance in the market). It may be miadi or darshani and can be transferred freely from one person to another by mere delivery but it is not payable to bearer. In some respects it is similar to a crossed cheque.

4. Namjog hundi: It is a hundi payable to the party named in the hundi or his order. Such a hundi is similar to a bill of exchange payable to order.

5. Dhanijog hundi: 'Dhani' in vernacular language means owner. Thus, a dhanijog hundi is one which is made payable to the owner, or a holder or bearer-owner. It is just like a bearer cheque and the holder of it becomes holder in due course if he takes it bona fide and for value.

6. Jokhmi hundi: The term 'Jokhmi' has been derived from the Hindi word 'jokhim' meaning 'risk'. Such a hundi is usually drawn against goods shipped on a vessel and implies a certain risk involved in the shipment of goods. Jokhmi hundi, in fact, is a combination of bill of exchange and insurance policy and payable only when the goods arrive in safe and sound condition. If the goods are lost in transit, the

consignor cannot claim payment of the hundi from the consignee, i.e., the drawee. Thus, a jokhmi hundi safeguards the interests of both, consignor and the consignee. It acts as a bill of exchange if the goods arrive safely and if the goods are lost or destroyed en route, such a bill works like an insurance coverage

7. Jawabee hundi: A hundi, which is in the form of letter or recommendation to a banker for payment of a certain sum of money to a specified person, is termed as jawabi hundi.

8. Zikri hundi: This is a hundi accepted for honour in writing on a Zikri chit (letter of protection) without being protested. It is drawn in the name of a specified person residing in the town or city where the hundi is payable. In case, acceptance is refused by the drawee or when a refusal is likely to occur, the hundi is furnished to the holder by some prior party to it.

9. Firmanjog hundi: The term Firman refers to order in vernacular language and therefore, a firmanjog hundi is made payable to the order of payee. It is just opposite of dhanijog hundi which is payable to the bearer only.

Renewal of Bill of Exchange

Bills of exchange have some specified time period. Drawee/acceptor has to make payments within that specified time period to Drawer/maker. But sometimes when they are not able to pay for the bill on the due date then he/she may ask the drawer to extend the period of credit.

If the drawer agrees then the drawer may cancel the old bill and draw a fresh bill for the extended period which the acceptor accepts. Cancelling the old bill and drawing of a fresh bill for an extended period is called Renewal of Bill. For the extended period, drawee is asked to pay interest which can be paid in cash or added to the amount of a new bill.

Making Entry of Renewal of Bills of Exchange

As when a new bill of exchange is issued, it affects both parties. Entry for renewal is passed in the books of the drawer as well as acceptor. If the drawer has discounted or dishonoured bill, the same entries are made as for dishonour.

Thereafter second entry is passed for interest. Interest may be paid in cash by cheque. If interest is paid in cash, then drawer debits the cash a/c and credits the interest a/c. If interest is paid by cheque then drawer debits the bank a/c and credits interest a/c.

On the other hand, acceptor debits the interest and credits the cash or bank a/c. For drawer, interest is the income and for acceptor, interest is an expense. Cash or cheque is received by the drawer and is paid by the acceptor.

If the acceptor does not pay interest on cash but agreed to pay later then instead of debiting cash/bank, drawer debits the amount of the acceptor. Where as acceptor credits the amount of drawer instead of cash/bank.

Because of the amount of interest drawer becomes the creditor and acceptor becomes the debtor. Interest is debited and credited in the same way whether paid in cash or not. A third entry is for renewal of the bill. Is dentist has been paid in the case then the bill of an amount of the new bill will be same as that of the old bill. If interest is not paid in cash then a new bill will include the old bill amount and interest.

126, Chandni Chowk,
Delhi-110 006
5th May, 2012.

₹ 10,000.00 P

Stamp

Three months after date, pay to us or our order a sum of Rupees Ten Thousand Only, for value received.

Accepted
For M/s Aggarwal Stores
(Signed) Nakul Gupta
5.5.2012
Partner

To
M/s Aggarwal Stores,
216, Malka Ganj,
Delhi-11007

For M/s Lakhmi Chand & Sons.
(Signed) Lakhmi Chand
(Lakhmi Chand)
Partner

Renewal in Case of Partial Payment

If acceptor is unable to pay for the bill in full, he/she can also pay partially. In this case, a new bill will be for the remaining amount. Interest will then be charged on the remaining amount for the extended period of credit. The amount of the new bill will include unpaid amount, interest and nothing charges if any.

First main entry is made to cancel the old bill. A second entry is made for partial payment. The third entry is made for interest. And the fourth entry is for drawing and accepting the new bill.

Renewal in Case of Dishonour of a Bill

Sometimes bill can be renewed by the drawer even after dishonour of bill. In this case, the acceptor is the debtor of the drawer for the amount of bill, noting charges and interest. If interest and noting charges or paid in cash by the acceptor, the drawer debits cash/bank and credits the interest and noting charges a/c.

On the other hand, acceptor debits the noting charges and interest a/c and credits the cash/ bank a/c. If these amounts are paid in cash, a fresh bill is drawn by the total of old bill amount, interest and noting charges.

Following entries are passed in this case:

In the Book of Drawer

1. Entry for Cancellation of the Bill:

   Acceptor's Personal A/c Dr

   To Bills Receivable A/c

2. Entry for Receipt of Cash:

   Cash A/c Dr

   To Acceptor's Personal A/c

3. Entry for Interest Received:

   Cash A/c Dr

   To Interest A/c

4. Entry for Interest not yet received but due:

   Acceptor's personal A/c Dr

   To Interest A/c

5. Entry for New Acceptance:

   Bills Receivable A/c Dr

   To Acceptor's Personal A/c

In the Books of Acceptor

1. Entry for Cancellation of Bill:

   Bills Payable A/c Dr

   To Drawer Personal A/c

2. Entry for part payment in cash:

   Drawer's Personal A/c Dr

   To Cash A/c

3. Entry for Interest Paid:

   Interest A/c Dr

   To Cash A/c

4. Interest not paid:

   Interest A/c Dr

   To Drawer's Personal A/c

5. Entry for Accepting New Bill:

   Drawer's Personal A/c Dr

   To Bills Payable A/c

Retirement of Bills of Exchange

It may happen sometimes that the drawee has surplus funds. So he may decide to pay the amount of the bill before the date of maturity. Thus, he asks the drawer or the holder whether he is ready to accept the payment before the due date of the bill. The drawer or the holder may agree to pre-payment. This is called the retirement of bills of exchange.

In order to encourage the drawee to pay the bill before the maturity date, the drawer gives him a discount. This discount is known as a rebate on bills. Thus, we calculate the rebate on bills at a certain rate of interest for the time between the date of payment and the date of maturity.

The rebate on bills is an expense of the drawer or the holder of the bill. While it is an income of the drawee or the payer. All journal entries are similar as in case of honor of the bill on the maturity date except for the rebate.

Journal Entry of Retirement of Bills of Exchange

Table: In the books of Drawer or Holder.

S.no	Particulars		Amount (Dr.)	Amount (Cr.)
1. The retirement of the bill	Bank/Cash A/c	Dr.	xxxx	
	Rebate on bills A/c	Dr.	xxxx	
	To Bills receivable A/c			xxxx
	(Being bill retired and rebate allowed)			

Table: In the books of Drawee or Payer.

S.no	Particulars		Amount (Dr.)	Amount (Cr.)
1. The retirement of the bill	Bills payable A/c	Dr.	xxxx	
	To Rebate on bills A/c			xxxx
	To Cash/ Bank A/c			xxxx
	(Being bill retired and rebate received)			

References

- Financial-accounting: accountingcoach.com, Retrieved 1 June, 2019
- Financial-accounting-definition-and-limitations, financial-accounting, accounting: yourarticlelibrary.com, Retrieved 18 January, 2019
- The-trial-balance-example-format: accountingtools.com, Retrieved 9 May, 2019
- Trial-balance, accounting: corporatefinanceinstitute.com, Retrieved 28 April, 2019
- Trial-balance: cleartax.in, Retrieved 23 July, 2019
- Trial-balance: accounting-simplified.com, Retrieved 3 May, 2019
- What-is-financial-capital-3305825: thebalance.com, Retrieved 28 January, 2019
- Debt-financing: upcounsel.com, Retrieved 13 February, 2019

- Equity-financing: upcounsel.com, Retrieved 11 July, 2019
- Cost-of-capital: businessjargons.com, Retrieved 15 August, 2019
- What-is-a-capital-surplus: accountingtools.com, Retrieved 18 March, 2019
- What-is-a-capital-expenditure: accountingtools.com, Retrieved 8 January, 2019
- Inventory: myaccountingcourse.com, Retrieved 14 June, 2019
- Bill-of-exchange-definition-and-parties-involved: paiementor.com, Retrieved 29 April, 2019
- Documentary-Bills, Banking-Credits-And-Finance, banking, finance: chestofbooks.com, Retrieved 30 August, 2019
- The-Documentary-Bill-Of-Exchange-Continued, Modern-Banking-Commercial-And-Credit-Paper, banking, finance: chestofbooks.com, Retrieved 5 June, 2019
- Definition-of-usance-bills, negotiable-instrument-act: bankingschool.co.in, Retrieved 2 March, 2019
- Accommodation-bills-meaning-and-dealing-methods-with-7-illustrations-2, Accommodation-bills, accounting: yourarticlelibrary.com, Retrieved 20 August, 2019
- Retirement-of-bills-of-exchange, bills-of-exchange-and-promissory-notes, principles-and-practice-of-accounting: toppr.com, Retrieved 21 July, 2019

3

Cost Accounting

The set of procedures which are used to record and report measurements of the cost of producing goods and services in detail is known as cost accounting. Some of the different types of costs which are studied within this field are direct cost, indirect cost, fixed cost and variable cost. The topics elaborated in this chapter will help in gaining a better perspective about cost accounting and cost accounting systems.

Cost

Cost is the monetary value of goods and services that producers and consumers purchase. In a basic economic sense, cost is the measure of the alternative opportunities foregone in the choice of one good or activity over others. This fundamental cost is usually referred to as opportunity cost. For a consumer with a fixed income, the opportunity cost of purchasing a new domestic appliance may be, for example, the value of a vacation trip not taken.

More conventionally, cost has to do with the relationship between the value of production inputs and the level of output. Total cost refers to the total expense incurred in reaching a particular level of output; if such total cost is divided by the quantity produced, average or unit cost is obtained. A portion of the total cost known as fixed cost—e.g., the costs of a building lease or of heavy machinery—does not vary with the quantity produced and, in the short run, does not alter with changes in the amount produced. Variable costs, like the costs of labour or raw materials, change with the level of output.

An aspect of cost important in economic analysis is marginal cost, or the addition to the total cost resulting from the production of an additional unit of output. A firm desiring to maximize its profits will, in theory, determine its level of output by continuing production until the cost of the last additional unit produced (marginal cost) just equals the addition to revenue (marginal revenue) obtained from it.

Types of Cost

Direct Cost

A direct cost is totally traceable to the production of a specific item, such as a product or service. For example, the cost of the materials used to create a product is a direct cost. There are very few direct costs. The cost of any consumable supplies directly used to manufacture a product can be considered a direct cost. However, production labor is frequently not a direct cost, because employees usually are not sent home if there is one less incremental item being produced; instead, they are paid for the duration of their work shifts, irrespective of the volume of production.

Other costs that are not direct costs include rent, production salaries, maintenance costs, insurance, depreciation, interest, and all types of utilities. Thus, when in doubt, assume that a cost is an indirect cost, rather than a direct cost.

For example, the materials used to produce an automobile are a direct cost, whereas the electrical cost of the metal stamping machine used to convert sheet metal into body panels for the automobile is not, because the machine must still (presumably) be powered up throughout the working day, irrespective of any changes in production volume.

Direct cost analysis can also be used outside the production department. For example, subtract the direct cost of goods sold to individual customers from the revenues generated by them, which yields the amount customers are contributing toward the company's coverage of overhead costs and profit. Based on this information, management may decide that some customers are unprofitable, and should be dropped.

However, there are a number of situations in which direct costing should not be used, and in which it will lead to incorrect behavior. Its single largest problem is that it completely ignores all indirect costs, which make up the bulk of all costs incurred by today's companies. This is a real problem when dealing with long-term costing and pricing decisions, since direct costing will likely yield results that do not achieve long-term profitability. For example, a direct costing system may calculate a minimum product price of $10.00 for a widget that is indeed higher than all direct costs, but which is lower than the additional overhead costs that are associated with the product line. If the company uses the $10.00 price for well into the future, then the company will experience losses because overhead costs are not being covered by the price.

Using just direct costs to derive the value of inventory is not allowed under generally accepted accounting principles and international financial reporting standards, on the grounds that it does not provide a comprehensive view of every cost being incurred to create a product.

Indirect Cost

Indirect costs are costs used by multiple activities, and which cannot therefore be assigned to specific cost objects. Examples of cost objects are products, services, geographical regions, distribution channels, and customers. Instead, indirect costs are needed to operate the business as a whole. It is useful to identify indirect costs, so that they can be excluded from short-term pricing decisions where management wants to set prices just above the variable costs of products. Indirect costs do not vary substantially within certain production volumes or other indicators of activities, and so are considered to be fixed costs. Examples of indirect costs are:

- Accounting and legal expenses
- Administrative salaries
- Office expenses
- Rent
- Security expenses
- Telephone expenses
- Utilities.

Fixed Cost

A fixed cost is a cost that does not change with an increase or decrease in the amount of goods or services produced or sold. Fixed costs are expenses that have to be paid by a company, independent of any specific business activities. In general, companies can have two types of costs, fixed costs or variable costs, which together result in their total costs.

Companies have a wide range of different costs associated with their business. These costs are broken out by indirect, direct, and capital costs on the income statement and notated as either short-term or long-term liabilities on the balance sheet. Together both fixed costs and variable costs make up the total cost structure of a company. Cost analysts are responsible for analyzing both fixed and variable costs through various types of cost structure analysis. In general, costs are a key factor influencing total profitability.

Companies have some flexibility in breaking down costs on their financial statements. As such fixed costs can be allocated throughout the income statement. The proportion of variable vs. fixed costs a company incurs and their allocations can depend on the industry they are in. Variable costs are costs directly associated with production and therefore change depending on business output. Fixed costs are usually negotiated for a specified time period and do not change with production levels. Fixed costs, however, can decrease on a per unit basis when they are associated with the direct cost portion of the income statement, fluctuating in the breakdown of costs of goods sold.

Fixed costs are usually established by contract agreements or schedules. These are base costs involved in operating a business comprehensively. Once established, fixed costs do not change over the life of an agreement or cost schedule. A company starting a new business would likely begin with fixed costs for rent and management salaries. All types of businesses have fixed cost agreements that they monitor regularly. While these fixed costs may change over time, the change is not related to production levels but rather new contractual agreements or schedules. Examples of fixed costs include rental lease payments, salaries, insurance, property taxes, interest expenses, depreciation, and potentially some utilities.

Financial Statement Analysis

Companies can associate both fixed and variable costs when analysing costs per unit. As such, cost of goods sold can include both variable and fixed costs. Comprehensively, all costs directly associated with the production of a good are summed collectively and subtracted from revenue to arrive at gross profit. Variable and fixed cost accounting will vary for each company depending on the costs they are working with. Economies of scale can also be a factor for companies who can produce large quantities of goods. Fixed costs can be a contributor to better economies of scale because fixed costs can decrease per unit when larger quantities are produced. Fixed costs that may be directly associated with production will vary by company but can include costs like direct labor and rent.

Fixed costs are also allocated in the indirect expense section of the income statement which leads to operating profit. Depreciation is one common fixed cost that is recorded as an indirect expense. Companies create a depreciation expense schedule for asset investments with values falling over time. For example, a company might buy machinery for a manufacturing assembly line that is expensed over time using depreciation. Another primary fixed, indirect cost is salaries for management.

Companies will also have interest payments as fixed costs which are a factor for net income. Fixed interest expenses are deducted from operating profit to arrive at net profit.

Any fixed costs on the income statement are also accounted for on the balance sheet and cash flow statement. Fixed costs on the balance sheet may be either short-term or long-term liabilities. Finally, any cash paid for the expenses of fixed costs is shown on the cash flow statement. In general, the opportunity to lower fixed costs can benefit a company's bottom line by reducing expenses and increasing profit.

Cost Structure Management

In addition to financial statement reporting, most companies will closely follow their cost structures through independent cost structure statements and dashboards. Independent cost structure analysis helps a company fully understand its variable vs. fixed costs and how they affect different parts of the business as well as the total business overall. Many companies have cost analysts dedicated solely to monitoring and analyzing the fixed and variable costs of a business.

Ratios

- Fixed cost ratio: The fixed cost ratio is a simple ratio that divides fixed costs by net sales to understand the proportion of fixed costs involved in production.
- Fixed charge coverage ratio: The fixed charge coverage ratio is a type of solvency metric that helps analyze a company's ability to pay its fixed-charge obligations. The fixed charge coverage ratio is calculated from the following equation:

  EBIT + fixed charges before tax / fixed charges before tax + interest

Other Considerations

- Breakeven analysis: Breakeven analysis involves using both fixed and variable costs to identify a production level in which revenue will equal costs. This can be an important part of cost structure analysis. A company's breakeven production quantity is calculated by:

  Breakeven quantity = fixed costs / (sales price per unit – variable cost per unit)

A company's breakeven analysis can be important for decisions on fixed and variable costs. Breakeven analysis also influences the price at which a company chooses to sell its products.

- Operating leverage: Operating leverage is another cost structure metric used in cost structure management. The proportion of fixed to variable costs will influence a company's operating leverage. Higher fixed costs help operating leverage to increase. With a higher operating leverage, companies can produce more profit per additional unit produced.

  Operating leverage = [Q (P-V)] / [Q (P-V)-F]

where:

  Q = number of units

P = price per unit

V = variable cost per unit

F = fixed costs

Variable Cost

Variable costs are corporate expenses that vary in direct proportion to the quantity of output. Unlike fixed costs, which remain constant regardless of output, variable costs are a direct function of production volume, rising whenever production expands and falling whenever it contracts.

Examples of common variable costs include raw materials, packaging, and labor directly involved in a company's manufacturing process.

The formula for calculating total variable cost is:

Total Variable Cost = Total Quantity of Output x Variable Cost Per Unit of Output

The term variable cost an accounting method related to reporting variable costs.

Example:

Let's assume XYZ Company has received an order for 5,000 widgets for a total sales price of $5,000 and wants to determine the gross profit that will be generated by completing the order. First, the variable costs per widget must be determined.

Let's assume the following:

Annual Widgets Produced: 100,000

Raw Materials Costs: $10,000

Direct Labor Costs: $50,000

From this information, we can conclude that each widget costs 10 cents ($10,000 / 100,000 widgets) in raw materials and 50 cents ($50,000 / 100,000 widgets) in direct labor costs. Using the formula above, we can calculate that XYZ Company's total variable cost on the order is:

5,000 x ($0.10 + $0.50) = $3,000

Therefore, the company can reasonably expect to earn a $2,000 gross profit ($5,000 - $3,000) from the order.

Importance of Variable Cost

While fixed costs, such as rent or other overhead, generally remain level, variable costs will correlate with the number of products manufactured. Because average variable costs differ widely among industries, comparisons are generally most meaningful among companies operating within the same industry.

When analyzing a company's income statement, it should be remembered that rising costs are not necessarily a troubling sign. Whenever sales rise, more units must first be produced (excluding the impact of stronger pricing), which in turn means that variable production costs must also increase. Thus, for revenues to climb, expenses must also rise accordingly.

It is important, though, that revenues increase at a faster rate than expenses. If, for example, a company reports volume growth of 8%, while cost of goods sold (COGS) only rises 5% over the same span, then costs have likely declined on a per unit basis. If a company can find ways to reduce the input costs associated with producing each item it sells, then its profitability will improve. One way to monitor this aspect of a company's business is to divide variable costs by total revenues to figure costs as a percentage of sales.

Variable costs frequently factor into profit projections and the calculation of break-even points for a business or project. Some costs change in a piecewise manner as output changes and therefore may not remain constant per unit of output. Also, note that many cost items have both fixed and variable components. For example, management salaries typically do not vary with the number of units produced. However, if production falls dramatically or reaches zero, then layoffs may occur. This is evidence that all costs are variable in the long run.

A company with a large number of variable costs (compared to fixed costs) may exhibit more consistent per-unit costs and hence more predictable per-unit profit margins than a company with fewer variable costs. However, a company with fewer variable costs (and hence a larger number of fixed costs) may magnify potential profits (and losses) because revenue increases (or decreases) are applied to a more constant cost level.

Operating Cost

Operating costs are key components of operating income calculation (and operating income is a crucial component of many financial measures). Thus, the lower a company's operating costs are, the more profitable it generally is.

Several things can affect operating costs (such as pricing strategy, prices for raw materials or labor costs), but because these items directly relate to the day-to-day decisions managers make, financial measures based on operating expenses are also measures of managerial flexibility and competency, particularly during rough economic times.

It is also important to note that some industries have higher operating costs than others. This is why comparing operating costs or income is generally most meaningful among companies within the same industry, and the definition of "high" or "low" costs should be made within this context.

Example:

Operating costs are expenses associated with running a business's core operations on a daily basis. Common examples are cost of goods sold and labor costs. Operating costs typically exclude interest expense, nonrecurring items (such as accounting adjustments, legal judgments or one-time transactions), and other income statement items not directly related to a company's core business operations.

Operating Costs Components

While operating costs generally do not include capital outlays, they can include many components of operating expenses including:

- Accounting and legal fees
- Bank charges
- Sales and marketing costs
- Travel expenses
- Entertainment costs
- Non-capitalized research and development expenses
- Office supply costs
- Rent
- Repair and maintenance costs
- Utility expenses
- Salary and wage expenses

Operating costs can include the cost of goods sold, which are the expenses directly tied to the production of goods and services. Some of the costs include:

- Direct material costs
- Direct labor
- Rent of the plant or production facility
- Benefits and wages for the production workers
- Repair costs of equipment
- Utility costs and taxes of the production facilities

Sunk Cost

A sunk cost is a cost that has already been incurred and cannot be recovered. A sunk cost differs from future costs that a business may face, such as decisions about inventory purchase costs or product pricing. Sunk costs (past costs) are excluded from future business decisions because the cost will be the same regardless of the outcome of a decision.

When making business decisions, organizations consider relevant costs, which include the future costs and revenue of one choice compared with another. To make an informed decision, a business only considers the costs and revenue that will change as a result of the decision; sunk costs that do not change are not considered.

Factoring in a Sell-or-process-further Decision

A manufacturing firm may have a number of sunk costs, such as the cost of machinery, equipment, and the lease cost of a factory. Sunk costs are excluded from a sell-or-process-further decision; this concept applies to products that can be sold as they are or can be processed further.

Assume, for example, that XYZ Clothing makes baseball gloves, and the company produces a basic model of glove that costs $50 per unit and sells for $70 per glove. The manufacturer can sell the basic model and earn a $20 profit, or it can continue production by adding $15 in costs and sell a premium model glove for $90. To make this decision, the firm compares the $15 additional cost with the $20 added revenue and decides to make the premium glove and earn $5 more in profit. The cost of the factory lease and the machinery are both sunk costs and are not part of the decision-making process.

Examples of Eliminated Sunk Costs

If a sunk cost can be eliminated, the cost becomes a relevant factor and should be a part of business decisions about future events. If, for example, XYZ Clothing is considering shutting down a production facility, any of the sunk costs that have end dates should be included in the decision. To make this decision, XYZ Clothing considers the revenue that would be lost if production ends and the material and labor costs that are eliminated. If, however, the factory lease ends in six months, the lease cost is no longer a sunk cost and should be included as an expense that can be eliminated. If the total costs are more than revenue, the facility should be closed.

Controllable costs

Controllable costs are those costs that can be altered in the short term. More specifically, a cost is considered to be controllable if the decision to incur it resides with one person. If the decision instead involves a number of individuals, then a cost is not controllable from the perspective of any one person. Also, if a cost is imposed on an organization by a third party (such as taxes), this cost is not considered to be controllable. Examples of controllable costs are:

- Advertising
- Bonuses
- Direct materials
- Donations
- Dues and subscriptions
- Employee compensation
- Office supplies
- Training

The reverse of a controllable cost is a fixed cost, which can only be altered over a long period of time. Examples of fixed costs are rent and insurance.

Uncontrollable Cost

Uncontrollable costs are business expenses that the manager doesn't have direct power over. In other words, the business manager doesn't have control over how these costs are incurred.

Most companies develop some type of evaluation system for their employees and managers. These systems are usually based on job performance. Managers are regularly evaluated on budgetary performance as well as the sales and income performance of their department. Most of the time these performance evaluations only take into consideration controllable costs.

Example:

A good example of an uncontrollable cost is insurance. A manager who runs a department on the factory floor does not have control over the liability insurance that the company buys. If several accidents happen within the company and the liability issuance increases, the manager shouldn't be penalized for the increased cost. Upper level executives usually set this insurance policy, so the factory floor manager doesn't have control over it.

Depreciation is another example of an uncontrollable cost. Even though a factory floor manager has control over the machines, maintenance costs, and upkeep, depreciation and accelerated depreciation is rarely set at the manager level. Depending on how much equipment was purchased for the year, depreciation can also eliminate all profits from the department.

Managers' profit performance evaluations usually do not include depreciation for this reason. It won't be fair to count these costs against a manager who has no control over them. Instead managers' performance is only judged based on controllable costs.

Standard Cost

A standard cost is described as a predetermined cost, an estimated future cost, an expected cost, a budgeted unit cost, a forecast cost, or as the "should be" cost. Standard costs are often an integral part of a manufacturer's annual profit plan and operating budgets.

When standard costs are used in a manufacturing setting, a product's standard cost for a future accounting period will consist of the following:

- Direct materials: A standard quantity of each material and a standard cost per unit of material.
- Direct labor: A standard quantity of labor and a standard cost per hour of labor.
- Manufacturing overhead: A budget for the fixed overhead, the standard variable overhead rate, and the standard quantity for applying a fixed and variable overhead rates.

In a standard costing system, the standard costs of the manufacturing activities will be recorded in the inventories and the cost of goods sold accounts. Since the company must pay its vendors and production workers the actual costs incurred, there are likely to be some differences. The differences between the standard costs and the actual manufacturing costs are referred to as cost variances and will be recorded in separate variance accounts. Any balance in a variance account indicates that the company is deviating from the amounts in its profit plan.

While standard costs can be a useful management tool for a manufacturer, the manufacturer's external financial statements must comply with the cost principle and the matching principle. Therefore, significant variances must be reviewed and properly assigned or allocated to the cost of goods sold and inventories.

Cost Accounting

Cost accounting is involved with the following:

- Determining the costs of products, processes, projects, etc. in order to report the correct amounts on a company's financial statements, and
- Assisting management in the planning and control of the organization,
- Preparing special analyses that assists in making the best decisions.

Examples of Cost Accounting

A significant part of cost accounting involves the unit cost of a manufacturer's products in order to report the cost of inventory on its balance sheet and the cost of goods sold on its income statement. This is achieved with techniques such as the allocation of manufacturing overhead costs and through the use of process costing, operations costing, and job-order costing systems.

Cost accounting assists management to plan and control the business through budgeting for operations, capital budgeting for expanding operations, standard costing and the reporting of variances, transfer pricing, etc.

Special analyses includes cost behavior, cost-volume-profit relationships, make or buy decisions, selling prices for products, activity-based costing, and more.

Cost accounting had its roots in manufacturing businesses. However, today it extends to service businesses. For example, a bank will use cost accounting to determine the cost of processing a customer's check and/or a deposit, maintaining a checking account, processing international wire transfers, servicing a mortgage loan, etc. This in turn may provide management with guidance in the pricing of various services.

Cost Accounting System

A cost accounting system is used by manufacturers to record production activities using a perpetual inventory system. In other words, it's an accounting system designed for manufacturers that tracks the flow of inventory continually through the various stages of production.

A typical cost accounting system works by tracking raw materials as they go through the production stages and slowly turn into finished goods in real time. When the raw materials are put into production, the system immediately records the use of the materials by crediting the raw materials account and debiting the goods in process account. Since most products go through many stages before they can be called finished goods, there are often several different work in process accounts.

Example:

As the materials move from one operation to the next, the cost accounting tracks the progress and updates it in the computerized system. This is extremely helpful for production managers and cost accountants, so they can see how much inventory is in every stage of production at any point in time.

It also allows companies to maintain just-in-time inventory systems where materials are only ordered from vendors and supplies on an as needed basis. No extra quantities are ordered and stored for processing at later point. The company only orders enough materials to fulfill the current customers' orders. This saves the company on many different costs including storage, security, and obsolescence.

The real time component of the system is its most valuable feature. Management can make decisions based on current data and don't have to wait for reports to be aggregated. Although important, this feature is not always easily achieved. Most companies either use a bar code system or implant each product with an RFID chip to track its location in the production process.

Manufacturers using job order cost accounting and process cost accounting can both benefit from cost accounting systems.

Activity-based Costing

The Activity-Based Costing (ABC) is a costing system which focuses on activities performed to produce products. ABC is that costing in which costs are first traced to activities and then to products. This costing system assumes that activities are responsible for the incurrence of costs and products create the demands for activities. Costs are charged to products based on individual product's use of each activity.

In traditional product costing system, costs are, first, traced not to activities but to an organisational unit, such as department or plant and then to products. ABC, as compared to traditional cost system is based on one fundamental difference. Under ABC, activity and product/service costs are determined based on the primary principle that activities consume resources (costs). Products and services (cost objects), in-turn, consume the activities. This principle is fundamentally different from traditional costing systems whose premise is that product/services consume resources directly, and activity costs are not calculated at all.

Stages and Flow of Costs in ABC

There are two primary stages in ABC— first, tracing costs to activities; second, tracing activities to products.

The different steps in the two stages of ABC are explained below:

Step 1: Identify the main activities in the organisation.

Examples include: Materials handling, purchasing, receipt, dispatch, machining, assembly and so on.

Step 2: Identify the factors which determine the costs of an activity. These are known as cost drivers. Examples include: number of purchase orders, number of orders delivered, number of set-ups and so on.

Step 3: Collect the costs of each activity. These are known as cost pools and are directly equivalent to conventional cost centres.

Stcp 4: Charge support overheads to products on the basis of their usage of the activity, expressed in terms of the chosen cost driver (s). For example, if the total costs of purchasing were Rs 2, 00,000 and there were 1,000 Purchase orders (the chosen cost driver), products would be charged Rs 200 per purchase order. Thus a batch generating 3 purchase orders would be charged 3 x Rs 200 = Rs 600 for Purchasing overheads.

ABC follows a two-stage cost assignment procedure and assigns resource costs such as factory overhead costs to activity cost centres or cost pools and then to cost objects to determine the amount of resource costs for each of the cost objects. That is, resources (costs) are assigned to activities. Activity cost is then assigned cost objects.

The flow of cost assignment in ABC is exhibited in Exhibit below:

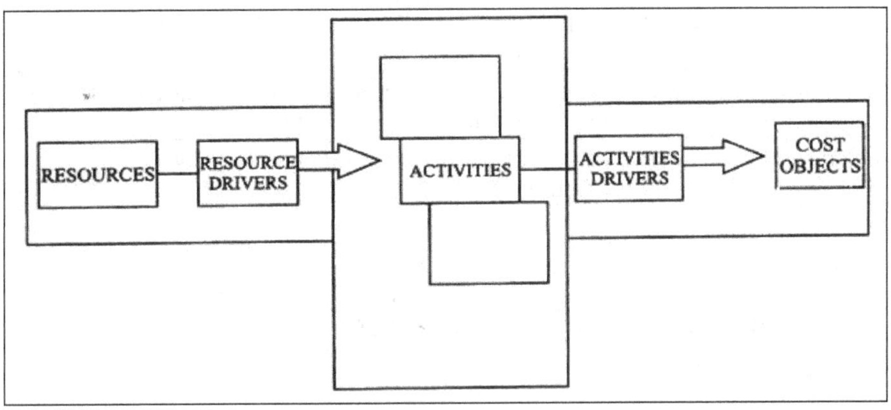

Exhibit: Cost assignment

Five basic Components of ABC

As displayed in Exhibit above, there are five basic components to the activity-based cost assignment:

1. Resources
2. Resource Drivers
3. Activities
4. Activity Cost Drivers, and
5. Cost Objects

Resources

Resources are what organizations spend their money on—the categories of costs that are recorded. Resource is defined as an economic or money element that is applied or used in the performance of activities. Salaries and materials, for examples, are resources used in the performance of activities. Additional examples of resources include repair, inspection, rent, depreciation, utilities, insurance, and supplies. Most ABC systems currently exclude costs like income taxes and interest expense that are not used in the performance of activities.

Resource Drivers

Resource drivers are the basis for tracing resources to activities. Resource driver is defined as a measure of the quantity of resource consumed by an activity. An example of a resource driver is the percentage of total square feet of space occupied by an activity. This factor is used to trace a portion of the cost of operating the facilities to the activity.

Examples of common resource drivers for salaries/wages, rent, equipment, depreciation, and utilities include the following:

Resource	Resource Driver
Salaries	Percentage of people's time spent on each activity. Headcount assignment. Hours spent on each activity.
Rent/facility costs	Square feet of facility consumed by each activity. Cubic feet of facility consumed by each activity.
Equipment depreciation	Specific analysis to associate equipment use to each activity. Machine time by activity.
Utilities (electric)	Kilowatt hours consumption by activity. Square feet of facility.

Activities

An activity is a unit of work. If you go to u restaurant for lunch/dinner, a waiter or waiters might perform the following units of work:

1. Seat customer and offer menu
2. Take your order
3. Send orders to kitchen
4. Bring food
5. Replenish beverages
6. Determine and bring bill
7. Collect money and give change
8. Clear table

Each of these is an activity and the performance of each activity consumes resources that cost money.

Activities represent work performed in an organization. The cost of activities is determined by tracing resource to activities using the resource drivers. An example of how the salaries of a receiving department of a manufacturing company might be traced to receiving department activities is illustrated. In this example, the resource is receiving department salaries.

The activities are as follows receive materials, unload trucks, move material, schedule receipts, expedite material, and resolve vender errors. The resource driver is a percentage of people's time devoted to each receiving department activity. While percentage of people's time was selected as the resource driver in this example, as an alternative, the head count of people assigned to each activity or the hours devoted to each activity could have been used as the resource driver.

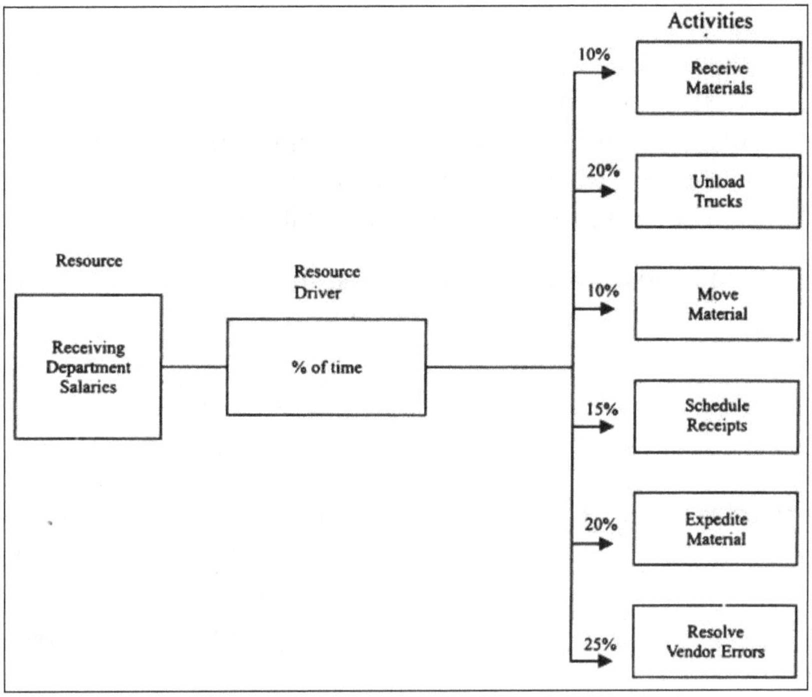

Exhibit: Resource driver example

Assuming that salaries were the only resource of the receiving department, calculating the cost of receiving department activities would be quite simple. All that is required is to multiply the percentage of people's time (resource driver) by the salary amount.

If receiving department salaries totaled $ 20 lakhs, the cost of each activity would be as follows:

1. Receive materials – $ 2, 00,000
2. Unload trucks – $ 4, 00,000
3. Move material – $ 2, 00, 000
4. Schedule receipts – $ 3, 00, 000
5. Expedite material – $ 4, 00, 000
6. Resolve Vendor Errors – $ 5, 00, 000
7. Total – $ 20, 00, 000

In practice, a single resource and resource driver would be rare. The receiving department of a large organization is likely to have multiple resource and resource drivers. Total activity cost would be determined by tracing each resource (using an appropriate resource driver) to the receiving department activities. Once determined, activity costs can be traced to cost objects using activity drivers.

Activity Cost Drivers

Like a resource driver that is used to trace resource to activities, an activity cost driver is used to trace activity costs to cost objects. Activity driver is defined as a measure of the frequency and intensity of the demands placed on activities by cost objects. An activity driver is used to assign costs to cost objects.

A cost driver is an activity which generates cost. A cost driver is a factor, such as the level of activity or volume, that causally affects costs (over a given time span). That is, a cause-and-effect relationship exists between a change in the level of activity or volume and a change in the level of the total costs of that cost object. Thus, cost drivers signify factors, forces or events that determine the costs of activities. Based on activity usage (consumption), activity costs are traced to cost objects.

In a manufacturing organization, the following are examples of some activity cost drivers:

Some Examples of Activity Cost Drivers:

1. Number of receiving orders for the receiving department.	12. Number of machine hours used on a product.
2. Number of purchase orders for the cost of operating the purchase department.	13. Number of set up hours.
3. Number of dispatch orders for the dispatch department.	14. Number of direct labour hours.
4. Number of units.	15. Number of sub-assemblies.
5. Number of setups.	16. Number of vendors.
6. Amount of labour cost incurred.	17. Number of purchasing and ordering hours.
7. Value of materials in a product.	18. Number of units scrapped.
8. Number of materials handling hours.	19. Number of labour transactions.
9. Number of inspections.	20. Number of customer orders processed.
10. Number of schedule changes.	21. Number of parts.
11. Number of parts received per month.	22. Number of employees.

It should be understand that direct costs do not need cost drivers as they can be traced directly to a product. Direct costs are themselves cost drivers. However, all other factory or manufacturing costs need cost drivers. The cost driver of variable costs is the level of activity or volume whose change causes the variable costs to change proportionately.

Costs that are fixed in the short run have no cost drivers in the short run but may have cost drivers in the long run. For instance, costs of testing personal computers (which comprise costs of testing department equipment and staff costs) may not change with changes in the volume of production.

Therefore, these costs would be fixed in the short run. In the long run. However, an organisation may need to increase/decrease testing department's equipment and staff to the levels needed to support future production volumes. So, in the long run, volume of production or activity becomes cost drivers of these testing and staff costs.

Selection of Activity Cost Drivers

In traditional product costing, the number of cost drivers used are few such as direct labour hours, machine hours, direct labour cost, units produced. But ABC may use a multitude of cost drivers that relate costs more closely to the resources consumed and activities occurring. There are difficulties in choosing realistic cost drivers. There are no simple rules that pertain to the selection of cost drivers.

The best approach is to identify the resources that constitute a significant proportion of the product costs and to determine their cost behaviour. When identifying and selecting activity drivers, match the activity to the activity level, which is defined as a description of how an activity is used by a cost object (product/service) or activity. Some activity levels describe the cost object that uses the activity and nature of its use.

Types of Cost Drivers

Customer demand is considered to be basic cost driver. Without customer demand for products or services, the organisation cannot exist. To serve customers, managers and employees make a variety of decisions and perform many actions/activities. These decisions and activities, undertaken to satisfy customer demand, drive costs.

Morse, Davis and Hart-graves suggest that cost drivers should be divided into three categories:

1. Structural Cost Drivers

   They are fundamental choices about the size and scope of operations and technologies employed in delivering products or services to customers. Decisions affecting structural cost drivers are made infrequently and once made, the organisation is committed to a course of action that will be difficult to change.

For a chain of super market stores, the following may be structural cost drivers:

- Determining the size of stores: This will affect the types of merchandise that can be provided to customers and operating costs.
- Determining the type of construction: A small size store will involve less cost. But it may not be suitable to store many other needed items.
- Determining the location of the store: Location in a high class shopping complex will cost more but will attract more customers.
- Determining the kind of technology used in the stores: A system involving clerks to keep all records of sales, purchases and inventory may be cheaper. A computerised systems in the beginning requires higher investment and fixed operating costs. But, later, it may be less expensive due to high sales volume. Also, it will provide latest information about all operations.

2. Organisational Cost Drivers

   They are choices concerning the organisation of activities and involvement of persons inside and outside the organisation in decision making. Like structural cost drivers, organisational cost drivers influence costs by affecting the type of activities and costs of activities performed to satisfy customer needs. Decisions that affect organisational cost drivers are made within the context of previous decisions affecting structural cost drivers. In a manufacturing organisation, previous decisions about plant, equipment and location are taken as given when decisions impacting organisational cost drivers are made.

In a manufacturing company, examples of organisational cost drivers are:

- Preferring a limited number of suppliers: This may be useful in ensuring proper supplies in proper quantities at proper time.
- Authorising employees to make decisions and giving them cost and other data: This will make employees customer-oriented, reduce costs and improve decision speed. Production workers, for example, may take steps to reduce manufacturing costs and defects and spoilage.
- Deciding components of a product to fit them in the most correct manner: This will save assembly time and cost and reduce defects.
- Deciding to manufacture a low-volume product on low speed, general purpose equipment; rather than high-speed, special purpose equipment.
- Deciding to reorganise the existing equipment in the factory so that sequential operations are nearer. This will reduce cost of moving inventory between different machines.

3. Activity Cost Drivers

   Activity cost drivers are specific units of work (activities) performed to serve customer needs that consume costly resources. The customer may be outside the organisation, such as a client of an advertising firm or inside the organisation, such as an accounting office that receives maintenance services. Because the performance of activities consumes resources and resources cost money, the performance of activities drives cost.

Cost Object

Cost objects, can be any customer, product, service, contract, project, or other work unit for which a separate cost measurement is desired. The most common cost object is product or service cost. Activity drivers are used to trace activity costs to cost objects. An example of how an activity of a sales department might be traced to customer segments (cost object) is illustrated.

In this example, the activity of the sales department is 'make sales calls'. The activity driver is the number of sales calls. If the objective was to determine the selling cost associated with costumer segments, then the cost objects might be large customers, medium-sized customers, and small customers. Assume that the make sales calls activity costs Rs 5, 00,000 and was the only activity of the department.

If the total sales calls made were 5,000, of which 1,000 were made on large customers, 500 on medium customers, and 3,500 on small customers, the cost of each customer segment would be:

- Large Customers – $ 1,00,000

- Medium Customers – $ 50,000
- Small Customers – $ 3, 50, 000
- Total Activity Cost – $ 5, 00, 000

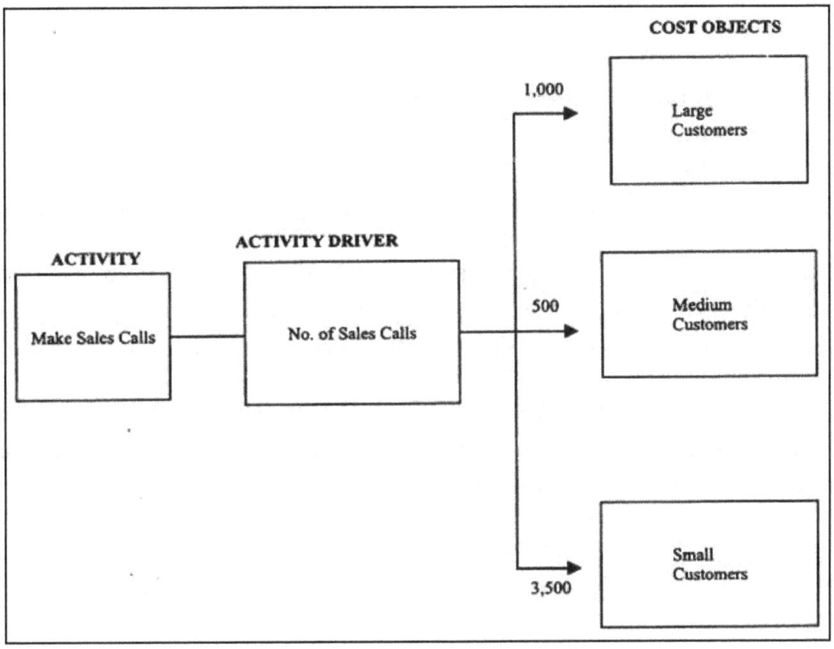

Exhibit: Activity driver example

Again, like the Resource Driver Example, single activities and activity drivers do not exist. It is only by tracing other sales department activities like prepare proposals, answer inquires, and take orders that the total cost for each of the customer segments identified as cost objects could be determined.

The foregoing examples were intended to be simple and to demonstrate the basic concepts of ABC. Applications of these concepts in practice can be quite complex. Even the simplest of ABC applications could involve 5 to 10 resources, 25 or more activities, and 10 to 25 cost objects.

That is why it is important to resist the urge for perfection by defining activities and drivers at too detailed a level, especially in the early stages of implementation. The goal of ABC is to provide relevant information useful for decision making, measuring performance, and effecting improvement.

Uses of Activity based Costing

The fundamental advantage of using an ABC system is to more precisely determine how overhead is used. Once you have an ABC system, you can obtain better information about the following issues:

- Activity costs: ABC is designed to track the cost of activities, so you can use it to see if activity costs are in line with industry standards. If not, ABC is an excellent feedback tool for measuring the on-going cost of specific services as management focuses on cost reduction.
- Customer profitability: Though most of the costs incurred for individual customers are simply product costs, there is also an overhead component, such as unusually high customer

service levels, product return handling, and cooperative marketing agreements. An ABC system can sort through these additional overhead costs and help you determine which customers are actually earning you a reasonable profit. This analysis may result in some unprofitable customers being turned away, or more emphasis being placed on those customers who are earning the company its largest profits.

- Distribution cost: The typical company uses a variety of distribution channels to sell its products, such as retail, Internet, distributors, and mail order catalogs. Most of the structural cost of maintaining a distribution channel is overhead, so if you can make a reasonable determination of which distribution channels are using overhead, you can make decisions to alter how distribution channels are used, or even to drop unprofitable channels.
- Make or buy: ABC provides a comprehensive view of every cost associated with the in-house manufacture of a product so that you can see precisely which costs will be eliminated if an item is outsourced, versus which costs will remain.
- Margins: With proper overhead allocation from an ABC system, you can determine the margins of various products, product lines, and entire subsidiaries. This can be quite useful for determining where to position company resources to earn the largest margins.
- Minimum price: Product pricing is really based on the price that the market will bear, but the marketing manager should know what the cost of the product is, in order to avoid selling a product that will lose company money on every sale. ABC is very good for determining which overhead costs should be included in this minimum cost, depending upon the circumstances under which products are being sold.
- Production facility cost: It is usually quite easy to segregate overhead costs at the plant-wide level, so you can compare the costs of production between different facilities.

Clearly, there are many valuable uses for the information provided by an ABC system. However, this information will only be available if you design the system to provide the specific set of data needed for each decision. If you install a generic ABC system and then use it for the above decisions, you may find that it does not provide the information that you need. Ultimately, the design of the system is determined by a cost-benefit analysis of which decisions you want it to assist with, and whether the cost of the system is worth the benefit of the resulting information.

Problems with Activity based Costing

Many companies initiate ABC projects with the best of intentions, only to see a very high proportion of the projects either fail or eventually lapse into disuse. There are several reasons for these issues, which are:

- Cost pool volume: The advantage of an ABC system is the high quality of information that it produces, but this comes at the cost of using a large number of cost pools – and the more cost pools there are, the greater the cost of managing the system. To reduce this cost, run an ongoing analysis of the cost to maintain each cost pool, in comparison to the utility of the resulting information. Doing so should keep the number of cost pools down to manageable proportions.

- Installation time: ABC systems are notoriously difficult to install, with multi-year installations being the norm when a company attempts to install it across all product lines and facilities. For such comprehensive installations, it is difficult to maintain a high level of management and budgetary support as the months roll by without installation being completed. Success rates are much higher for smaller, more targeted ABC installations.
- Multi-department data sources: An ABC system may require data input from multiple departments, and each of those departments may have greater priorities than the ABC system. Thus, the larger the number of departments involved in the system, the greater the risk that data inputs will fail over time. This problem can be avoided by designing the system to only need information from the most supportive managers.
- Project basis: Many ABC projects are authorized on a project basis, so that information is only collected once; the information is useful for a company's current operational situation, and it gradually declines in usefulness as the operational structure changes over time. Management may not authorize funding for additional ABC projects later on, so ABC tends to be "done" once and then discarded. To mitigate this issue, build as much of the ABC data collection structure into the existing accounting system, so that the cost of these projects is reduced; at a lower cost, it is more likely that additional ABC projects will be authorized in the future.
- Reporting of unused time: When a company asks its employees to report on the time spent on various activities, they have a strong tendency to make sure that the reported amounts equal 100% of their time. However, there is a large amount of slack time in anyone's work day that may involve breaks, administrative meetings, playing games on the Internet, and so forth. Employees usually mask these activities by apportioning more time to other activities. These inflated numbers represent misallocations of costs in the ABC system, sometimes by quite substantial amounts.
- Separate data set: An ABC system rarely can be constructed to pull all of the information it needs directly from the general ledger. Instead, it requires a separate database that pulls in information from several sources, only one of which is existing general ledger accounts. It can be quite difficult to maintain this extra database, since it calls for significant extra staff time for which there may not be an adequate budget. The best work-around is to design the system to require the minimum amount of additional information other than that which is already available in the general ledger.
- Targeted usage: The benefits of ABC are most apparent when cost accounting information is difficult to discern, due to the presence of multiple product lines, machines being used for the production of many products, numerous machine setups, and so forth – in other words, in complex production environments. If a company does not operate in such an environment, then it may spend a great deal of money on an ABC installation, only to find that the resulting information is not overly valuable.

Project Accounting

Project accounting is a specialised form of accounting that corresponds to the ever-evolving needs of project delivery, which helps adequately track, report and analyse financial results and implications. This includes the practice of creating financial reports specifically designed to track the financial progress of projects, which can then be used by managers to aid project management.

Traditionally, project accounting and its principles were largely used to track and report predominantly large construction, engineering and government projects. Today, project management delivery methodologies have expanded into several other sectors, including financial, technology and legal. Subsequently, project accounting has needed to follow to cover these areas to ensure corresponding financial tracking and financial implications are understood and considered.

The need for project accounting arose as a specialised field from the nature of projects being treated as separate temporary individualised entities set up for the purpose of delivering one or more business products. As the nature of each project may be different from the business-as-usual activities run by the business, existent management accounting and financial accounting skills were recognised as insufficient to accurately advise on the treatment and financial reporting of a project. Hence, a new field emerged within the accounting sphere – project accounting.

Project accounting therefore includes:

- A separate accounting system or cost centre to track and report project specific transactions, with project revenues, costs, assets and liabilities identified and allocated to the project.
- Frequent reporting, with the frequency often increasing as the project approaches completion.
- A layer of simplified reporting, including key performance indicators relevant to whether the project is on or off track. For instance traffic lights on a dashboard.
- A process for identifying project related transactions in the main accounting system and allocating or apportioning these to the project accounting system.
- Forecasting of costs to complete the project. Key stakeholders are often not only focused on the costs incurred to date, but also those committed and the expected final cost.

Projects differ from the day-to-day business-as-usual (BAU) activities in that they frequently cross organisational boundaries, may last for anything from a few days or weeks to a number of years, during which time budgets may also be revised many times. They may also be one of a number of projects that make up a larger overall project or program.

Consequently, in a project management environment costs (both direct and overhead) and revenues are also allocated to projects, which may be subdivided into a work breakdown structure, and grouped together into project hierarchies. Project accounting permits reporting at any such level that has been defined, and often allows comparison with historical as well as current budgets.

Project accounting is commonly used by government contractors, where the ability to account for costs by contract (and sometimes contract line item, or CLIN) is usually a requirement for interim payments.

Percentage-of-completion is frequently independently assessed by a project manager, program management officer (PMO) and project accountant. It includes the continuous recognition of revenues and income related to longer-term projects. By doing this, the seller is able to identify some gain or loss relevant to a project in every accounting period that is ongoing active. Funding advances and actual-to-budget cost variances are calculated using the project budget adjusted to percent-of-completion.

Where labor costs are a significant portion of overall project cost, it is usually necessary for employees to fill out a timesheet in order to generate the data to allocate project costs.

The capital budget processes of corporations and governments are chiefly concerned with major investment projects that typically have upfront costs and longer term benefits. Investment go/no-go decisions are largely based on net present value assessments. Project accounting of the costs and benefits can provide crucially important feedback on the quality of these important decisions.

An interesting specialised form of project accounting is production accounting, which tracks the costs of individual movie and television episode film production costs. A movie studio will employ production accounting to track the costs of its many separate projects.

Role of the Project Accountant

The project accountant requires the knowledge of management accounting and financial accounting. They require an understanding of the complexities of cross-functional involvement, as well as, project delivery frameworks and methodologies used by the business. Within a project delivery framework, the project accountant plays a dual role of:

- Gatekeeper reporting into the business the true and fair view of how the project is tracking financially; and
- Advisor advising the project team as to the financial treatment and implications of the various decisions being made, their impact on both the project and the business.

The key benefit of this is the project accountant ultimately plays a Translator role between the project and other finance/accounting functions.

The role of a project accountant depends on the project needs, but as a basic function, the project accountant position is accountable for monitoring the progress of projects, investigating variances, approving expenses, and ensuring that project billings are issued to customers and payments collected.

In Australia, a project accountant earns an average salary of AU$81,830 per year, with salaries ranging between AU$59,769 - AU$123,896. Most people working in this field move to a different position after approximately 20 years. The jobs that normally increase pay towards this job is Budget Managing and Cost Accounting. Experience has a moderate effect on income for this job.

Percentage of Completion Method

The percentage-of-completion method permits companies to record profits as development is made toward the finishing of the project. This method is not to be used when compelling uncertainty's about the percentage of completion of the remaining costs to be incurred. The method instead works at its finest when it is rationally likely to estimate the stages of the project in process.

The percentage-of-completion may be measured in any of the resulting ways:

- Cost-to-cost method: This is an example of the contract cost acquired to date the total expected cost. The price of the products already bought for a contract however have not yet been installed should not be added in the perseverance of the percentage of completion of a project, not unless they were particularly created for the contract. Also, assign the cost of equipment over the contract course, rather than direct, unless title to the supplies is being transported to the customer.
- Efforts-expended method: This is the share of effort consumed to date in comparison to the total effort expected for the agreement. e.g. the percentage of completion may possibly be established on direct work hours, machine hours, or material size.
- Units-of-delivery-method: This is the portion of units delivered to the buyer to the overall number of units to be brought under the terms of a contract. It should only be in use when the builder produces a number of units to the requirements of a buyer. The recognition is established on:
    - For revenue, the contract price of units delivered.
    - For expenses, the costs reasonably allocable to the units delivered.

However, the necessary steps are the following:

- Subtract the total predicted contract costs from total approximated revenues to appear at the total estimated gross margin.
- Measure the range of process toward completion, using one of the methods mentioned above.
- Increase the total likely contract revenue by the estimated finishing percentage to arrive at the total amount of revenue that can be acknowledged.
- Subtract the contract revenue allowed to date through the foregoing period from the complete amount of revenue that be accepted. Recognise the development in the current accounting period.
- Consider the cost of the received revenue in the same manner. This means raising the same percentage of completion by the total supposed contract cost, and subtracting the amount formerly realised to arrive at the cost of collected revenue to be recognised in the current accounting period.

Calculations

The following calculation is used to determine the completion percentage:

Percent Complete = Cost Incurred to Date / Total Cost Estimate.

The current period revenue to be recognised during production would then be:

Current Period Revenue = (Percent Complete x Total Contract Revenue) - Revenue Recognised in Prior Periods.

Production Accounting

Production Accounting involves the person who is essential in the film industry to manage the finances and financial records during the film production. Working in this position requires being in close association with the producer and the production office for the development of the film budget and to arrange schedules. Further into this role, as the accountant for a film, day-to-day duties are expected such as the normal accounting tasks of an office and maintaining the budget by recording the expenses accumulated to make secure they do not go over the allocated budget.

Other duties of the production accountant include:

- Managing the payroll.
- Managing the petty cash.
- Analysing costs.
- Provide weekly cash reports.
- Estimating future costs.

Standard Cost Accounting

Standard costing is a technique which uses standards for costs and revenues for the purpose of control through variance analysis. Standard is a predetermined measurable quantity set in defined conditions against which actual performance can be compared, usually for an element of work, operation or activity.

Objectives of Standard Costing

The objectives of standard costing technique are as follows:

- To provide a formal basis for assessing performance and efficiency.
- To control costs by establishing standards and analysis of variances.
- To enable the principle of 'management by exception' to be practised at the detailed, operational level.
- To assist in setting budgets.
- The standard costs are readily available substitutes for actual average unit costs and can be used for stock and work-in-progress valuations, profit planning and decision making and as a basis of pricing where 'cost-plus' systems are used.
- To assist in assigning responsibility for nonstandard performance in order to correct deficiencies or to capitalise on benefits.
- To motivate staff and management.
- To provide a basis for estimating.

- To provide guidance on possible ways of improving performance.

One cannot have perfect and effective system of budgetary control without standard costing, and standard costing cannot be implemented without proper budgetary control system. The budgetary control system and standard costing are both supplementary and complementary to each other.

The use of standard costing is useful for MIS, profit planning, inventory control, product pricing, decision making, cost control etc. Both standards and budgets are concerned with setting performance and cost levels for control purposes. They are similar in principle although they differ in scope. Standards are unit concept, i.e., they apply to particular products, to individual operations or processes.

Budgets are concerned with totals they lay down cost limits for function and departments and for the firm as a whole. In order to enable an organization to set up or install standard costing system the management has to finalize and prescribe various forms, methods and systems keeping in mind the nature, size and technicalities of the business and motivate responsible persons.

Types of Standards

- Current Standard: Current standard is a standard established for use over a short period of time, related to current conditions. The problem with this type of standard is that it does not try to improve on current levels of efficiency.
- Basic Standard: Basic standard is standard established for use over a long period from which a current standard can be developed. The main disadvantage of this type of standard is that because it has remained unaltered over a long period of time, it may be out of date. The main advantage is in showing the changes in trend of price and efficiency from year to year.
- Ideal Standard: Ideal standard is a standard which can be attained under the most favourable conditions. No provision is made, e.g., for shrinkage, spoilage or machine breakdowns. Users believe that the resulting unfavourable variances will remind management of the need for improvement in all phases of operations. Ideal standards are not widely used in practice because they may influence employee motivation adversely.
- Attainable Standard: Attainable standard is a standard which can be attained if a standard unit of work is carried out efficiently, on a machine properly utilized or material properly used. Allowances are made for normal shrinkage, waste and machine breakdowns. The standard represents future performance and objectives which are reasonably attainable.

Besides having a desirable motivational impact on employees, attainable standards serve other purposes, e.g., cash budgeting, inventory valuation and budgeting departmental performance. If correctly set attainable standards are the best type of standards to use, since they provide employees with a realistic target. Attainable standards have the greatest motivational impact on the workforce.

Setting Standards

In order to use predetermined standard costs, standards have to be set for each element of cost for each line of product manufactured or service supplied. Standard cost shows what the cost should be keeping in mind the most favourable production conditions, and on the assumption that plant will operate at maximum possible efficiency.

The collaboration of all functional departments is a must in setting standards. The quantities, price and rates, qualities or grades, terms of purchase, product substitution etc. have to be kept in mind while setting standards.

The success of standard cost system depends on the reliability, accuracy and acceptance of the standards. Standards must be set and the system implemented whatever may be faults or delay or cost, otherwise the whole exercise will go waste.

The methodology used in conventional approach to variance analysis is as follows

- Setting of standards and construction of a budget based on them.
- Comparison of actual with budgeted outcomes.
- Factoring the variance into individual components and investigation of the significant differences.

In this approach the standards are related to expectations over the budget period and do not necessarily reflect optimal performance. Usually it is believed that standards should be reasonably attainable in the circumstances envisaged.

Thus in this context conventional variance analysis is a postmortem exercise. If the standards are tight then this will have a disincentive effect, whereas if the standards are loose then this results in complacency.

The behavioural aspects and implications are generally ignored while setting the standards, which cause the arbitrary investigation of variances. It does not give adequate guidance regarding cost-benefit of variances investigated or cost of correcting errors. Thus the conventional analysis is more a postmortem.

The following aspects need to be given consideration while setting the standards:

- Standard setting and variance analysis should be sufficiently refined to provide adequate information.
- Qualitative information is not given proper attention.
- The standard costing system should provide for opportunity costs and profit forgone.

The conventional standard cost system is criticized because of using crude variance classifications, in appropriate measurements, calculation of redundant variances, ignoring variances related important control areas. The standard costing system should give due importance to interdependence between different responsibility centres rather than traditional variance analysis.

Standard Costing System during Inflation

The inflationary tendency in the economy will cause fall in purchasing power of money thereby affects the accounting for real value. In inflationary conditions the results shown in financial statements do not represent the correct view of activities carried on in the business concern. Any decision taken or estimates made without inflation would not be correct. The expectations of the investors are more in the inflationary conditions.

If an investor expects 8% in an inflation free world, he would expect 12% rate of return on investment in a world subject to inflation pressures. The rate of inflation will have its impact on future cash-flows and profitability of the concern. Before any estimates made or standards set, the difference between money rate of interest and real rate of interest, the difference between them should be taken as rate of inflation.

The Practical Approach for Adjusting Inflation is as Follows:

- Predict the cash-flows in nominal rupees and use the nominal discount rate.
- Predict cash-flows in real rupees and use a nominal discount rate.

The correct treatment of inflation, therefore, requires the assumptions about inflation which enter the cash-flow forecasts and discount rate calculations. Uncertainty in standard costing can be caused by inflation, technological change, economic and political factors etc. Standards, need to be continually updated and revised.

Standard Cost Card

After setting standard for each element of cost, a standard cost card is prepared showing therein the unit standard cost for each element of cost. Standard margin per unit and standard selling prices, standard materials, labour and factory overhead costs are kept on a standard cost card that shows the itemized cost of each materials and labour operation as well as the overhead cost. A standard cost card gives the standard unit cost of a product.

Responsibility for Setting Standards

The line managers who have to work with and accept the standards must be involved in establishing them. There are strong behavioural and motivational factors involved in this process. The line managers must be involved in the critical part of standard setting. The human aspects of budgeting apply equally to standard costing.

The Cost Accountant has to determine the units of products to be made by producing cost centres and work to be performed by service cost centres. After application of service cost centres rates to production cost centres, a standard overhead rate has to be determined for each production cost centre.

After the standards have been fixed, the management is interested in calculation of variance from the standards with the purpose of making the members of various management levels to know what the variances are, and who is responsible for it.

The purpose of setting standards is to fix yardsticks for measuring the performance of various activities and helps in responsibility accounting. Overhead recovery rates has to be determined in advance and applied on that basis to product/cost centres. There is always a difference in actual expenditure and overheads absorbed.

Problems in Setting Standard Costs

The problems involved in setting standard costs, apart from the inevitable problems of forecasting errors, include the following:

- Deciding how to incorporate inflation into planned unit costs.
- Agreeing a labour efficiency standard for example should current times, expected times or ideal times be used in the labour efficiency standard?
- Deciding on the quality of materials to be used, because a better quality of material will cost more, but perhaps reduce material wastage.
- Deciding on the appropriate mix of component materials, where some change in the mix is possible.
- Estimating materials prices where seasonal price variations or bulk purchase discounts may be significant.
- Possible behavioural problems. Managers responsible for the achievement of standards might resist the use of a standard costing control system for fear of being blamed for any adverse variances.
- The cost of setting up and maintaining a system for establishing standards.

Advantages of Standard Costing

A standard costing system has many advantages which include the following:

- Budgets are compiled from standards.
- Standard costing highlights areas of strengths and weaknesses.
- Actual costs can be compared with standard costs in order to evaluate performance.
- The setting of standards should result in the best resources and methods being used and thereby increase efficiency.
- Standard costs can be used to value stock and provide a basis for setting wage incentive schemes.
- Standard costing simplifies bookkeeping, as information is recorded at standard, instead of a number of historic figures.
- It acts as a form of feed forward control that allows an organization to plan the manufacturing inputs required for different levels of output.
- It act as a form of feedback control by highlighting performance that didn't achieve the standard predicted, thus altering decision makers to situations that may be out of control and in need of corrective action.
- It motivates workers by acting as challenging, specific goals that are intended to guide behaviour in the desired directions.

- It helps to trace/allocate manufacturing costs to each individual unit produced.
- It operates via the management by exception principle, where only those variances (differences between actual and expected results) which are outside certain tolerance limits are investigated, thereby economizing on managerial time and maximizing efficiency.
- Control action is immediate, e.g., as soon as material is issued from stores to production it can be compared with the standard material which should have been used for the actual production.
- Transfer prices are based on standard rather than actual costs. If the latter were used inefficiencies in the form of excess costs might be passed on from one division to another division.
- The process of setting, revising and monitoring standards encourages reappraisal of methods, materials and techniques so leading to cost reductions.

Throughput Accounting

Throughput Accounting (TA) can be understood as a simplified accounting system based on Theory of Constraints (ToC) principles. TA makes growth-driven management and decision making simpler and understandable even for people not familiar with traditional accounting.

Beyond simplifying, TA has a different approach compared to traditional accounting. The latter will focus on cost control (cost of goods sold) and minimizing the unit cost while TA strives to maximize profit.

Throughput Accounting sets the base for Throughput Analysis, helping to make decisions in the ToC way.

Throughput Accounting will probably not replace GAAP in short nor medium term, but provides a limited set of simple KPIs, sufficient to:

- Manage and make decisions in a growth-oriented and ToC way.
- Allow faster reporting and near to real-time figure-based management.
- Help people in operations to understand the basics of accounting.
- Set a common base for controllers and operations to discuss decisions, investments, etc.

Throughput Accounting uses 3 KPIs and 2 ratios:

Throughput (T)

Throughput, defined as the rate of producing goal units (usually money) and translates as revenue or sales minus totally variable expenses in accounting terms.

Totally variable expenses can be simplified to the cost of direct materials because labor is nowadays paid on a (relatively) fixed amount per time period, hence a constant expense to be considered as part of Operating Expenses.

Operating Expenses (OE)

Operating Expenses are all expenses, except the totally variable expenses, required to run and maintain the system of production. Operating Expenses are considered fixed costs, even so they may have some variable cost characteristics.

Investments (I)

Investments, formerly call Inventories, is the amount of cash invested (formerly "tied") into the system in order to turn as much of the Investments into Throughput as possible. This encompasses the stored raw material waiting to be transformed into sellable products as well as investments in capacities / capabilities to produce more units.

Net Profit (NP)

Net Profit is defined as Throughput minus Operating Expenses, or Sales – Total Variable Costs – Operating Expenses.

Return on Investment (ROI)

Return on Investment is the Net Profit compared to Investments (ROI = NP/I).

Drivers for Achieving the Goal

Throughput Accounting offers a simplified way to identify and use the drivers to achieve the Goal, assuming the Goal is to make money now and in the future.

In a very simple way this can be summarized by the following picture which means strive to maximize Throughput while minimize the Operating Expenses and Investments.

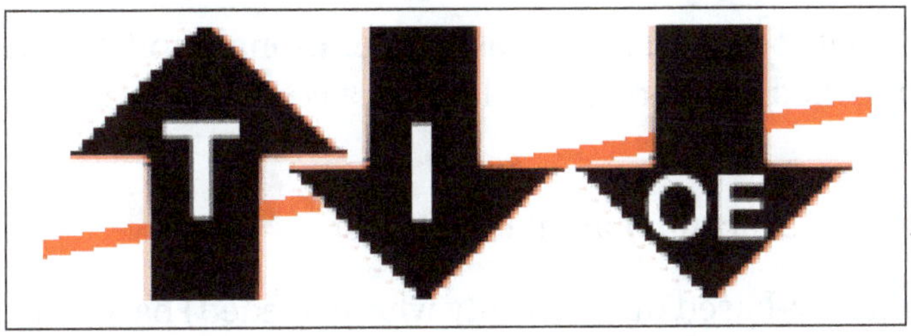

ToC practitioners recognize that Throughput has no limit while Operating Expenses and Investments have limits beyond which no safe operations can be further envisioned. The priority focus on improving T (focusing on the constraint exploitation) rather to go for all-out cost cutting explains the (usually) superior results when going the ToC way compared to unfocused improvements. Throughput Accounting KPIs can be presented in a Dupont-inspired model in order to make the levers and consequences clear.

Throughput Analysis

Beyond the simplification compared to traditional accounting, Throughput Accounting sets the base for Throughput Analysis, helping to make decisions in the ToC way.

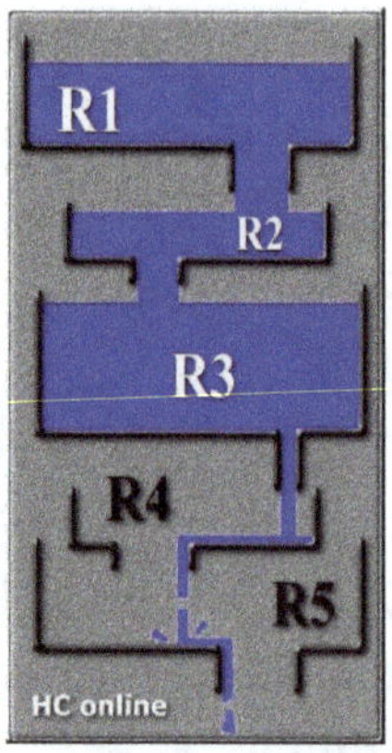

It becomes obvious then that utmost attention must be paid to maximize the passing of the highest profit generating products through the constraint. The decision making is then based on the Throughput per constraint minute rate. The higher the T/mn, the better.

Resource Consumption Accounting

Resource Consumption Accounting (RCA) is a management theory describing a dynamic, integrated, and comprehensive management accounting approach that provides managers with decision support information for enterprise optimization. RCA is a relatively new management accounting approach based largely on the German management accounting approach Grenzplankostenrechnung (GPK) and also allows for the use of activity-based drivers.

Concepts of Resource Consumption Accounting

RCA concepts that distinguish it from other management accounting approaches include the following:

1. Germany's GPK method of quantity-based operational modeling using fixed and proportional costs established at the resource level in a company (i.e., cost center/resource pools or value streams");
2. Gordon Shillinglaw's concept of attributable cost;
3. Flexible use of activity-based drivers (only where needed) based on specific, and restrictive rules;
4. Value chain integration of management accounting into operational systems;
5. Use of fundamental operations transactions as the primary source for financial and quantitative data (rather than the general ledger);
6. Replacing the principle of variability with the principle of responsiveness for operational modeling;
7. Support for a multi-level, contribution margin-based profit & loss statement that supports managerial decision making without the cost distortions and complexity of inappropriate (not based on the principle of causality) allocations of cost.

Core Elements of RCA

There are three core elements that enable RCA to lay a very different foundation for its cost model:

1. The view of resources – Resources and their costs are considered foundational to proper cost modeling and decision support. An organization's cost and revenues are all a function of the resources that produce them.
2. Quantity-based modeling – The entire model is constructed using operational quantities. Operational data is the foundation of value creation and the leading indicator of economic outcomes.
3. Cost behavior – Value is added as a veneer to the quantity-based model and costs/dollars behavior is determined by the behavior of resource quantities as they are applied to value creating operations within an organization.

Additional Information

The goals of the RCA Institute, in promoting the acquisition of knowledge and skills to apply RCA, include the following:

1. Improve management accounting knowledge and practice by clarifying and embracing sound principles that will enhance enterprise decision making and the public welfare through optimum resource usage.
2. Advance the knowledge and practice of Resource Consumption Accounting (RCA) through:
    - A community of active, high quality practitioners and academics.
    - Consistent and disciplined practice centered on a core body of RCA knowledge that is not diluted by wide variations in use or form.
    - Education of adopters, practitioners and vendors and the certification of vendors' products and services.
    - Increased adoption of RCA, over the long-term, as the dominant management accounting approach in business, government, and non-profit organizations.

The RCA Institute library contains an annotated bibliography that is currently divided into four sections:

1. RCA theory,
2. Management accounting landscape and management accounting philosophy,
3. RCA related research and
4. Other materials.

This annotated bibliography provides more information for recommended reading and some guidance on how to get the most out of the information that is there.

Target Costing

Target costing is a system under which a company plans in advance for the price points, product costs, and margins that it wants to achieve for a new product. If it cannot manufacture a product at these planned levels, then it cancels the design project entirely. With target costing, a management team has a powerful tool for continually monitoring products from the moment they enter the design phase and onward throughout their product life cycles. It is considered one of the most important tools for achieving consistent profitability in a manufacturing environment.

The primary steps in the target costing process are:

1. Conduct research: The first step is to review the marketplace in which the company wants to sell products. the design team needs to determine the set of product features that customers are most likely to buy, and the amount they will pay for those features. the team must learn about the perceived value of individual features, in case they later need to determine what impact there will be on the product price if they drop one or more features. it may be necessary to later drop a product feature if the team decides that it cannot provide the feature while still meeting its target cost. at the end of this process, the team has a good idea of the target price at which it can sell the proposed product with a certain set of features, and how it must alter the price if it drops some features from the product.

2. Calculate maximum cost: The company provides the design team with a mandated gross margin that the proposed product must earn. by subtracting the mandated gross margin from the projected product price, the team can easily determine the maximum target cost that the product must achieve before it can be allowed into production.

3. Engineer the product: The engineers and procurement personnel on the team now take the leading role in creating the product. the procurement staff is particularly important if the product has a high proportion of purchased parts; they must determine component pricing based on the necessary quality, delivery, and quantity levels expected for the product. they may also be involved in outsourcing parts, if this results in lower costs. the engineers must design the product to meet the cost target, which will likely include a number of design iterations to see which combination of revised features and design considerations results in the lowest cost.

4. Ongoing activities: Once a product design is finalized and approved, the team is reconstituted to include fewer designers and more industrial engineers. the team now enters into a new phase of reducing production costs, which continues for the life of the product. For example, cost reductions may come from waste reductions in production (known as kaizen costing), or from planned supplier cost reductions. These ongoing cost reductions yield enough additional gross margin for the company to further reduce the price of the product over time, in response to increases in the level of competition.

The design team uses one of the following approaches to more tightly focus its cost reduction efforts:

1. Tied to components: The design team allocates the cost reduction goal among the various product components. This approach tends to result in incremental cost reductions to the same components that were used in the last iteration of the product. This approach is

commonly used when a company is simply trying to refresh an existing product with a new version, and wants to retain the same underlying product structure. The cost reductions achieved through this approach tend to be relatively low, but also result in a high rate of product success, as well as a fairly short design period.

2. Tied to features: The product team allocates the cost reduction goal among various product features, which focuses attention away from any product designs that may have been inherited from the preceding model. This approach tends to achieve more radical cost reductions (and design changes), but also requires more time to design, and also runs a greater risk of product failure or at least greater warranty costs.

Of these methods, companies are more likely to use the first approach if they are looking for a routine upgrade to an existing product, and the second approach if they want to achieve a significant cost reduction or break away from the existing design.

What if the project team simply cannot meet the target cost? Rather than completing the design process and creating a product with a substandard profit margin, the correct response is to stop the development process and move on to other projects instead. This does not mean that management allows its project teams to struggle on for months or years before finally giving up. Instead, they must come within a set percentage of the cost target on various milestone dates, with each successive milestone requirement coming closer to the final target cost. Milestones may occur on specific dates, or when key completion steps are reached in the design process, such as at the end of each design iteration.

Though management may cancel a design project that cannot meet its cost goals, this does not mean that the project will be permanently shelved. Instead, management should review old projects at least once a year to see if the circumstances have changed sufficiently for them to possibly become viable again. A more precise review approach is to have each project team formulate a set of variables that should initiate a product review if a trigger point is reached (such as a decline in the price of a commodity that is used in the product design). If any of these trigger points are reached, the projects are immediately brought to the attention of management to see if they should be revived. Such a revival should take into consideration any changes in the market prices of comparable products since the project was last examined.

Target costing is most applicable to companies that compete by continually issuing a stream of new or upgraded products into the marketplace (such as consumer goods). For them, target costing is a key survival tool. Conversely, target costing is less necessary for those companies that have a small number of legacy products that require minimal updates, and for which long-term profitability is more closely associated with market penetration and geographical coverage (such as soft drinks).

The target costing concept has limited application in a services business where labor comprises the primary cost.

Target costing is an excellent tool for planning a suite of products that have high levels of profitability. This is opposed to the much more common approach of creating a product that is based on the engineering department's view of what the product should be like, and then struggling with costs that are too high in comparison to the market price.

Life Cycle Costing

Life cycle costing is the process of compiling all costs that the owner or producer of an asset will incur over its lifespan. The concept applies to several decision areas. In capital budgeting, the total cost of ownership is compiled and then reduced to its present value in order to determine the expected return on investment (ROI) and net cash flows. This information is a key part of the decision to acquire an asset. In the procurement area, the purchasing staff seeks to examine the total cost of ownership of an asset in order to place orders for those items that are the least expensive, in aggregate, to install, operate, maintain, and dispose of. In the engineering and production areas, life cycle costing is used to develop and manufacture goods that will have the least cost to the customer to install, operate, maintain, and dispose of. In the customer service and field service areas, life cycle costing is focused on minimizing the amount of warranty, replacement, and field service work that must be performed on products over their useful lives.

Life cycle costing is more heavily used by businesses that place an emphasis on long-range planning, so that their multi-year profits are maximized. An organization that does not pay attention to life cycle costing is more likely to develop goods and acquire assets for the lowest immediate cost, not paying attention to the heightened servicing costs of these items later in their useful lives.

Output Costing

Unit or output costing is that method of costing in which cost are ascertained per unit of a single product in a continuous manufacturing activity. Per unit cost is calculated by dividing total production cost by number of units produced. This method is also known as single costing. This method is known as 'single costing' as industries adopting this method manufacture, in most cases, a single variety of product.

This method is also known as 'unit costing', as not only the cost of the total output, but also the cost per unit of output is ascertained under this method. Under this method cost units are identical. This method is also called 'output costing', as cost is ascertained for the total output of a product.

Features of Output Costing

Output costing has certain characteristics features:

The important features of output costing are:

1. Output costing is the method of costing adopted in concerns where there is a production of single product or a few grades of the same product differing only in size, shape or quality by continuous process of manufacture. The units of production or output are identical and the costs of units are physical and natural.

2. Under this method, the cost per unit of output, say, per ton, per barrel, per kilogram, per metre, per quintal, per bag, etc. is ascertained. The cost per unit of output is ascertained by dividing the total cost incurred on a product during a given period of time by output produced during the period.

Where the products manufactured are of different grades, first, the costs of products are ascertained grade-wise, and then the total cost of each grade of the product is divided by the number of units of that grade so as to ascertain the cost per unit of each grade of the product.

3. Equality of cost is an important feature of this method. That is, under this method, cost units, which are identical, will have identical cost.

4. Under this method, the cost of product is ascertained at the end of the accounting period.

5. Under this method, the cost information relating to a product may be presented in the form of either cost sheet or production account.

6. This method is the simplest method of all the methods of costing; in the sense that the cost collection and the cost ascertainment are quite simple.

7. The cost per unit of output, determined under single. Costing enables the management to make real comparison between different periods and between different firms within the same industry, as the unit of output is a common factor between different periods and between different firms within the same industry.

Objectives of Output Costing

Output costing has the certain objectives:

They are:

1. To ascertain the total cost of the output as well as the cost per unit of output.
2. To ascertain the profit or loss on production.
3. To analyse the expenditure by nature, classify them into element of cost and know the extent to which each element of cost contributes to the total cost.
4. To facilitate comparison of the cost of one period with the cost of another period to know the efficiency or otherwise of the production.
5. To facilitate the preparation of tender or quotation.
6. To control the cost of the product through comparative study of the costs of any two periods or through the comparison of the actual costs with the pre-determined standard cost.

Important Items Regarding Preparation of Statement of Cost and Cost Sheet:

Normal Loss of Materials

This type of loss is unavoidable and arises due to the nature of material. For example – loss by evaporation of liquid materials, loss due to loading and unloading of materials, etc. This loss is not deducted from the cost of material rather it is charged to the output because it is a principle of costing that all normal expenses which are necessarily to be incurred should be included in the cost of production.

Therefore, in order to absorb normal material losses in cost, the rates of usable materials are inflated so that such losses are covered. In other words, such normal loss should be ignored and this will get automatically charged to output.

Abnormal Loss of Materials

Abnormal losses are those losses which arise due to abnormal reasons such as loss by theft, loss by fire, careless handling etc. The cost of materials abnormally lost should be deducted from the value of materials purchased so that output is charged only for the materials used in production. Abnormal losses are charged to Costing Profit and Loss Account.

Wages of Normal Idle Time

Normal idle time is inherent in any work situation and cannot be reduced. The cost of normal idle labour time is charged to the cost of production. Hence, wages of normal idle time is not subtracted from the labour cos.

Wages of Abnormal Idle Time

Abnormal idle time arises due to unanticipated causes such as strikes, lockouts, fire, accidents, major machine break-down, earthquakes, etc. Loss of time due to such abnormal causes cannot be planned. Such causes are sudden and non-frequent.

The cost of abnormal idle time is not included in cost of production. The wages paid for abnormal idle time should be debited to Costing P/L A/c. Hence, wages of abnormal idle time is subtracted from the labour cost.

Sale of Scrap, Defective, Salvage or Residue

If clear information is given, then adjustment of these sales will be made accordingly. But, if it is not clear that what the nature of scrap defective, etc., the sale value of scrap etc. is deducted before computing factory cost.

Defective or Rejected Work

Sometimes, under production process there might be defective goods. The production not conforming to the standard set is known as defective. If such goods cannot be rectified, then it may be sold in the market at lower rate. Whatever the amount is collected from such sale is deducted from the factory cost. Similarly the defective units are also deducted from the number of units produced.

On the other hand, the defective units which can be rectified by incurring extra expenses, then such extra expenses incurred on such a rectification can be added in factory overhead as an extra factory overhead. After that the saleable units and their costs can be determined.

Cash Discount and Trade Discount

Cash discount is not considered as the part of cost of production, since it is of financial nature. Whereas, trade discount is treated as sales promotion expense and is included in selling and distribution expenses or may be deducted from gross sales.

Allocation of Joint Expenses

In absence of clear-cut information factory overhead is allocated on the basis of wages ratio and office and administration expenses and selling and distribution expenses on the basis of works cost ratio.

Packing Charges

Treatment of packing charges depends upon its nature. If, in absence of packing, goods cannot be sold, then it should be treated as direct expense (i.e. packing of mustard oil etc.). Packing charges in respect of partly finished goods are considered as factory overhead. In the same way, packing expenses concerned with finished goods are included in selling and distribution expenses.

Cost Collection or Cost Accumulation

Usually the following procedure is adopted under output costing for the cost accumulation of the various elements of cost:

Material

As materials both direct and indirect are issued to production against properly authorised material requisitions. The direct and indirect material costs can be ascertained through material requisitions.

Through the analysis of material requisitions, the quantities of direct and indirect materials issued to production can be ascertained, and on the basis of the prevalent method of pricing material issues, the direct and indirect material costs can be ascertained.

Accounting of Materials

Materials are dealt in cost accounting as follows:

1. The direct material costs are taken as a part of Prime Cost.
2. Indirect material costs are charged to Factory Overheads.
3. Normal loss of materials is adjusted by inflating the issue price of materials.
4. Abnormal loss of materials is not taken into account in the cost of production. It is charged to the Costing Profit and Loss Account.

Labour

The labour costs are collected periodically through pay rolls kept separately for each section or type of work without the detailed job cards or chits required in job costing.

Treatment of Labour Cost in Cost Accounting

Labour cost is dealt as follows:

1. Direct labour costs are treated as a part of Prime Cost.
2. Indirect labour costs are charged to Factory Overheads.

Direct Expenses

Direct expenses or chargeable expenses are separately collected from the financial record where the actual direct expenses incurred are recorded.

The main expenses under this head are:

1. Royalty
2. Architect and surveyor's fees
3. Expenses of drawing and designs
4. Excise duty etc.

Treatment

It is treated as a part of Prime Cost.

Overheads

Where cost finding is undertaken at the end of long interval, i.e., at the end of the year, after the overheads incurred are actually recorded in the financial book, the actual overheads incurred during the year are collected from the financial records.

The actual overheads collected from the financial records are analysed into three broad categories, viz.:

1. Factory Overheads,
2. Office and Administration Overheads, and
3. Selling and Distribution Overheads and are treated as such for cost finding.

Process Costing

Process costing is an accounting methodology that traces and accumulates direct costs, and allocates indirect costs of a manufacturing process. Costs are assigned to products, usually in a large batch, which might include an entire month's production. Eventually, costs have to be allocated to individual units of product. It assigns average costs to each unit, and is the opposite extreme of Job costing which attempts to measure individual costs of production of each unit. Process costing is usually a significant chapter. It is a method of assigning costs to units of production in companies producing large quantities of homogeneous products.

Process costing is a type of operation costing which is used to ascertain the cost of a product at each process or stage of manufacture. CIMA defines process costing as "The costing method applicable where goods or services result from a sequence of continuous or repetitive operations or processes. Costs are averaged over the units produced during the period". Process costing is suitable for industries producing homogeneous products and where production is a continuous flow. A process can be referred to as the sub-unit of an organization specifically defined for cost collection purpose.

Importance of Process Costing

Costing is an important process that many companies engage in to keep track of where their money is being spent in the production and distribution processes. Understanding these costs is the first step in being able to control them. It is very important that a company chooses the appropriate type of costing system for their product type and industry. One type of costing system that is used in certain industries is process costing that varies from other types of costing (such as job costing) in some ways. In process costing unit costs are more like averages, the process-costing system requires less bookkeeping than does a job-order costing system. Thus, some companies often prefer to use the process-costing system.

When is Process Costing Applied?

Process costing is appropriate for companies that produce a continuous mass of like units through series of operations or process. Also, when one order does not affect the production process and a standardization of the process and product exists. However, if there are significant differences among the costs of various products, a process costing system would not provide adequate product-cost information. Costing is generally used in such industries such as petroleum, coal mining, chemicals, textiles, paper, plastic, glass, food, banks, courier, cement, and soap.

Reasons for use

Company units of product in a given period of time:

- Products are manufactured in large quantities, but products may be sold in small quantities, sometimes one at a time (automobiles, loaves of bread), a dozen or two at a time (eggs, cookies), etc.
- Product costs must be transferred from Finished Goods to Cost of Goods Sold as sales are made. This requires a correct and accurate accounting of product costs per unit, to have a proper matching of product costs against related sales revenue.
- Managers need to maintain cost control over the manufacturing process. Process costing provides managers with feedback that can be used to compare similar product costs from one month to the next, keeping costs in line with projected manufacturing budgets.
- A fraction-of-a-cent cost change can represent a large dollar change in overall profitability, when selling millions of units of product a month. Managers must carefully watch per unit costs on a daily basis through the production process, while at the same time dealing with materials and output in huge quantities.
- Materials part way through a process (e.g. chemicals) might need to be given a value, process costing allows for this. By determining what cost the part processed material has incurred such as labor or overhead an "equivalent unit" relative to the value of a finished process can be calculated.

Process Cost Procedures

There are four basic steps in accounting for Process cost:

- Summarize the flow of physical units of output.

- Compute output in terms of equivalent units.
- Summarize total costs to account for and Compute equivalent unit costs.
- Assign total costs to units completed and to units in ending work in process inventory.

The journal entries for process costing are the same as those for job-order costing with one exception. The entry to transfer cost from one work-in-process account to another is:

- Work-in-process inventory-second department Debit (Left)
- Work-in-process-first department Credit (Right)

Example: Micro Labs Company produces house paint in two processing departments: the Mixing Department which mixes the paint colors and the Finishing Department which puts the paint in containers and labels them. The following information related to the company's operation for October follows:

A) Raw materials were issued for use in production: Mixing department, $551,000, and the Finishing department, $629,000. B) Direct labor costs incurred: Mixing department $230,000, and Finishing department $270,000. C) Manufacturing overhead cost applied: Mixing department $665,000, and Finishing department, $405,000. D) The cost of the mixed paint transferred from the Mixing department to the Finishing department was $1,850,000. E) Paint that had been prepared for shipping was transferred from the Finishing department to Finished Goods. Cost of the transferred paint was $3,200,000.

Required: Prepare journal entries to record items A) through E) above.

Solution:

–Work in Process – Mixing	551,000	
–Work in Process – Finishing	629,000	
–Raw Materials		1,180,000
–Work in Process – Mixing	230,000	
–Work in Process – Finishing	270,000	
–Wages and Salaries Payable		500,000
–Work in Process – Mixing	665,000	
–Work in Process – Finishing	405,000	
–Manufacturing Overhead		1,070,000
–Work in Process – Finishing	1,850,000	
–Work in Process – Mixing		1,850,000
–Finished Goods	3,200,000	
–Work in Process – Finishing		3,200,000

Example: Larney Corporation uses process costing. A number of transactions that occurred in June are listed below. As follows:

A) Raw materials that cost $38,200 are withdrawn from the storeroom for use in the Mixing Department. B) Direct labor costs incurred $36,500,in the Mixing Department. C) Manufacturing overhead of $42,100 is applied in the Mixing Department. D) Units with a carrying cost of $112,400 finish processing in the Mixing Department and are transferred to the Drying Department for further processing. E) Units with a carrying cost of $143,800 finish processing in the Drying Department, the final step in the production process, and are transferred to the finished goods warehouse. F) Finished goods with a carrying cost of $138,500

Required: Prepare journal entries to record items A) through F).

Solution:

–work in process-mixing department	$38,200	
—raw materials		$38,200
–work in process	$36,500	
–salaries/wages payable		$36,500
–work in process-mixing department	$42,100	
–manufacturing overhead		$42,100
–work in process-drying department.	$112,400	
–work in process mixing department		$112,400
–finished goods	$143,800	
–work in process-drying department		$143,800
–costs of goods sold	$138,500	
–finished goods		$138,500

Operation Cost in Batch Manufacturing

Batch costing is a modification of job costing. When production is repetitive nature and consists of a definite number of articles, batch is used. In batch costing, the most important problem is to determine the optimum size of the batch that follows the fact that production of two elements of costs:

- Set up costs which are generally fixed per batch.
- Carrying costs which vadetermination of batch quantity requires considerations of some factors:
  - Setting up costs per batch.
  - Cost of manufacturing such as (direct materials cost + direct wages + direct overhead) per piece.
  - Cost of storage.
  - Rate of interest on the capital invested in product and rate of demand for product.

Service Costing

The term service costing or operating costing refers to the computation of the total operational cost incurred on each unit of the intangible product. These intangible products or services can be either in the form of internal services that are carried out by industries as supporting activities for the manufacturing of goods; or external services that are offered as a significant product to the customers by the service sector companies.

Service costing is an essential concept since every service organization needs to ascertain its business overheads, to ensure fair pricing of the products, i.e., services; and for keeping a control over its fixed and variable costs.

Features of Service Costing

The costing in a service industry can be better understood with the help of the following characteristics:

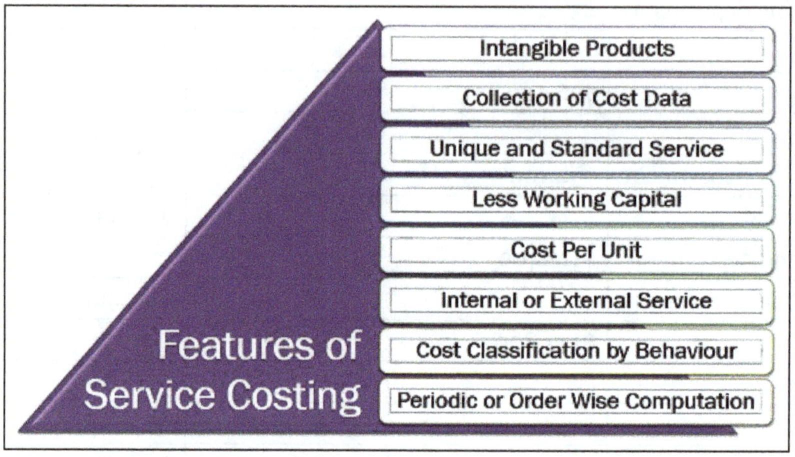

- Intangible Products: Service costing deals with the operating cost of products which does not have any physical form but satisfies consumer needs and wants.
- Collection of Cost Data: The documents used for service costing of products include cost sheet, bills payables, daily log sheet, etc.
- Unique and Standard Service: The services so offered by such organizations are specialized and exclusive.
- Less Working Capital: The service costing involves less working capital since the direct cost of raw material and other direct expenses is comparatively low.
- Cost Per Unit: The cost per unit is mainly calculated in service costing, where the cost unit is determined by the type of service industry the business belongs to, and it usually differs from company to company. Like, in the case of goods transport it is 'tonne-miles'; whereas, in boilers, it is 'per cubic centimetre-litre'.
- Internal or External Service: The service costing can be performed internally, to determine the operating cost of the supporting activities in manufacturing industries; or it can be carried out externally, by the companies dedicated to rendering services.
- Cost Classification by Behaviour: In the operating cost sheet format, all the business costs are classified according to their behaviour, i.e., fixed costs, semi-variable costs and variable costs.
- Periodic or Order Wise Computation: The service costing records the overheads at regular intervals, i.e., monthly or yearly but for operating cost of vehicles like tractors and JCB machines, order wise computation is adopted.

Cost Unit in Service Costing

To measure the cost of business operations in a service industry is a complex activity where all the cost parameters are to be considered while deciding a suitable unit for costing.

Following are the two different kinds of cost unit ascertained under service costing:

Simple Cost Unit

The cost unit which uses only one single parameter for measurement of the service cost is termed as a simple cost unit.

The different types of service organizations and their simple cost units are mentioned below:

Nature of Service Organization	Cost Unit
Water Supply	Per Kiloliter
Canteen	Per Meal / Per Person / Per Staff
Road Maintenance	Per Kilometer
Street Lighting	Per Lamp / Per Point
Boiler House	Per 1000 Ibs
Gas	Per Cubic Meter / Per Kilogram
Private Transport	Per Kilometer / Per Hour / Per Trip / Per Passenger

Composite Cost Unit

The most commonly used cost unit in service costing is the composite cost unit where two parameters are considered, and the measurement of both the parameters are combined to form a single cost unit.

Following are the different types of service organizations and their composite cost units:

Nature of Service Organization	Cost Unit
Hospital	Per Bed-Day / Per Patient-Day
Hotel	Per Room-Day / Per Room-Night / Per Bed-Day
Electricity	Per Kilowatt-Hour
Entertainment in Cinema or Theater	Per Ticket-Show
Boiler House	Per Cubic Centimeter-Liter
Passenger Transport	Per Passenger-Kilometer / Per Passenger-Mile
Goods Transport	Per Tonne-Mile / Per Quintal-Kilometer

Calculation of Cost per Unit: The formula for computing the cost of each service unit (i.e., cost per unit) is given below:

$$\text{Cost Per Service Unit} = \frac{\text{Total Costs for the Period}}{\text{Number of Services Units in the Period}}$$

Format of Service Costing

Transport is one of the significant service industry these days, and it is essential to have an insight of the proforma for determining the operating costing of such organizations:

Operating cost sheet of...
For the period...

Cost unit...
No. of cost units...

Particulars	Total ($)	Per units ($)
Fixed Costs:		
Licence fee	X	X
Garage rent	X	X
Interest on capital	X	X
Motor vehicle Tax / road Tax	X	X
Administration cost/general supervision	X	X
Insurance	X	X
Deprecation	X	X
(A)Total	X	X
Semi-variable cost:	X	X
Overhauling	X	X
Repairs and maintenances	X	X
Tyres and tubes	X	X
Painting	X	X
(B) Total	X	X
Variable cost	X	X
Driver's wages	X	X
Conductor's wages	X	X
Petrol/ diesel	X	X
Engine oil	X	X
Grease/ Lubricating	X	X
(C) Total	X	X
Grand total (A+B+)	X	X

Types of Service Costing

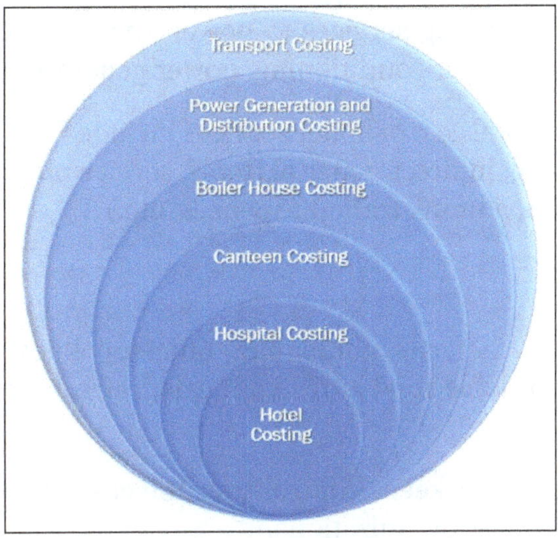

Types of Services Costing

When we talk about services, our mind recalls the multiple intangible products we use on a day to day basis. But do you know that all these services have different cost units and elements during computation?

This is because each of these services is unique and involves a variety of different type of overheads. Thus, the service costing for each kind of service organization varies and can be classified as follows:

Transport Costing

The costing in the transport industry meets multiple objectives. These objectives can be segregated as follows by the type of transport service an organization provides:

- Private Transport: When the vehicle is hired individually for private tours, service costing is used to determine the hiring charges to be applied.
- Passenger Transport: It also ascertains the cost of conveyance, per passenger up to to a certain distance in case of public or passenger transport companies.
- Goods Transport: When we talk about goods transport services, the cost of carrying a defined quantity of goods up to a particular distance is also decided through service costing.

The common objectives of transport costing include a comparison between two different vehicles or group of vehicles and; whether to use an alternative source of transport or own vehicle, in terms of cost involved.

Power Generation and Distribution Costing

The powerhouses produce energy in the form of electricity through water, gas or sunlight. The cost of power generation services majorly includes fixed costs, i.e., interest on capital, depreciation, repairs and maintenance, administration expenses; and variable costs such as steam consumed, labour wages, lubricants, coal, etc.

Boiler House Costing

The boiler house provides supporting services to power and electricity generation units, in the form of steam which is used in the air conditioning, power generation and air compression.

The overheads involved in the total cost of boiler services include fuel (coal, oil), direct and indirect labour, water and its processing, indirect material (tools, service material), maintenance and fixed costs (rent, taxes, depreciation, administration expenses, etc.)

Canteen Costing

The government organizations, factories, companies, offices, colleges, schools and even hospitals have canteens to provide affordable foodstuff like meals, refreshment, snacks, etc. to the staff, students and patients.

The canteen manager or supervisor keeps control over the costs and performs service costing to ascertain revenue of these business organizations.

The costs involved in canteen services include the cost of material, labour, services, consumable stores and miscellaneous overheads.

Hospital Costing

The services provided by the medical organizations like hospitals health centres, nursing homes, medical camps and clinics require cost analysis, which is possible through service costing.

The hospital cost includes fixed charges such as labour salaries, maintenance charges, rent, administration expenses and other overheads. Also, the variable charges like medicines, bed charges, doctors fees, etc. are involved in the total cost.

Hotel Costing

The hotels provide accommodation to the guests as services; thus, it involves a high maintenance cost along with the fixed cost. The fixed cost includes depreciation, staff salaries, interest on capital, taxes, etc. Whereas, variable cost involves electricity charges, temporary staff salary, etc.

Example:

XYZ Transport Co. provides the following data for the month ending on January 31, 2019:

Particulars	Vehicle
No. of Vehicles	5
Cost of Each Vehicle	₹200000
Garage Rent (Monthly)	₹5000
Depreciation	12% p.a.
Insurance (Yearly)	₹28800
Licence Fee	₹3000

Overhauling (Monthly)	₹7500
Diesel	₹50 per trip each way
General Supervision	₹7200 p.a.
Drivers' Wages (Monthly)	₹10000
Engine Oil (Monthly)	₹1500

We have assumed that the licence fee was calculated on a monthly basis. Also, each vehicle has the capacity of 2-tonne of goods. If,

- Each vehicle covers a distance of 100 miles each way daily to and from the city;
- Each vehicle runs on an average of 20 days a month; and
- While going to the city, the capacity was full and while returning the capacity is 25% occupied.

Find out the following:

- Operating cost per tonne-mile; and
- Rate per trip to be charged, if the company plans to make 40% profit on freightage.

Computation

Operating cost sheet of XYZ & Co.
For the month ending January 31.2019

Cost/ unit: ₹2.00
No. of cost units: 25000 tonne- miles

Particulars	Total ($)	Per units ($)
Fixed Cost:		
Garage rent	3000	0.12
General supervision	5000	0.20
Insurance	600	0.02
Depreciation	2400	0.10
Total	10000	0.84
Semi-variable cost:		
Overhauling	7500	0.30
Total	7500	0.30
Variable costs:		
Driver's Wages	10000	0.40
Diesel	10000	0.40
Engine oil	1500	0.06
Total	21500	0.86
Grant Total(A+B+C)	50000	2.00

No. of Cost Units

On the first way of the trip: 100% capacity was occupied, i.e., 2-tonnes,

No. of Cost Units=Distance×Capacity Occupied×Working Days×No. of Vehicles,

No. of Cost Units=100×2×20×5=20000 tonne-miles.

On the second way of the trip: 25% capacity was occupied, i.e., 0.5-tonnes; Similarly, No. of Cost Units=100×0.5×20×5=5000 tonne-miles.

Hence,

Total No. of Cost Units=20000+5000=25000 tonne-miles.

General Supervision

It is given annually, therefore;

Monthly expense on general supervision=7200/12=₹600.

Insurance

It is given annually, therefore;

Monthly expense on insurance=28800/12=₹2400.

Depreciation

It is given annually, therefore;

Monthly depreciation=(Total Cost of 5 Vehicles×Rate of Depreciation)/(100×12);

Monthly depreciation=(1000000×12)/(100×12)=₹10000.

Diesel

Monthly expense on diesel=Cost per Trip×No. of Ways per Trip×No. of Working Days×No. of Vehicles;

Monthly expense on diesel=50×2×20×5=₹10000.

Non-integral System

Non-integral system is a system of accounting under which two separate sets of account books are maintained—one for cost accounts and the other for financial accounts. In other words, cost accounts are maintained separately from financial accounts.

Since separate ledgers are maintained for cost and financial accounts in this system, the cost accountant is responsible for recording of the cost accounting transactions and the financial accountant is responsible for financial transactions.

Non-integral system of accounting is also known as non-integrated system or Inter-locking system or Cost Ledger Accounting system. CIMA, London defines Non-integral system as a system in which the cost accounts are distinct from financial accounts, the two sets of accounts being kept continuously in agreement by the use of control accounts or made readily reconcilable by other means.

Basic Features of Non-Integral System

- Separate ledgers are maintained for cost and financial accounts.
- Like financial accounting, it is also based on double entry system.
- There are no personal accounts because cost accounts do not show relationship with outsiders.
- Cost accounts are concerned with impersonal accounts i.e., real and nominal accounts.
- In real accounts, only stocks are shown in cost accounts.
- Transactions affecting the nominal accounts are recorded separately in detail. Thus cost accounting department is concerned mainly with the ascertainment of income and expenditure of business.
- Under this system one main ledger (i.e., Cost Ledger) and various subsidiary ledgers are maintained.
- Since the system is not properly integrated, some items may appear in financial ledgers only, while some other items appear only in cost ledger.
- The profit or loss disclosed by the two sets of accounts for a particular period will never be the same and as such a reconciliation of costing profit or loss with that of financial accounts is essential.

Ledgers under Non-integral Accounts

The principal financial ledgers are:

- General Ledger: It contains all real, nominal and personal accounts except trade debtors and trade creditors account.
- Debtors Ledger: It has personal accounts of trade debtors.
- Creditors Ledger: It has personal accounts of trade creditors.
- The principal cost ledgers are:
- Cost Ledger: It is the principal ledger in cost books which controls all other ledgers in the costing department. It contains all impersonal accounts and is similar to General Ledger of financial accounts.
- Stores Ledger: It is a subsidiary ledger. It contains all stores accounts.

- Work-in-Progress Ledger: It is a subsidiary ledger. It contains a separate account for each job in progress. Each such account is debited with the materials costs, wages and overheads chargeable to the jobs and credited with the cost of work completed. The balance in this account shows the cost of uncertified work.
- Finished Goods Ledger: It is a subsidiary ledger. It contains accounts of completely finished goods and jobs. The cost ledger is made self-balancing by opening a control account for each of the above subsidiary ledgers.

Practical Problems Relating to Non-integral System

Problem:

Pass Journal Entries in the cost books (non-integrated system) for the following transactions:

- Worth Rs. 25000 returned to the stores from job.
- Gross total wages paid Rs. 48,000. Employer's contribution to P.F and State Insurance amount to Rs. 2,000. Wages analysis book detailed Rs. 20,000 towards direct labour, Rs. 12,000 towards indirect factory labour, Rs 10,000 towards salaries etc. to office staff and Rs. 8,000 for salaries etc. to selling and distribution staff.

Solution:

Journal entries in the cost books (non- integrated system)				
Date	Particulars	L.F	Dr. $	Cr. $
	Store Ledger Control A/c Dr. To Work-in -progress ledger control A/c (Material returned to stores from job)		25,000	25,000
	Wages control A/c Dr. To General Ledger Adjustment A/c (Payment of gross wages including employer's contribution to P.F and State Insurance)		50,000	50,000
	Work-in -progress Ledger Control A/c Dr. Factory Overhead Control A/c Dr. Administration Overhead Control A/c Dr. Selling and Dist. Overhead Control A/c Dr. To Wages Control A/c (Amount of wages allocated to WIP and respective overhead control accounts.)		20,000 12,000 10,000 8,000	50,000

Problem:

Pass journal entries in the cost books, maintained on non-integrated system, for the following:

1. Issue of material	: Direct $ 5,50,000, indirect	$ 1,50,000
2. Allocation of wagas	: Direct $ 2,00,000 indirect	$ 40,000
3. Under / Over – absorbed overheads	:Factory (over) $ 20,000	
	Administration (under)	
	:$ 10,000	

Solution

Entries in the cost books (Non- integrated systems)				
Date	Particulars	L.F	Dr. $	Cr. $
	1. Work-in-Progress Ledger control A/c Dr. Factory Overhead Control A/c Dr. To Strores Ledger control A/c (Issue of direct and indirect material)		5,50,000 1,50,000	 7,00,000
	2. Work-in-Progress Ledger Control A/c Dr. Factory Overhead Control A/c Dr. To Wages Control A/c (Allocation of direct and indirect wages)		2,00,000 40,000	 2,40,000
	3. Factory Overhead Control A/c Dr. To Costing Profit and Loss A/c (Over absorption of factory overhead transferred to Costing Profit and Loss A/c)		20,000	 20,000
	4. Costing Profit and Loss A/c Dr. To Administration Overhead Control A/c (Under-Absorption of Administration overhead transferred to Costing Profit and Loss A/c)		10,000	 10,000

Problem:

Assuming non-Integrated accounting system, pass journal entries in the cost books for the following transactions:

Issue of material	: Direct $5,00,000, indirect	$ 1,00,000
Allocation of wagas and salaries	: Direct labour	$ 1,20,000
	Indirect factory labour	$ 40,000
	Salaries to office staff	$ 90,000
Over – absorption of factory overheads	: $ 10,000	

Solution:

Journal entries in the cost books (non- integrated system)

Date	Particulars	L.F	Dr. $	Cr. $
	1. Work-in-Progress Ledger control A/c Dr. Factory Overhead Control A/c Dr. To Strong ledger Control A/c (Issue of direct and indirect material)		5,00,000 1,00,000	 6,00,000
	2. Work-in-Progress Ledger Control A/c Dr. Factory Overhead Control A/c Dr. Office and Adm: Overhead Control A/c Dr. To Wagas Control A/c (Allocation of direct and indirect wages)		1,20,000 40,000 90,000	 2,50,000
	3. Factory Overhead Control A/c Dr. To Costing Profit and Loss A/c (Over absorption of factory overhead transferred to costing profit and loss A/c)		10,000	 10,000

Cost Allocation

Cost allocation is the assigning of a cost to several cost objects such as products or departments. The cost allocation is needed because the cost is not directly traceable to a specific object. Since the cost is not directly traceable, the resulting allocation is somewhat arbitrary. Because of the arbitrariness, some people describe cost allocation as the spreading of a cost.

Accountants have made efforts to improve the cost allocation techniques. Over time, manufacturers' overhead allocations have moved from a plant-wide rates to departmental rates. Some allocations that were allocated on the basis of direct labor hours are now based on machine hours. In order to improve those bases of allocations, some accountants are implementing activity based costing. The goal is to reduce the arbitrariness by identifying the various root causes of the overhead costs.

Examples of Cost Allocations

The following are only a few of the many cost allocations that occur in some companies or organizations:

- The cost of a manufacturing building is allocated to each of the years that the building is expected to be used. Each year's depreciation is allocated to the departments that use the building. Each department's allocated cost is then allocated/assigned to the products that are processed in the department.
- The electricity that is used in the production facility as measured by a single meter is allocated to the departments using the electricity. Each department's electricity is then allocated/assigned to the products processed in the department.
- The cost of raw land that was purchased for $1 million is going to be developed into 80 residential lots of various sizes and 10 business lots of different sizes. The $1 million cost must be allocated to the resulting 90 lots in a meaningful way so that the developer can report the profit of selling two residential lots and the largest of the business lots. The basis for the allocation is likely to be the net realizable values of the lots.
- The annual salary and benefits of an employee that spends time in three main functions of a nonprofit organization.

Revenue Expenditure

A revenue expenditure is a cost that is charged to expense as soon as the cost is incurred. By doing so, a business is using the matching principle to link the expense incurred to revenues generated in the same reporting period. This yields the most accurate income statement results. There are two types of revenue expenditure:

- Maintaining a revenue generating asset: This includes repair and maintenance expenses, because they are incurred to support current operations, and do not extend the life of an asset or improve it.

- Generating revenue: This is all day-to-day expenses needed to operate a business, such as sales salaries, rent, office supplies, and utilities.

Other types of costs are not considered to be revenue expenditures, because they relate to the generation of *future* revenues. For example, the purchase of a fixed asset is categorized as an asset and charged to expense over multiple periods, to match the cost of the asset against. These expenditures are known as capital expenditures.

References

- What-are-direct-costs: accountingtools.com, Retrieved 2 February, 2019
- What-are-indirect-costs: accountingtools.com, Retrieved 22 June, 2019
- Fixedcost: investopedia.com, Retrieved 11 January, 2019
- Variable-costs: investinganswers.com, Retrieved 17 May, 2019
- Controllable-costs: accountingtools.com, Retrieved 19 January, 2019
- Uncontrollable-costs, accounting: myaccountingcourse.com, Retrieved 2 March, 2019
- What-is-a-standard-cost: accountingcoach.com, Retrieved 23 June, 2019
- What-is-cost-accounting: accountingcoach.com, Retrieved 25 April, 2019
- Gofman, Dina; Duggineni, Lourdes (28 Aug 2016). "Why your finance team might cut your project budget?". projectaccounting.com.au. Retrieved 10 Nov 2017
- Standard-costing-meaning-and-objectives-cost-accounting, standard-costing, cost-accounting: accountingnotes.net, Retrieved 22 March, 2019
- Target-costing: accountingtools.com, Retrieved 20 August, 2019
- Service-costing: theinvestorsbook.com, Retrieved 23 April, 2019
- Non-integral-system-cost-accounting, cost-book-keep, cost-accounting: accountingnotes.net, Retrieved 7 February, 2019
- What-is-cost-allocation: accountingcoach.com, Retrieved 29 May, 2019
- Revenue-expenditure: accountingtools.com, Retrieved 9 July, 2019

4

Auditing: Types and Processes

The process of systematically and independently examining the books, accounts and documents of an organization to determine the accuracy of the financial statements and non-financial disclosures is known as auditing. Some of the different types of audits are financial audit, cost audit and internal audit. This chapter has been carefully written to provide an easy understanding of these varied types of auditing.

Auditing is the process of assessment and ascertaining of financial, operational, and strategic goals and processes in organizations to determine whether they are in compliance with the stated principles in addition to them being in conformity with organizational and more importantly, regulatory requirements. Indeed, among the objectives of auditing ,conformance with regulatory norms and rules and regulations is indeed one of the drivers behind auditing and historically and traditionally, has been the main reason why organizations get their financial statements, operational process, and strategic imperatives audited.

The purpose of auditing is to perform an objective examination and evaluation of the financial statements of an organization or an individual to make sure that their records are a fair and accurate representation of the transactions they claim to represent. An audit can be conducted internally by employees of a business or an outside firm. Having audits done by an outside party can be helpful as it removes any biases when it comes to the state of a company's financials. Outside auditors can be candid about their findings without affecting daily work relationships.

Audit

The term 'audit' means an unbiased examination of the financial statements, i.e. account books and other relevant documents such as vouchers, invoices, bills, receipts, etc., of a business entity, regardless of the size, nature, orientation and legal structure, carried out by an auditor so as to give an opinion on the financial statement. The auditor can satisfy himself, by ensuring that:

- The financial statements of the company are prepared in reference to the entries in the account books.
- Sufficient documents and vouchers back the entries made in the books of account.
- During the process of compilation, no entries are omitted or skipped in the books of accounts.
- The financial statement clearly communicates the information.
- There must have proper classification, description and disclosure of the amounts in the financial statement, adhering to the accounting standards.
- The financial statement shows a clear view of the operational results, i.e. profits and losses and assets and liabilities of the entity.

Objectives of Audit

- To gain considerable assurance that the financial statement of the entity does not have any material misstatement, that may influence the decision of the stakeholders.
- To present a report on the financial statements so examined by the auditor, with respect to the findings of the auditor.

The audit is not a mandatory requirement for all categories of business entities or institution. So, based on this, there are two types of audit, i.e. audit required by law and voluntary audit.

Features Covered under Audit

- Examining the Accounting and the internal control system and procedures of the organization.
- Confirming the validity, reliability and authenticity of transactions.
- Scrutinizing the vouchers and supporting documents.
- Checking arithmetic accuracy of the accounts.
- Determining whether distinction has been made between capital and revenue natured items.
- Making a comparison of the items covered in the financial statement with those of the account books.
- Verifying the assets and liabilities.
- Confirming the statutory requirements of the body corporate.
- Reporting to the requisite authority

Audit Process

The following are the steps of the audit process, along with the auditee's involvement and responsibilities during each of these steps:

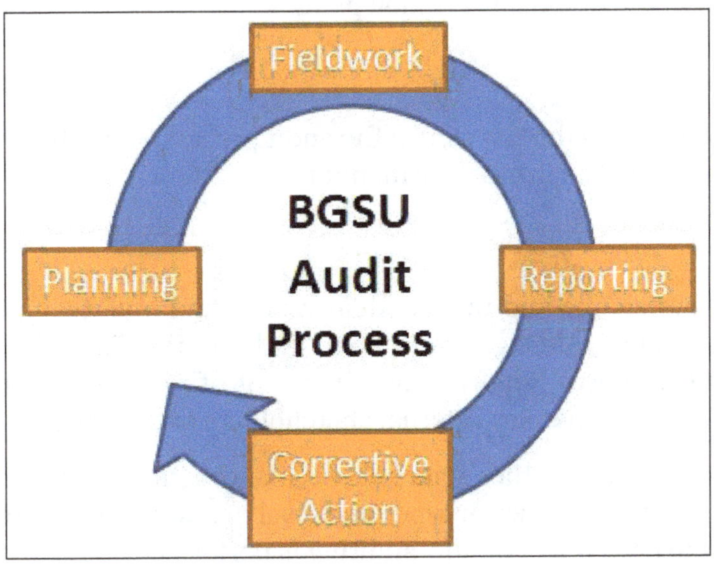

Pre-planning

Pre-planning provides a preliminary understanding of the risks, responsibilities and key processes of the operation being audited. Pre-planning is generally completed during the annual audit plan development process or prior to "Audit Kick-off".

During pre-planning, the auditor will meet with the head of the department to gain a general understanding of the scope and scale of your operations. The auditor may also request a site tour or introduction of key staff.

Planning

Planning involves developing a detailed understanding of the operation's processes. Planning generally involves face-to-face interviews, sample data extraction and development of a testing plan for fieldwork.

During planning, the auditor may want to interview various employees of the department, shadow them through transactions or ask for a limited amount of data. Employees may also need to assist in providing access to applications or locations.

Fieldwork

During fieldwork, transactional or analytical analyses will be performed to determine the adequacy of controls.In fieldwork, employees may need to provide the auditor with additional data or answer follow-up questions. If issues are identified, key individuals will work with the auditors to ensure that findings are accurate and needed feedback is timely.

Reporting

Documentation of any identified findings will be summarized in a report to management. The report will identify those issues requiring resolution. During the reporting phase, department supervisors and employees will be active participants in ensuring the report is factually accurate, and that issues requiring feedback have well-defined action plans.

Corrective Action

The Corrective Action process is the last step of the audit process. It has been established to ensure that identified issues are resolved in a timely manner.

Types of Audits

The audit is an art of systematic and independent review and investigation on Financial Statements, Management Accounts, Management Reports, Accounting Records, Operational Reports, Revenues Reports, and Expenses Reports, etc. The result of reviewing and investigation will be reported to shareholders and other key internal stakeholders of the entity.

Audit reports sometime submit to other stakeholders like government, banks, creditors or public. The audit is classified into many different types and level of assurance according to the objectives, scopes, purposes and the procedures of how auditing is performed.

The execution of a financial statements auditing is normally in accordance with International Standards on Auditing (ISA) as well as other local auditing standards. There are many types of audit including financial audit, operational audit, statutory audit, compliance audit and so on.

We will explain the some types of audits being performed in the current audit industry or practices.

Financial Audit

Financial auditing refers to an accounting process applied in business. The process involves using an individual body for evaluating the financial transactions and statements of a business. The ultimate purpose of financial audit is presenting an accurate amount of the business transactions of a company. Besides, it ensures that the accounts presented to the public and shareholders are accurate and justified. The results of financial audit are useful for banks, shareholders, and anybody else with an interest in the company.

Basic Procedures for a Financial Audit

Generally, four key phases are outlined for financial audit process. These phases include planning the audit, determining the working of internal control, testing significant assertions about the data and evaluating compliance, and reporting the evaluations.

These phases are explained below for your reference:

- Planning: The process of financial audit begins with a plan that involves the method of collecting data to form an opinion about the organization or company's financial status. A way is planned to collect a sample reflecting a point in time in the life of the company or organization. The financial transactions and documents are then looked at. It is noteworthy that the sample should show compliance with GAAP.
- Internal controls: The next step involves giving a look at the internal controls. The auditor demands info, looks closely at the records, and watches financial procedures in action. Without these steps, the auditor cannot give a statement about the financial status of the organization.
- Testing: Testing implies checking whether the internal controls are working or not. An auditor requests more info, returns to the company for more inspections, and watches how financial procedures are being performed. If the evidence demonstrates GAAP compliance, the auditor determines that the company successfully detects and prevents the errors.
- Reporting: The final step in financial audit involves giving a conclusion on how the company adheres to accounting standards. The audit from a CPA gives the organization an unqualified approval, a qualified approval, a disclaimer, or an adverse finding. The unqualified approval is considered as the best result and the adverse finding is considered to be the worst result.

Financial Statement Audit

A financial statement audit is the examination of an entity's financial statements and accompanying disclosures by an independent auditor. The result of this examination is a report by the auditor, attesting to the fairness of presentation of the financial statements and related disclosures. The auditor's report must accompany the financial statements when they are issued to the intended recipients.

The purpose of a financial statement audit is to add credibility to the reported financial position and performance of a business. The Securities and Exchange Commission requires that all entities that are publicly held must file annual reports with it that are audited. Similarly, lenders typically require an audit of the financial statements of any entity to which they lend funds. Suppliers may also require audited financial statements before they will be willing to extend trade credit (though usually only when the amount of requested credit is substantial).

Audits have become increasingly common as the complexity of the two primary accounting frameworks, Generally Accepted Accounting Principles and International Financial Reporting Standards, have increased, and because there have been an ongoing series of disclosures of fraudulent reporting by major companies.

The primary stages of an audit are:

1. Planning and risk assessment: Involves gaining an understanding of the business and the business environment in which it operates, and using this information to assess whether there may be risks that could impact the financial statements.
2. Internal controls testing: Involves the assessment of the effectiveness of an entity's suite of controls, concentrating on such areas as proper authorization, the safeguarding of assets, and the segregation of duties. This can involve an array of tests conducted on a sampling of transactions to determine the degree of control effectiveness. A high level of effectiveness allows the auditors to scale back some of their later audit procedures. If the controls are ineffective (i.e., there is a high risk of material misstatement), then the auditors must use other procedures to examine the financial statements. There are a variety of risk assessment questionnaires available that can assist with internal controls testing.
3. Substantive procedures: Involves a broad array of procedures, of which a small sampling are:
   - Analysis: Conduct a ratio comparison with historical, forecasted, and industry results to spot anomalies.
   - Cash: Review bank reconciliations, count on-hand cash, confirm restrictions on bank balances, issue bank confirmations.
   - Marketable securities: Confirm securities, review subsequent transactions, verify market value.
   - Accounts receivable. Confirm account balances, investigate subsequent collections, test year-end sales and cutoff procedures.
   - Inventory: Observe the physical inventory count, obtain confirmation of inventories held at other locations, test shipping and receiving cutoff procedures, examine paid supplier invoices, test the computation of allocated overhead, review current production costs, trace compiled inventory costs to the general ledger.

- Fixed assets: Observe assets, review purchase and disposal authorizations, review lease documents, examine appraisal reports, recalculate depreciation and amortization.
- Accounts payable: Confirm accounts, test year-end cutoff.
- Accrued expenses: Examine subsequent payments, compare balances to prior years, recompute accruals.
- Debt: Confirm with lenders, review lease agreements, review references in board of directors minutes.
- Revenue: Examine documents supporting a selection of sales, review subsequent transactions, recalculate percentage of completion computations, review the history of sales returns and allowances.
- Expenses: Examine documents supporting a selection of expenses, review subsequent transactions, confirm unusual items with suppliers

Cost Audit

Cost Audit is an audit process for verifying the cost of manufacture or production of any article, on the basis of accounts as regards utilisation of material or labour or other items of costs, maintained by the company. In simple words the term cost audit means a systematic and accurate verification of the cost accounts and records and checking of adherence to the objectives of the cost accounting.

Objectives of Cost Audit

The following are some of the objectives for which cost audit is under taken:

1. To establish the accuracy of costing data. This is done by verifying the arithmetical accuracy of cost accounting entries in the books of accounts.
2. To ensure that cost accounting principles are governed by the management objectives and these are strictly adhered in preparing cost accounts.
3. To ensure that cost accounts are correct and also to detect errors, frauds and wrong practice in the existing system.
4. To check up the general working of the costing department of the organization and to make suggestions for improvement.
5. To help the management in taking correct decisions on certain important matters i.e. to determine the actual cost of production when the goods are ready.
6. To reduce the amount of detailed checking by the external auditor if effective internal cost audit system is in operation.

Scope of Cost Audit

The cost audit extents to the verification and checking of the following areas:

Services

Utilization of power, fuel, water, steam and electricity and that of material, labour and other costs like overheads allocated to the service department.

Wages and Salaries

Maintenance of employment and attendance records, overtime and idle time records, allocation of wages and salaries among various departments and those connected with the capital work.

Overhead

The overheads like production, administration, selling and distribution should be allocated on a reasonable basis. The cost auditor ensures a fair and equitable distribution of overheads between various departments, reconciliation of the cost records with that of financial records, overhead recovery rates, and basis for allocation of cost between fixed and variable.

Depreciation

Maintenance of fixed assets registers with quantitative details, situation, method of calculating depreciation, allocation of depreciation in respect of the common assets.

Production

Daily production reports, summaries from daily to monthly, monthly to yearly and comparison with past records and budgeted targets including abnormal losses, work in-progress, etc.

Work-in-progress

Maintenance of records viz., job cards, work order, cost ledger, etc. and their valuation method.

Stock Verification

Inventory records for stock – both finished and unfinished products, spares and stores, tools, machinery spares, etc. their values, issue procedure and balances.

Utilization of Capacity

Plant utilization and capacity utilization are not considered in detail in financial audit. Under this category the cost auditor's examination covers the following aspects – total available hours, standards hours, planned hours, and actual hours worked. Practical capacity, standard capacity, expected capacity, and actual capacity utilized.

Besides, the cost auditor's examination covers various other aspects viz., royalty payments, company policies with regard to inventory management, productivity, internal control, internal audit, cost reduction, export performance, bottlenecks in the production process, inter-company transactions, etc. Hence, from the practical utility point of view, the scope of cost audit is much wider than the financial audit.

Internal Audit

Internal audit can be defined as the evaluation, monitoring, and analysis of activities associated with the operations of a company, also counting the business structure, information systems, and employee behavior. An internal audit is designed in a way to review the activities performed by a company to recognize the probable threats to the company's health and profitability, in addition to making suggestions for reducing risk related with those threats so as to mitigate the costs.

The internal audit forms an important component of an organization's risk management for they are helpful to the companies in identifying issues before they take the form of substantial problems. Moreover, these are also helpful in identifying the risky behavior by individual employees and threats created by external parties, like attempts to steal intellectual property.

Objectives of Internal Audit

The key purpose of internal audit is helping the management in addition to keeping proper control over business activities. Other important objectives of internal audit include:

- Determining the reliability and integrity of information through the evaluation of internal control systems and the integrity of financial and operating info generated from those systems.
- Determining the compliance of company operations existing with procedures, policies, laws and regulations.
- Determining the safeguard of assets in addition to verifying the existence of these assets.
- Appraising the economy and efficiency of resource utilization, including financial and physical resources.
- Reviewing operations and programs for consistency with well established management goals and objectives.
- Assisting members of an organization in performing their responsibilities effectively and successfully by providing them with appraisals, analysis, recommendations, and other related info concerning the activities under review.

Advantages of Internal Audit

The key advantages of internal audit include:

- Internal audit leads to detection of errors which are rectified during external audit.
- There is no additional cost involved in the process as it is performed by the company employees.

Since internal audit is a continuous procedure which involves regular checking of records thus ensuring the accounting staff to keep the records intact.

Operational Audit

Operational audit is types of audit services that the review is mainly focused on the key processes, procedures, system, as well as internal control which the main objective is to improve the productivity, as well as efficiency and effectiveness of the operation.

Operation audit has also targeted the leak of key control and processes that cause waste of resources and then recommend for improvement.

Operational audit is the part of internal audit and their main aim is to add value to the business their professional services. Systematic and highly discipline is also the part that help to make sure the operational audit add value to the organization.

Types of Operations to be Audited

There are many areas that internal auditors perform their operational audit. And before the reviewing could be performed, internal audit need to identify the audit-able areas, and process first. Those could be identify by obtained input form managements of the companies.

For example, chief of operation might raise some concern about the wrong information could be provide to customer by sales team. Finance director might raise some concern related to miss match between invoices with good delivery noted.

For this case, sales processes and issuing invoices process might need to review. Auditor could also identify the processes or operation to be audited by themselves through obtaining an understanding about the big picture of business first.

Then, they could identify the key processes and well as business units that related. Once all of these are identify, auditor should perform the assessment to identify the related to risks that related to control and processes.

Operational Auditing Process

The process of operational auditing is not much difference to others audit that perform by internal auditor. Those include planning, execution, reporting and follow up:

- Planning: Auditor need to obtain an understanding about the business as well as operation. Then, they need to make assessment and target which key operation should they perform.
- Execution: Validating the key control and operation involve obtaining the key documents, observing how certain key control are performing and inspecting certain documents like sales invoices, goods delivery note.
- Reporting: Once the key operation and control is validated, report need to be prepared and submit to audit committee.
- Follow up: Same like others internal audit, any key finding and recommendations that

prepare by auditor need to follow up whether those key findings are mitigated by related management, or department.

Objectives of an Operational Audit

The operational audit is a great alternative to detect shortcomings in time and transform the activity of the company into a profitable process, which is ultimately what matters most to a company: doing more with the least amount of resources possible:

- Analyze administrative, managerial and operational aspects on which the appropriate modifications will be made in order to improve business operations.
- Identify which areas should reduce costs and support the processes with the greatest needs.

There are many companies that go wrong, but they do not know how to detect the reason. That's where the operational audit comes into play. This will detect the weak point of the business with total certainty, establish the measures to which the company should be supported and, thus, finally achieve to overcome and successfully achieve their objectives.

Advantages of Operational Audit

Regarding the advantages of the company being subjected to an operational audit, we find:

- The company obtains an objective and realistic opinion. This will have important effects in the control of inventories in the short / medium term: increase in production, speed in sales (sales plan), cost reduction, etc.
- Long-term money savings it is a great investment, but with great positive results visible over time.

Disadvantages of Operational Audit

- It is a process that costs money; so many companies are reluctant or simply cannot afford it.
- It requires a relatively long period of time to complete, since it is an analysis and exhaustive examination of the company's operations with which to detect productive improvements.
- Difficulty in finding important deficiencies

Challenges of an Operational Audit

An operational audit, involves a review of the processes and procedures at the heart of the business, to analyse the performance and consider ways to improve.

An operational audit, according to a specific area of activity, is organized in two phases:

- An analysis of the functions of the company in order to understand the functioning of the organization: At the heart of this phase, processes and procedures are identified and analyzed. Their correct application is evaluated. This phase also makes it possible to establish a matrix of processes and their interdependencies, for example to avoid redundant processes.

- An analysis of the efficiency of the processes: This phase consists in analyzing the performance of a process by analyzing its revenues (direct and indirect) and its costs (direct and indirect).

External Audit

An external audit is an examination that is conducted by an independent accountant. This type of audit is most commonly intended to result in a certification of the financial statements of an entity. This certification is required by certain investors and lenders, and for all publicly-held businesses.

The objectives of an external audit are to determine:

- The accuracy and completeness of the client's accounting records;
- Whether the client's accounting records have been prepared in accordance with the applicable accounting framework; and
- Whether the client's financial statements present fairly its results and financial position.

There are other types of external audits that may be targeted at specific issues concerning a client's accounting records, such as an examination that searches for the existence of fraud.

Reasons for an External Audit

When contracted from the business controllers, the external audit process happens for 2 reasons. First, the company can receive more efficiency by using an external auditor. This could happen for many reasons: company employees are already occupied on other tasks, external auditors are better trained for the purpose, internal fraud may prevent an internal audit from being valuable, and more. In any event, the company will use an external auditing company to find the answer to certain questions about their accounting. The external audit plan by professional companies may be concerned with missing funds, providing a second opinion, or merely auditing the Accounting Cycle which a company follows.

Second, an external audit *report* may occur when a governmental entity questions part of the financial statements of a company. In this instance, an external audit will not be voluntary. The IRS or a court usually mandates it. There are many reasons why an external audit will occur under these situations: the IRS questions the financial statements of a company, the IRS may detect internal fraud, the company may not be creating GAAP compliant statements, a court authorizes the audit because they suspect funds may have been spent on illegal activities, and more. External audit fees are usually paid by the business being audited. The exception to this is that if they find illegal activity; then the business may be charged with the costs of the external audit.

External Audit Example

Dwayne owns a healthcare research company. His business, fueled by his years of experience in healthcare research, provides analysis of samples sent by doctors offices as well as hospitals.

Dwayne knows the operations of his business left and right. Recently, Dwayne's business has come under an IRS audit. The IRS suspects that he may be excluding some of their profits from the books to be in a lower tax bracket. Dwayne is afraid that the audit will expose problems which he is not responsible for.

After some time, Dwayne is acquitted of any wrong-doing. The auditor has found that this is not the case: his company temporarily took less profit due to the recent recession. Dwayne is relieved to hear this as he continues his work.

Dwayne made sure to comply with the auditors requests. The reason for this is two fold: he knew he was innocent and wanted to present a reputable picture to the IRS. In doing this he made his experience much more pleasant than it might have been.

Dwayne now appreciates the auditor because he was merely doing his job. Dwayne, the average patriotic American, respects the auditor as an accountant. He is glad to help in preventing fraud in even his own business.

Process Audit

A process audit is an examination of results to determine whether the activities, resources and behaviours that cause them are being managed efficiently and effectively. A process audit is not simply following a trail through a department from input to output - this is a transaction audit. Processes generate results therefore for an audit to be a process audit it has to establish whether the results are being generated by an effectively managed process.

Procedures Audits	Process Audits
Identifies what tasks are being performed.	Identifies what objectives are required to be achieved.
Identifies who performs the tasks.	Identifies the factors affecting success.
Identifies the procedures governing the tasks.	Establishes what the process is for achieving the objectives.
Establishes whether the procedures are being followed.	Verifies that the controls in place are consistent with the success factors.
Establishes whether the person is trained to perform the task.	Establishes the competences and capabilities required to deliver the process outputs.
Verifies that the documentation is current and the equipment is calibrated.	Establishes that competence and capability is being assessed effectively.
Verifies that the working conditions are suitable.	Establishes what results are being achieved.
Establishes where the inputs come from and where the outputs go to.	Establishes how outputs are being measured.
Verifies that the personnel making acceptance decisions are authorised to do so.	Verifies the integrity of the results.
Verifies maintenance of records.	Establishes that improvement in performance, efficiency and effectiveness is pursued.
Establishes that performance, efficiency and effectiveness is reviewed.	
Verifies conformity with ISO 9001.	

What is an Effectively Managed Process?

An effective process is one that achieves the results that are intended – i.e. the objectives. An effectively managed process is a process in which the activities, resources and behaviours are planned, organized and controlled in a way that the outputs achieve specified objectives as illustrated right:

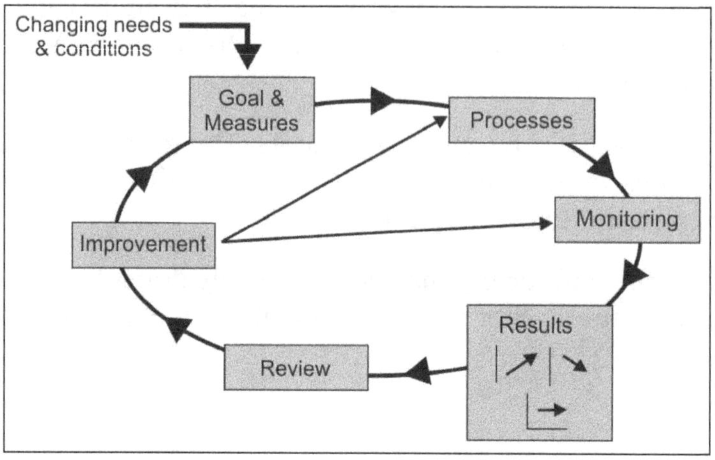

Difference between Process Audit and Procedure Audit

Process audits focus on results and this is the principal difference between procedures audits that in general focus on tasks.

Product Audit

The product audit is the assessment of the final product/service and its qualification for use evaluated versus the intent of the purpose of the product/service. It ensures a thorough inspection of a final product before delivery to a supplier or a customer. By thoroughly inspecting the final product, it aims at improving quality, increasing profitability, and enhancing customer satisfaction and loyalty. It is necessary for a product to go through this process in order to determine if it meets specifications. The Product Audit ultimately serves as a benefit to the suppliers and customers by ensuring quality which results in higher customer satisfaction.

Benefits of Product Audits

- Assists companies and businesses to determine if a company or organization is doing what it says it is.
- Helps businesses and organizations management to address non conformance and take corrective action that leads to company improvement.
- Establish quality in as far as their businesses are concerned and also the creation of a quality system that is vital if products are to be of the highest quality.
- Assists businesses and companies in conducting their own internal audits before involving external auditors.

- Increases customer satisfaction especially where customers have requested an audit or a product because of some consistent problems with the product.
- Helps the upper management of businesses and organizations in the drafting of a quality policy.
- Performs random sampling to determine if they are an accurate representation of a company's quality system.
- Document and describe specific activities and tasks within the organization that assists in ensuring high quality products.
- Determine and distinguish the difference between observation and non conformance in as far as quality of products is concerned.
- Constantly measures the effectiveness of current processes and strives to meet more difficult objectives that satisfy customers.
- Assists with how to gather information that pertains to the quality of a product process of a quality system.
- Helps a forum where the audit team and the auditee are able to meet and discuss the results of a product audit.
- Have an objective assessment of the effectiveness of the quality systems, especially when the product audit is conducted by an external auditor.
- Assists businesses and organizations in conducting internal audits of products by the organization's own staff, which is a requirement of ISO 9000.
- Addresses product quality issues adequately so that products are able to sell and have a competitive edge over competing products.

Information Technology Audit

An information technology audit, or information systems audit, is an examination of the management controls within an Information technology (IT) infrastructure. The evaluation of obtained evidence determines if the information systems are safeguarding assets, maintaining data integrity, and operating effectively to achieve the organization's goals or objectives. These reviews may be performed in conjunction with a financial statement audit, internal audit, or other form of attestation engagement.

IT audits are also known as automated data processing audits (ADP audits) and computer audits. They were formerly called electronic data processing audits (EDP audits).

Purpose

An IT audit is different from a financial statement audit. While a financial audit's purpose is to evaluate whether the financial statements present fairly, in all material respects, an entity's financial position, results of operations, and cash flows in conformity to standard accounting practices, the purposes of an IT audit is to evaluate the system's internal control design and effectiveness. This includes, but is not limited to, efficiency and security protocols, development processes, and IT governance or oversight. Installing controls are necessary but not sufficient to provide adequate security. People responsible for security must consider if the controls are installed as intended, if they are effective, or if any breach in security has occurred and if so, what actions can be done to prevent future breaches. These inquiries must be answered by independent and unbiased observers. These observers are performing the task of information systems auditing. In an Information Systems (IS) environment, an audit is an examination of information systems, their inputs, outputs, and processing.

The primary functions of an IT audit are to evaluate the systems that are in place to guard an organization's information. Specifically, information technology audits are used to evaluate the organization's ability to protect its information assets and to properly dispense information to authorized parties. The IT audit aims to evaluate the following:

Will the organization's computer systems be available for the business at all times when required? (known as availability) Will the information in the systems be disclosed only to authorized users? (known as security and confidentiality) Will the information provided by the system always be accurate, reliable, and timely? (measures the integrity) In this way, the audit hopes to assess the risk to the company's valuable asset (its information) and establish methods of minimizing those risks.

Types of IT Audits

Various authorities have created differing taxonomies to distinguish the various types of IT audits. Goodman & Lawless state that there are three specific systematic approaches to carry out an IT audit:

- Technological innovation process audit: This audit constructs a risk profile for existing and new projects. The audit will assess the length and depth of the company's experience in its chosen technologies, as well as its presence in relevant markets, the organization of each project, and the structure of the portion of the industry that deals with this project or product, organization and industry structure.
- Innovative comparison audit: This audit is an analysis of the innovative abilities of the company being audited, in comparison to its competitors. This requires examination of company's research and development facilities, as well as its track record in actually producing new products.
- Technological position audit: This audit reviews the technologies that the business currently has and that it needs to add. Technologies are characterized as being either "base", "key", "pacing" or "emerging".

Others describe the spectrum of IT audits with five categories of audits:

- Systems and Applications: An audit to verify that systems and applications are appropriate, are efficient, and are adequately controlled to ensure valid, reliable, timely, and secure input, processing, and output at all levels of a system's activity. System and process assurance audits form a subtype, focussing on business process-centric business IT systems. Such audits have the objective to assist financial auditors.

- Information Processing Facilities: An audit to verify that the processing facility is controlled to ensure timely, accurate, and efficient processing of applications under normal and potentially disruptive conditions.
- Systems Development: An audit to verify that the systems under development meet the objectives of the organization, and to ensure that the systems are developed in accordance with generally accepted standards for systems development.
- Management of IT and Enterprise Architecture: An audit to verify that IT management has developed an organizational structure and procedures to ensure a controlled and efficient environment for information processing.
- Client/Server, Telecommunications, Intranets, and Extranets: An audit to verify that telecommunications controls are in place on the client (computer receiving services), server, and on the network connecting the clients and servers.

And some lump all IT audits as being one of only two type: "general control review" audits or "application control review" audits.

A number of IT audit professionals from the Information Assurance realm consider there to be three fundamental types of controls regardless of the type of audit to be performed, especially in the IT realm. Many frameworks and standards try to break controls into different disciplines or arenas, terming them "Security Controls", "Access Controls", "IA Controls" in an effort to define the types of controls involved. At a more fundamental level, these controls can be shown to consist of three types of fundamental controls: Protective/Preventative Controls, Detective Controls and Reactive/Corrective Controls.

In an IS, there are two types of auditors and audits: internal and external. IS auditing is usually a part of accounting internal auditing, and is frequently performed by corporate internal auditors. An external auditor reviews the findings of the internal audit as well as the inputs, processing and outputs of information systems. The external audit of information systems is frequently a part of the overall external auditing performed by a Certified Public Accountant (CPA) firm.

IS auditing considers all the potential hazards and controls in information systems. It focuses on issues like operations, data, integrity, software applications, security, privacy, budgets and expenditures, cost control, and productivity. Guidelines are available to assist auditors in their jobs, such as those from Information Systems Audit and Control Association.

IT Audit Process

The following are basic steps in performing the Information Technology Audit Process:

- Planning IN
- Studying and Evaluating Controls
- Testing and Evaluating Controls
- Reporting

- Follow-up
- Reports

Information Security

Auditing information security is a vital part of any IT audit and is often understood to be the primary purpose of an IT Audit. The broad scope of auditing information security includes such topics as data centers (the physical security of data centers and the logical security of databases, servers and network infrastructure components), networks and application security. Like most technical realms, these topics are always evolving; IT auditors must constantly continue to expand their knowledge and understanding of the systems and environment& pursuit in system company.

Principles of an IT Audit

The following principles of an audit should find a reflection:

- Timeliness: Only when the processes and programming is continuously inspected in regard to their potential susceptibility to faults and weaknesses, but as well with regard to the continuation of the analysis of the found strengths, or by comparative functional analysis with similar applications an updated frame can be continued.
- Source openness: It requires an explicit reference in the audit of encrypted programs, how the handling of open source has to be understood. E.g. programs, offering an open source application, but not considering the IM server as open source, have to be regarded as critical. An auditor should take an own position to the paradigm of the need of the open source nature within cryptologic applications.
- Elaborateness: Audit processes should be oriented to certain minimum standard. The recent audit processes of encrypting software often vary greatly in quality, in the scope and effectiveness and also experience in the media reception often differing perceptions. Because of the need of special knowledge on the one hand and to be able to read programming code and then on the other hand to also have knowledge of encryption procedures, many users even trust the shortest statements of formal confirmation. Individual commitment as an auditor, e.g. for quality, scale and effectiveness, is thus to be assessed reflexively for yourself and to be documented within the audit.

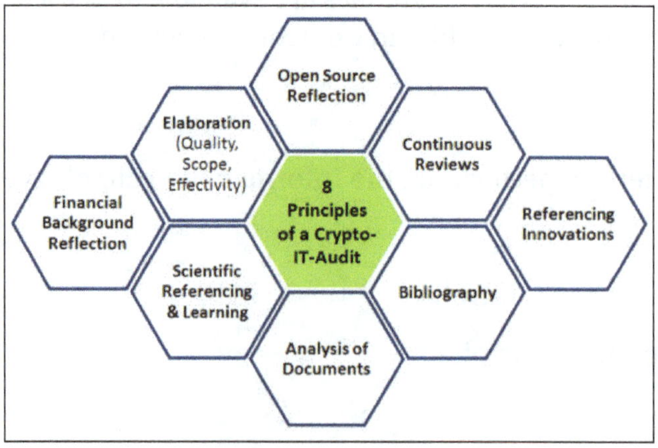

- The financial context: Further transparency is needed to clarify whether the software has been developed commercially and whether the audit was funded commercially (paid Audit). It makes a difference whether it is a private hobby / community project or whether a commercial company is behind it.
- Scientific referencing of learning perspectives: Each audit should describe the findings in detail within the context and also highlight progress and development needs constructively. An auditor is not the parent of the program, but at least he or she is in a role of a mentor, if the auditor is regarded as part of a PDCA learning circle (PDCA = Plan-Do-Check-Act). There should be next to the description of the detected vulnerabilities also a description of the innovative opportunities and the development of the potentials.
- Literature-inclusion: A reader should not rely solely on the results of one review, but also judge according to a loop of a management system, to ensure, that the development team or the reviewer was and is prepared to carry out further analysis, and also in the development and review process is open to learnings and to consider notes of others. A list of references should be accompanied in each case of an audit.
- Inclusion of user manuals & documentation: Further a check should be done, whether there are manuals and technical documentations, and, if these are expanded.
- Identify references to innovations: Applications that allow both, messaging to offline and online contacts, so considering chat and e-mail in one application - as it is also the case with GoldBug - should be tested with high priority (criterion of presence chats in addition to the e-mail function). The auditor should also highlight the references to innovations and underpin further research and development needs.

This list of audit principles for crypto applications describes - beyond the methods of technical analysis - particularly core values, that should be taken into account.

Emerging Issues

There are also new audits being imposed by various standard boards which are required to be performed, depending upon the audited organization, which will affect IT and ensure that IT departments are performing certain functions and controls appropriately to be considered compliant.

Web Presence Audits

The extension of the corporate IT presence beyond the corporate firewall (e.g. the adoption of social media by the enterprise along with the proliferation of cloud-based tools like social media management systems) has elevated the importance of incorporating web presence audits into the IT/IS audit. The purposes of these audits include ensuring the company is taking the necessary steps to:

- Rein in use of unauthorized tools (e.g. "shadow IT")
- Minimize damage to reputation
- Maintain regulatory compliance
- Prevent information leakage

- Mitigate third-party risk
- Minimize governance risk

The use of departmental or user developed tools has been a controversial topic in the past. However, with the widespread availability of data analytics tools, dashboards, and statistical packages users no longer need to stand in line waiting for IT resources to fulfill seemingly endless requests for reports. The task of IT is to work with business groups to make authorized access and reporting as straightforward as possible. To use a simple example, users should not have to do their own data matching so that pure relational tables are linked in a meaningful way. IT needs to make non-normalized, data warehouse type files available to users so that their analysis work is simplified. For example, some organizations will refresh a warehouse periodically and create easy to use "flat' tables which can be easily uploaded by a package such as Tableau and used to create dashboards.

Enterprise Communications Audits

The rise of VOIP networks and issues like BYOD and the increasing capabilities of modern enterprise telephony systems causes increased risk of critical telephony infrastructure being misconfigured, leaving the enterprise open to the possibility of communications fraud or reduced system stability. Banks, financial institutions, and contact centers typically set up policies to be enforced across their communications systems. The task of auditing that the communications systems are in compliance with the policy falls on specialized telecom auditors. These audits ensure that the company's communication systems:

- Adhere to stated policy
- Follow policies designed to minimize the risk of hacking or phreaking
- Maintain regulatory compliance
- Prevent or minimize toll fraud
- Mitigate third-party risk
- Minimize governance risk

Enterprise communications audits are also called voice audits, but the term is increasingly deprecated as communications infrastructure increasingly becomes data-oriented and data-dependent. The term "telephony audit" is also deprecated because modern communications infrastructure, especially when dealing with customers, is omni-channel, where interaction takes place across multiple channels, not just over the telephone. One of the key issues that plagues enterprise communication audits is the lack of industry-defined or government-approved standards. IT audits are built on the basis of adherence to standards and policies published by organizations such as NIST and PCI, but the absence of such standards for enterprise communications audits means that these audits have to be based an organization's internal standards and policies, rather than industry standards. As a result, enterprise communications audits are still manually done, with random sampling checks. Policy Audit Automation tools for enterprise communications have only recently become available.

Compliance Audit

Compliance audit is essentially about comprehensively reviewing whether a company is adhering to the regulatory related guidelines or not. IT, security and independent accounting consultants conduct an evaluation of the thoroughness and strength of preparations pertaining to compliance. Auditors conduct a review of the security related policies, procedures pertaining to risk management and user access controls throughout the compliance audit course.

Thus, a compliance audit helps in determining whether an entity is following all the rules laid down in the contract or agreement or not. Entities enter into agreements or prepare contracts for a number of business related purposes. These contracts and agreements are reviewed carefully and also audited to make sure no misstatements or fraud exists as the entity meets the obligations pertaining to the contract. Accounting entities or a certified public accountant is held responsible for carrying out the compliance audit on company agreements and contracts.

A compliance audit is an independent evaluation to ensure that an organization is following external laws, rules, and regulations or internal guidelines, such as corporate bylaws, controls, and policies and procedures. Compliance audits may also determine if an organization is conforming to an agreement, such as when an entity accepts government or other funding. Although most people are familiar with financial audits, such as those for public companies through the Sarbanes-Oxley Act (SOX) or individual or corporate tax audits through the Internal Revenue Service (IRS), compliance audits are not merely financial. Audits may also review IT and other security issues, compliance with HR laws, quality management systems, and other areas. Compliance plays a crucial role in GRC, which stands for governance, risk, and compliance.

Compliance is important for many reasons. Aside from signifying levels of professional standards, like the ISO 9000, ISO 14000, and other guidelines, noncompliance with regulatory guidelines may bring sanctions and penalties. Penalties for noncompliance with federal regulations, such as Sarbanes-Oxley, are specified through the Federal Sentencing Guidelines Act and apply fines based on a formula that calculates the most recent offenses and determines whether the organization employs a compliance officer who communicates regulatory needs to the organization.

Boards of directors are also often accountable for operations and need to see audit reports. If a regulatory agency does investigate, proof of a compliance program is important to show that the organization has controls and other mechanisms that can detect deficiencies and even illegal activity.

Depending on the circumstances, the audit may be conducted by an employee, such as an internal auditor, a certified public accountant, a third-party auditor, or a government auditor. In many circumstances, auditors may seek the expert advice of outside specialists, such as lawyers.

Audits provide recommendations on ways to make improvements or corrective actions and to prevent future deficiencies or nonconformities. Audits review for effectiveness to determine the number of compliant versus non-compliant processes. Audits also help organizations to stay in compliance with frequently changing federal regulations. In addition, audits identify areas of risk for noncompliance within the organization and report these appraisals to management and the appropriate regulatory entity as applicable.

Challenges of Compliance Auditing

Compliance can seem to present organizations with a predicament in which they are liable for penalties whether they work to comply or not. Deficiencies discovered in a regulatory audit may be subject to fines. However, any deficiencies that are not discovered in an audit may still subject an organization to a third-party lawsuit. Deficiencies disclosed in self-auditing and self-reporting can still garner significant penalties.

Compliance Test

Used in many industries, including software development, a compliance test is a non-functional test that is performed to ensure that something meets the specified standards and requirements for the deliverable.

Compliance Test in Auditing

In auditing, a compliance test confirms the presence of controls and their application. Substantive tests verify the integrity of controls and the actual accuracy of documents, such as balanced accounting sheets.

Auditor's Report

Auditor's report reflects the validity and reliability of a company's financial statements and is prepared by an independent practicing Chartered Accountant. Audit reports enumerates on whether or not the financial statements prepared by a business comply with GAAP (Generally Accepted Accounting Principles) standards. In addition, it points out any misrepresentations of financial information. The content of an Auditor's Report needs to be clear and precise, providing sufficient evidence to justify the auditor's opinion.

Audit Opinion

There are four types of audit opinion. Based on the audit, in the audit report, the Auditor would provide one of the following types of audit opinion.

Unqualified Opinion

This is also called clean opinion and is the best type of report that a business can receive. It shows that the reports fully comply with GAAP standards and are free of any misrepresentations.

Qualified Opinion

This shows that no misrepresentations are identified, but the records have not been maintained in accordance with GAAP.

Adverse Opinion

This, on the other hand, is the worst type of report. It identifies that the reports have been grossly misrepresented either due to error or fraud. It also shows that the records do not conform to GAAP. In such a case, the business would have to correct the mistakes and have it re-audit.

Disclaimer of Opinion

This states that the auditor is not able to complete a satisfactory report due to absence of any appropriate financial details. Therefore, the auditor issues a disclaimer of opinion, stating that an opinion of the firm's financial status cannot be determined.

Uses of Auditor's Reports

The following are some of the major uses of an Auditor's Report:

Assurance to Stakeholders

Auditor's reports are very useful for shareholders and potential investors to understand the true financial status of a company as it provides assurance from a professional auditor. This helps investors to make a fair investment decision because many do not have an in-depth financial knowledge to identify fraud in financial reports.

Verification of Internal Controls

Auditors have the knowledge and access to internal financial details to identify any fraudulent activities carried out while preparing financial statements. It is also used by government bodies to check if the financial operations of a company are genuine. Other users of the report include management, board of directors, banks, etc.

Credibility Check

The report is beneficial to banks and other creditors to ascertain the true financial health of a company. The credibility and reliability of a company is reflected in its auditor's report by checking the true performance, which will determine the ability of the company to repay loans.

Fraud Prevention

The auditor's report is extremely important to prevent fraud, as it encourages companies to prepare its financial statements with fairness and accuracy. To achieve audit level accuracy, the company would need to maintain quality internal accounting systems and employ qualified accountants. Efficient audit systems help a company to identify weaknesses and find solutions to fix them.

Limitations of Auditor's Reports

Undetected Fraud

Although audit checks are used to identify fraud, it is likely that some complicated fraud remain undetected by auditors. They cannot completely eliminate fraud. In some cases, misrepresentations of financial data occur as a result of human error, which can be counted as fraud. It is sometimes difficult for auditors to distinguish between fraud and error. Furthermore, audit results vary from one auditor to another based on the efficiency of audit methodology used and the way it is practiced by each auditor.

Emphasis on Financial Aspects

Audits focus on the financial aspects of a company's operations. Non-financial aspects are ignored while determining the credibility and reliability of a company, which might show a false image of the entity to its shareholders and other users.

Inefficient Internal Controls

The efficiency of auditing is commonly affected by the standards of a company's internal financial control. In many cases, higher level authorities in a company override controls by incorrectly recording transactions or concealing certain activities. Such internal inefficiencies challenge the efficiency of auditing.

Audit Report Format

The following is the overall structure of an audit report. You can also download the following Audit Report formats:

- Audit Report Format – Unqualified Opinion
- Audit Report Format – Qualified Opinion

Title of Audit Report

Provide an appropriate title is to be given in order to distinguish the independent auditor's report from reports and statement issued by others.

For example, the title could be 'Independent Auditor's Report:

Addressee

Specify the party, such as the local government or shareholders, to whom the report is addressed.

For example, in a company's audit report, the report would be addressed to the Members of the Company.

Introductory Paragraph

In the introductory paragraph, the names of the financial statements audited should be provided. This usually includes the profit and loss account, balance sheet, cash flow statement, statement of changes in equity and other supportive books that were used in the preparation of financial reports.

Example: We have audited the accompanying standalone financial statements of XXX COMPANY LIMITED ("the Company"), which comprise the Balance Sheet as at 31st March, 20XX, the Statement of Profit and Loss, the Cash Flow Statement for the year then ended, and a summary of the significant accounting policies and other explanatory information.

Management's Responsibility

In this part, the Auditor clearly mentions that it is the responsibility of the management to prepare the financial statements and maintain internal controls.

Example: It is the responsibility of the management to prepare its financial statements in compliance with the financial reporting framework. It needs to establish appropriate systems to minimize error, also to detect and mitigate fraud. Efficient internal controls are to be implemented and governed by management to establish quality control throughout its operations to increase accuracy in all departments.

Auditor's Responsibility

In this part, the Auditor emphasises his/her responsibility with respect to the audit.

Example: The auditor is responsible for conducting audit in accordance with established Standards on Auditing and to express a true opinion on the financial statements. In order to check whether the financial statements are free of any misrepresentations, the auditor needs to collect reasonable evidence to support an opinion. It is the responsibility of the auditor to plan and perform the audit with professional integrity. In failing to do so, the auditor will be liable for damages to the company.

Auditor's Opinion

In this topic, the Auditor expresses his opinion on the financial statements which could be unqualified, qualified, and adverse or disclaimer.

Example (if the opinion is unqualified): In our opinion and to the best of our information and according to the explanations given to us, the aforesaid standalone financial statements give the information required by the Act in the manner so required and give a true and fair view in conformity with the accounting principles generally accepted in India, of the state of affairs of the Company as at 31st March, 20XX, and its profit/loss and its cash flows for the year ended on that date.

Other Reporting Responsibilities (Optional)

This optional section can be used to mention the responsibilities other than the main responsibilities under the Standards on Audit.

Signature of the Auditor

The report is signed in the personal name of the auditor and in the name of the audit firm. The auditors also need to mention the registration number of the firm as allotted by ICAI, in the audit reports that they signed.

Date of the Auditor's Report

The report should not be dated any earlier than the final date on which the auditor has obtained sufficient appropriate audit evidence and has submitted it.

Place of Signature

The location is usually the name of the city, where the auditor signed the report.

Audit Risk

Audit risk is the risk that auditors issued the incorrect audit opinion to the audited financial statements. For example, auditor issued an unqualified opinion to the audited financial statements even though the financial statements are materially misstated. Or the qualified opinion is issued as the result of immateriality found in financial statements which the correct opinion should be unqualified.

Audit risks come from two main different sources: Clients and Auditors themselves. The risks are classified into three different types: Inherent risks, Control Risks, and Detection Risks.

The auditor is required to assess the risks of material misstatements in the financial statements as per requirement from ISA 315 Identifying and Assessing the Risks of Material Misstatement Through Understanding the Entity and Its Environment. The procedures that auditors use to perform risks assessment are an inquiry, inspection, observation, and analytical procedures.

Model and Calculation of Audit Risks

Audit risk can be presented by the risks model as the combination of inherent risks, control risks, and detection risks. As mention above, inherent risks and control risks are control by clients whereas detection risks are control by auditors. All of these three risks are discussed below:

Here is the formula:

$$\text{Audit risk} = \text{Inherent risk} \times \text{control risk} \times \text{detection risk}$$

Just because the model use multiplies here it does not mean that the need to be multiple to get audit risk. Detection Risk alone could also make high audit risk.

Inherent Risks

Inherent risk refers to the risk that could not be protected or detected by the entity's internal control. This risk could happen as the result of the complexity of client nature of business or transactions. Sometime, that nature of business could link to the complexity of financial transactions and require high involvement with judgment.

The risk is normally high if the transaction or even involve highly with human judgment. For example, the exposure in the complex derivative instrument. This kind of risk could also be affected by the external environment; for example, climate change, political problem, or some other PESTEL effect on the business.

Auditor required to assess those kinds of risks and set up audit procedures to address inherent risks properly. For example, the auditor needs to set up a proper audit plan, audit approach and audit strategy to that all relevance inherent risks that might affect the financial statements are identify and rectify on time.

Those include the sufficient time for the audit team to work on the significant areas or having a member that have a deep understanding of the business as well as accounting transactions of the auditing financial statements.

In case auditor being aware that the potential client has high exposure to inherent risks, and auditor also know that the current resources are not capable to handle such client, the audit should not accept the engagement. This procedure could help the auditor to minimize audit risks that come from inherent risks.

Control Risks

Control risk or internal control risk is the risk that current internal control could not detect or fail to protect significant error or misstatement in the financial statements.

Basically, managements are required to set up and assess the effectiveness and efficiency of internal control over financial reporting to make sure that financial statements are free from material misstatements.

If the control is weak, there is a high chance that financial statements are materially misstated, and there is subsequently high chance that auditors could not detect all kind of those misstatements. That means to control risk could lead to audit risk.

The auditor needs to understand and assess the client's internal control over financial reporting conclude whether those control could be relied on or not. If the client internal control seems to be strong, then the audit needs to confirm if the control is worked by testing internal control.

There are certain ways that auditors could use to help them to minimize the control risks that result from poor internal control. For example, auditors should have proper risks assessment at the planning stages. These risks assessment required auditors to understand not only the nature of the business, but also internal control activities that link to financial reporting.

Mostly, COSO frameworks are the popular frameworks that use by most of the international audit firms to documents and assess internal controls. Once the internal over financial statements and risks are properly assessed, the audit programs are properly tailored, then Control Risks are minimized.

Detection Risk

Detection risk is the risk that auditor fails to detect the material misstatement in the financial statements and then issued an incorrect opinion to the audited financial statements. The common cause of detection risk is improper audit planning, poor engagement management, wrong audit methodology, low competency and lack of understanding of audit client. Detection risk is occurred because of auditor part rather than the client part.

Detection risk could be the result of poor audit planning. For example, if audit planning is poor, not all kind of risks are defined and the audit program that use to detect those risks is to deploy incorrectly. Then, the result is the material misstates are not detected.

There are certain guidelines that could help auditors to minimize detection risks so that the audit risks are also subsequently minimized. At the time planning, auditors should set the right audit strategy, employed the right audit approach, and having a strong strategic audit plan.

Those including having a good understanding of the nature of the business, the complexity of the business operation, the complexity of the client's financial statements, and deep understanding of the client's internal control over financial reporting. Clear understanding about audit objective and scope of audit could help auditors to set audit approach and tailors the right audit program.

Having a strong audit team could also help auditors to minimize detection risks. For example, having enough team members and those team member have good experiences and knowledge related to clients' business and financial statements.

Need to Perform a Risk Assessment

Auditor requires performing risks assessments to make sure that all possible risks of misstatements that might happen to the financial statements are identified.

This is normally performed during and after the audit plan. If certain risks are identified during the cause of audit, the auditor should perform additional assessments to figure out the real size of the risks.

The auditor should assess audit risks before audit engagements by understanding the nature of the business that its client operating in, and the complexity of financial reporting in that sector.

This might help them to understand more about the audit risks and let them ready to detect these risks. The different industry might face different challenging in financial reporting. For example, the financial reporting of the merchandising company might be easy than financial reporting in agriculture or oil.

The auditor should also assess audit risks at the time they prepare the audit plan. Normally, this is done by using a control framework like COSO to assess.

At this stage, the auditor might obtain an understanding in detail of client nature of the business, major internal control over financial reporting, financial reporting system and many more. Auditor will also assess the leadership of the management team as well as the entity's culture.

Calculation of Audit Risk

We have mentioned the audit risks model and by that, you might think of the way to casting audit risk. Before we say whether or not audit risk is calculable,

The audit risks model is:

$$\text{Audit Risks} = \text{Inherent Risk} \times \text{Control Risk} \times \text{Deletion Risk}$$

This formula seems to tell us that the audit risks are quantifiable yet it does not.

This formula is just the concept. The thing is if either one is high the likelihood that auditor issued incorrect opinion is also hight.

Difference between Audit Risk and Fraud Risk

Let assume you already have a better understanding of audit risks and let check above if you still not sure. Now, let talk about fraud risks. Fraud risk is the risks that financial statements have material misstatement without detection by both auditor and management.

Management has the primary role and responsibility to design the control that could prevent and detect fraud. They also have the primary responsibility to investigate fraud. The auditor is not responsible for fraud but they are responsible for providing reasonable assurance to the users of financial statements. Based on the audit standard, the auditor needs to assess the risks of fraud that might happen as well as the materiality.

Audit Sampling

Audit sampling is the application of audit procedures to less than 100% of the total population and all the items in the population have the same chance to be selected.

This is to ensure that the items that selected represent the total population which enables auditors to draw their conclusion and express their opinion based on their predetermined objective.

Audit sampling is really important because it doesn't only help auditors to gather the sufficient and appropriate audit's evidence to draw the audit's opinion, but also play the very important part on the audit's works' efficiency and effectiveness. That mean auditor is not required to check 100% of object or items to let them express their opinion.

To ensure that the selected items could represent the total population, the selection process and methods should not involve too much from human judgments and should be avoiding bias from auditors.

They only perform their review and verification on the selected items and then express their opinion on the entire population. In general, audit sampling can be performed in two different types.

First, statistical and second is non-statistical sampling. These two types of sampling contain many other methods .

Objectives and Purpose of Audit Sampling

Audit sampling is a very important part of audit works. No matter it is a financial audit, internal audit and other kinds of audit, audit sampling still need to be used by auditors. Audit sampling also part of the audit standards requirements and it could help auditors to meet their objective with less effort.

The following are the purposes and objectives of audit sampling:

- To gather audit evidence in order to conclude audit opinion.
- To reduce the works yet audit yet still help audit to reach its conclusion.
- To provide the basis for the auditor to conclusion audit opinion.
- To detect any kind of error or fraud that could happen in the company as well as financial statements.

- To prove auditors have done their jobs base on the required auditing standards.
- Use as a tool for investigations.

Two Types of Audit Sampling

Statistic Audit Sampling

Statistic audit sampling is the sampling approach where auditor uses random sampling to select the items from the total population use the probabilities technique to measure the result of the testing and make a conclusion.

Using statistical sampling is very important to help the auditor to manage and control the audit's risk. This because statistic, we use data and probabilities to select the items from the total population and those data are not prejudged and unbiased by auditors.

This statistic sampling normally performs where the total population is more than 100 items. Based on experiences, there are many different tools available in the market that we use could use to perform audit sampling. And, if you don't have the tool, you can use the function in excel instead of software.

For example, auditor verifying the addition of the fixed asset during the year and the total purchase transactions are more than 100 items. You are an auditor and is assigning to perform testing on fixed assets addition. Statistical sampling is highly recommended in the audit program. And random sampling is the methods you decided to use.

In the statistical sampling, you can consider select 10 items from total population randomly or you can set internal every item that reaches the interval set. That means every item among 100 items has the same chance to be selected for verification. Once you completed your testing, and got the result and then make a conclusion base on the result.

So, this is how statistical sampling looks like and how it is using. The two important things you need to remember about statistical sampling are the items are selected randomly and the conclusion is made based on the result of testing. If either of these two things is not meet, then the sampling is called non-statistic.

Non-statistic Audit Sampling

Non-statistical sampling by the ways is different from the statistic. Based on the theory from IFRS, any method that not mean the criteria of the statistic is non-statistic. That means you have to be very clear and understand well about statistic audit sampling. There are two importance thinks that you can use to identify whether the sampling is systematic or not.

The first one is the selection of data or items are not random. That means the selections are based on judgment. Second, the result of testing from that selections is not using to conclude for the nature of the entire population.

The auditor might not use statistic audit sampling to select items for testing. Instead, they might select the items based on:

- Value of items, for example, the top ten highest value.

- Select the items that higher than a certain amount or value. For example, any items higher than 200,000 USD.
- Items that contain information or data they want to assess. For example, any purchasing transactions from supplier name Dalata Ltd.

These methods of sampling are called non-statistic.

Five Methods of Audit Sampling Selection

- Random selection: It is the type of sampling that provides an equal opportunity to all items or units in the total population. This kind of selection could use in excel or other generating tools.
- Systematic selection: Involves selecting items using a constant interval between selections, the first interval having a random start. When using systematic selection, auditors must ensure that the population does not structure in such a manner that the sampling interval corresponds with a particular pattern in the population.
- Haphazard: Selection may be an alternative to the random selection provided auditors satisfy that the sample is representative of the entire population. This method requires care to guard against making a selection which is biased, for example towards items which are easily located, as they may not be representative. It should not be used if auditors are carrying out statistical sampling.
- Block selection: Maybe use to check whether certain items have particular characteristics. For example, an auditor may use a sample of 50 consecutive cheques to test whether cheques are signed by authorized signatories rather than picking 50 single cheques throughout the year. Block sampling may; however, produce samples that are not representative of the population as a whole, particularly if errors only occurred during a certain part of the period, and hence the errors found cannot be projected onto the rest of the population.
- Monetary Unit Sampling is a type of value-weighted selection in which sample size, selection, and the evaluation result in a conclusion in monetary amounts. Monetary unit sampling is a kind of systematic audit sampling.

References

- What-is-auditing-its-types-and-purposes: managementstudyguide.com, Retrieved 12 August, 2019
- What-is-auditing, accounting, hub: freshbooks.com, Retrieved 15 April, 2019
- Auditing: businessjargons.com, Retrieved 9 February, 2019
- The-audit-process, internal-auditing: bgsu.edu, Retrieved 28 July, 2019
- Financial-audit, audit: readyratios.com, Retrieved 13 January, 2019
- What-is-a-financial-statement-audit: accountingtools.com, Retrieved 17 August, 2019
- Cost-audit-meaning-scope-objectives: accountlearning.com, Retrieved 7 May, 2019
- Internal-audit, audit: readyratios.com, Retrieved 11 July, 2019

- Process-auditing: transition-support.com, Retrieved 16 March, 2019
- Product-audits, auditing: enhancequality.com, Retrieved 6 January, 2019
- Richard A. Goodman; Michael W. Lawless (1994). Technology and strategy: conceptual models and diagnostics. Oxford University Press US. ISBN 978-0-19-507949-4. Retrieved May 9, 2010
- Compliance-audit, audit: readyratios.com, Retrieved 16 June, 2019
- Compliance-auditing: smartsheet.com, Retrieved 26 February, 2019
- Auditors-report: indiafilings.com, Retrieved 28 March, 2019

5

Financial Statements

The reports which are prepared by the management of a company to show the financial performance and position at any given time are known as financial statements. Some of the major components of financial statements are income statement, balance sheet and cash flow statement. All these diverse components of financial statements have been carefully analyzed in this chapter.

A financial statement is a collection of data organized according to logical and consistent accounting procedures. Its purpose is to convey an understanding of some financial aspects of a business firm. It may show a position at a moment in time, as in the case of a balance sheet, or may reveal a series of activities over a given period of time, as in the case of an income statement.

Thus, the term 'financial statements' generally refer to the two statements:

1. The position statement or the balance sheet; and
2. The income statement or the profit and loss account.

These statements are used to convey to management and other interested outsider the profitability and financial position of a firm.

Financial statements are the outcome of summarizing process of accounting.

Nature of Financial Statements

The financial statements are prepared on the basis of recorded facts. The recorded facts are those which can be expressed in monetary terms. The statements are prepared for a particular period, generally one year. The transactions are recorded in a chronological order, as and when the events happen.

The accounting records and financial statements prepared from these records are based on historical costs. The financial statements, by nature, are summaries of the items recorded in the business and these statements are prepared periodically, generally for the accounting period.

The American Institute of Certified Public Accountants states the nature of financial statements as "Financial Statements are prepared for the purpose of presenting a periodical review of report on progress by the management and deal with the status of investment in the business and the results achieved during the period under review. They reflect a combination of recorded facts, accounting principles and personal judgments."

The American Accounting Association expresses in its statement, "Every corporate statement should be based on accounting principles which are sufficiently uniform, objective and well understood to justify opinions as to the condition and progress of business enterprise. Its basic assumption was that the purpose of periodic financial statements of a corporation is to furnish information that is necessary for the formation of dependable judgments."

The following points explain the nature of financial statements:

Recorded Facts

The term 'recorded facts' refers to the data taken out from the accounting records. The records are maintained on the basis of actual cost data. The original cost or historical cost is the basis of recording various transactions. The figures of various accounts such as cash in hand, cash in bank, bills receivables, sundry debtors, fixed assets etc. are taken as per the figures recorded in the accounting books. The assets purchased at different times and at different prices are put together and shown at cost prices. As recorded facts are not based on replacement costs, the financial statements do not show current financial condition of the concern.

Accounting Conventions

Certain accounting conventions are followed while preparing financial statements. The convention of valuing inventory at cost or market price, whichever is lower, is followed. The valuing of assets at cost less depreciation principle for balance sheet purposes is followed.

The convention of materiality is followed in dealing with small items like pencils, pens, postage stamps, etc. These items are treated as expenditure in the year in which they are purchased even though they are assets in nature. The stationery is valued at cost and not on the principle of cost or market price whichever is less. The use of accounting conventions makes financial statements comparable, simple and realistic.

Postulates

The accountant makes certain assumptions while making accounting records. One of these assumptions is that the enterprise is treated as a going concern. The other alternative to this postulate is that the concern is to be liquidated, this, is untenable if management shows an intention to liquidate the concern. So the assets are shown on a going concern basis. Another important assumption is to presume that the value of money will remain the same in different periods.

Though there is a drastic change in purchasing power of money the assets purchased at different times will be shown at the amount paid for them. While preparing profit and loss account, the revenue is treated in the year in which the sale was undertaken even though the sale price may be received in a number of years. The assumption is known as realization postulate.

Personal Judgments

Even though certain standard accounting conventions are followed in preparing financial statements but still personal judgment of the accountant plays an important part. For example, in applying the cost or market value whichever is less to inventory valuation the accountant will have to use his judgment in computing the cost in a particular case. There are a number of methods for valuing stock, viz.; last in first out, first in first out, average cost method, standard cost, base stock method, etc.

The accountant will use one of these methods for valuing materials. The selection of depreciation method, to use one of the several methods for estimating uncollectible debts, to determine the period for writing off intangible assets are some of the examples where judgment of the accountant will play an important role in choosing the most appropriate course of action.

Objectives of Financial Statements

Financial statements are the sources of information on the basis of which conclusions are drawn about the profitability and financial position of a concern. They are the major means employed by firms to present their financial situation of owners, creditors and the general public. The primary objective of financial statements is to assist in decision making.

The Accounting Principles Board of America (APB) states the following objectives of financial statements:

1. To provide reliable financial information about economic resources and obligations of a business firm.
2. To provide other needed information about changes in such economic resources and obligations.
3. To provide reliable information about changes in net resources (resources less obligations) arising out of business activities.
4. To provide financial information that assists in estimating the earning potentials of business.
5. To disclose, to the extent possible, other information related to the financial statements that is relevant to the needs of the users of these statements.

Importance of Financial Statements

Management

The financial statements are useful for assessing the efficiency for different cost centres. The management is able to exercise cost control through these statements. The efficient and inefficient spots are brought to the notice of the management. The management is able to decide the course of action to be adopted in future.

Creditors

The trade creditors are to be paid in a short period. This liability is met out of current assets. The creditors will be interested in current solvency of the concern. The calculation of current ratio and liquid ratio will enable the creditors to assess the current financial position of the concern in relation to their debts.

Bankers

The banker is interested to see that the loan amount is secure and the customer is also able to pay the interest regularly. The banker will analyze the balance sheet to determine financial strength of the concern and profit and loss account will also be studied to find out the earning position.

A banker has a large number of customers and it is not possible to supervise their business activities. It is through the financial statements that a banker can keep a watch on the business plans and performances of its customers. These statements also help the banker to determine the amount of securities it will ask from the customers as a cover for the loans.

Investors

The investors include both short-term and long-term investors. They are interested in the security of the principal amount of loan and regular interest payments by the concern. The investors will study the long-term solvency of the concern with the help of financial statements. The investors will not only analyze the present financial position but will also study future prospects and expansion plans of the concern. The possibility of paying back the loan amount in the face of liquidation of the concern is also taken into consideration.

Government

The financial statements are used to assess tax liability of business enterprises. The government studies economic situation of the country from these statements. These statements enable the government to find out whether business is following various rules and regulations or not. These statements also become a base for framing and amending various laws for the regulation of business.

Trade Associations

These associations provide service and protection to the members. They may analyze the financial statements for the purpose of providing facilities to these members. They may develop standard ratios and design uniform system of accounts.

Stock Exchange

The stock exchanges deal in purchase and sale of securities of different companies. The financial statements enable the stock brokers to judge the financial position of different concerns. The fixation of prices for securities, etc., is also based on these statements.

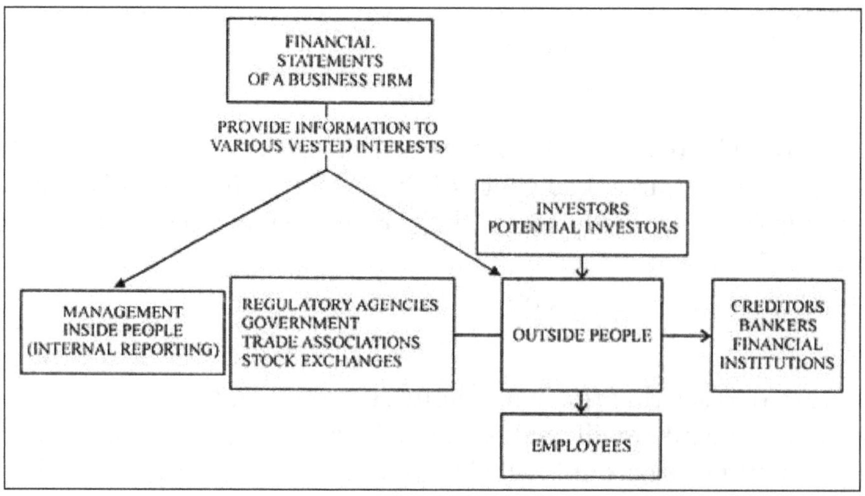

Income Statement

The income statement, also called the profit and loss statement, is a report that shows the income, expenses, and resulting profits or losses of a company during a specific time period. The income statement is the first financial statement typically prepared during the accounting cycle because the net income or loss must be calculated and carried over to the statement of owner's equity before other financial statements can be prepared.

The income statement calculates the net income of a company by subtracting total expenses from total income. This calculation shows investors and creditors the overall profitability of the company as well as how efficiently the company is at generating profits from total revenues.

The income and expense accounts can also be subdivided to calculate gross profit and the income or loss from operations. These two calculations are best shown on a multi-step income statement. Gross profit is calculated by subtracting cost of goods sold from net sales. Operating income is calculated by subtracting operating expenses from the gross profit.

Unlike the balance sheet, the income statement calculates net income or loss over a range of time. For example annual statements use revenues and expenses over a 12-month period, while quarterly statements focus on revenues and expenses incurred during a 3-month period.

Purpose of Income Statement

What is an Income Statement used for?

there are several different types of income statements that are created for different reasons. For example, the year-end statement that is prepared annually for stockholders and potential investors doesn't do much good for management while they are trying to run the company throughout the year. Thus, interim financial statements are prepared for management to check the status of operations during the year. Management also typically prepares departmental statements that break down revenue and expense numbers by business segment.

In the end, the main purpose of all profit and loss statements is to communicate the profitability and business activities of the company with end users. Each one of these end users has their own use for this information. Let's look at who uses the P&L and what they use it for.

Who uses an Income Statement?

There are two different groups of people who use this financial statement: internal users and external users.

Internal users like company management and the board of directors use this statement to analyze the business as a whole and make decisions on how it is run. For example, they use performance numbers to gauge whether they should open new branch, close a department, or increase production of a product.

External users like investors and creditors, on the other hand, are people outside of the company who have no source of financial information about the company except published reports.

Investors want to know how profitable a company is and whether it will grow and become more profitable in the future. They are mainly concerned with whether or not investing their money is the company with yield them a positive return.

Creditors, on the other hand, aren't as concerned about profitability as investors are. Creditors are more concerned with a company's cash flow and if they are generating enough income to pay back their loans.

Competitors are also external users of financial statements. They use competitors' P&L to gauge how well other companies are doing in their space and whether or not they should enter new markets and try to compete with other companies.

Format of Income Statement

There are two income statement formats that are generally prepared.

- Single-step income statement – The single step statement only shows one category of income and one category of expenses. This format is less useful of external users because they can't calculate many efficiency and profitability ratios with this limited data.
- Multi-step income statement – The multi-step statement separates expense accounts into more relevant and usable accounts based on their function. Cost of goods sold, operating and non-operating expenses are separated out and used to calculate gross profit, operating income, and net income.

In both income statement formats, revenues are always presented before expenses. Expenses can be listed alphabetically or by total dollar amount. Either presentation is acceptable.

P&L expenses can also be formatted by the nature and the function of the expense.

All income statements have a heading that display's the company name, title of the statement and the time period of the report. For example, an annual income statement issued by ABC Inc. would have the following heading:

- ABC Inc.
- Income Statement.
- For the Year Ended December 31, 2015.

Income Statement Example

Single Step Income Statement

Paul's Guitar loop, inc. Income Statement For the Year Ended December 31, 2015		
Revenues		
Merchandise Sales	$ 24,800	
Music Lesson Income	3,000	
Total Revenues		$ 27,800
Expenses		

Cost of Goods Sold	10,200	
Depreciation expense	2,000	
Wage expense	750	
Rent expense	500	
Interest expense	500	
Supplies expense	500	
Utilities expense	400	
Total Expenses		14,850
Net Income		$ 12,950

As you can see, this example income statement is a single-step statement because it only lists expenses in one main category. Although this statement might not be extremely useful for investors looking for detailed information, it does accurately calculate the net income for the year.

Components of an Income Statement

The income statement may have minor variations between different companies, as expenses and income will be dependent on the type of operations or business conducted. However, there are several generic line items that are commonly seen in the income statement.

The most common income statement items include:

Revenue/Sales

Sales Revenue is the company's revenue from sales or services, displayed at the very top of the statement. This value will be gross of the costs associated with creating the goods sold or in providing services. Some companies have multiple revenue streams that add to a total revenue line.

Cost of Goods Sold (COGS)

Cost of Goods Sold (COGS) is a line-item that aggregates the direct costs associated with selling products to generate revenue. This line item can also be called Cost of Sales if the company is a service business. Direct costs can include labor, parts, materials, and an allocation of other expenses such as depreciation.

Gross Profit

Gross Profit Gross profit is calculated by subtracting Cost of Goods Sold (or Cost of Sales) from Sales Revenue.

Marketing, Advertising and Promotion Expenses

Most businesses have some expenses related to selling goods and/or services. Marketing, advertising, and promotion expenses are often grouped together as they are similar expenses, all related to selling.

General and Administrative Expenses

SG&A Expenses include the selling, general, and the administrative section that contains all other indirect costs associated with running the business. This includes salaries and wages, rent and office expenses, insurance, travel expenses, and sometimes depreciation and amortization, along with other operational expenses. Entities may, however, elect to separate out depreciation and amortization in its own section.

EBITDA

EBITDA, while not present in all income statements, stands for Earnings before Interest, Tax, Depreciation, and Amortization. It is calculated by subtracting SG&A expenses (excluding amortization and depreciation) from gross profit.

Depreciation and Amortization Expense

Depreciation and amortization are non-cash expenses that are created by accountants to spread out the cost of capital assets such as Property, Plant, and Equipment (PP&E).

Operating Income (or EBIT)

Operating Income represents what's earned from regular business operations. In other words, it's the profit before any non-operating income, non-operating expenses, interest or taxes are subtracted from revenues. EBIT is a term commonly used in finance and stands for Earnings Before Interest and Tax.

Interest

Interest Expense: It is common for companies to split out interest expense and interest income as a separate line item in the income statement. This is done to be able to reconcile the difference between EBIT and EBT. Interest expense is determined by the debt schedule.

Other Expenses

Businesses often have other expenses that are unique to their industry. Other expenses may include things such as fulfillment, technology, research and development (R&D), stock based compensation (SBC), impairment charges, gains/losses on the sale of investments, foreign exchange impacts, and many more expenses that are industry or company-specific.

EBT (Pre-tax Income)

EBT stands for Earnings before Tax, also known as pre-tax income, and is found by subtracting interest expense from Operating Income. This is the final subtotal before arriving at net income.

Income Taxes

Income Taxes refer to the relevant taxes charged on pre-tax income. The total tax expense can consist of both current taxes and future taxes.

Net Income

Net Income is calculated by deducting income taxes from pre-tax income. This is the amount that flows into retained earnings on the balance sheet, after deductions for any dividends.

Example of an Income Statement

Below is an example of Amazon's consolidated statement of operations, or income statement, for the years ended December 31, 2015 – 2017. Take a look at the P&L and then read a break down of it below:

Year Ended December 31,			
	2015	2016	2017
Net product sales	$ 79.268	$ 94.665	$ 118,573
Net services sales	27,738	41,322	59,293
Total net sales	107,738	135,987	177,866
Operating expense			
Cost of sales	71,651	88,265	111,93
Fulfilment	13,410	17,619	25,249
Marketing	5,254	7,233	10,069
Technologies and content	12,540	16,085	22,620
General and administrative	1,747	2,432	3,674
Other operating expense, net	171	167	214
Total operating expenses	104,773	131,801	173,760
Operating income	2,233	4,186	4,106
Interest income	50	100	202
Interest expense	(459)	(484)	(848)
Other income (expenses) ,net	(256)	90	346
Total non-operating income (expenses)	(665)	(294)	(300)
Income before income taxes	1,568	3,892	3,806
Provision for income taxes	(950)	(1,425)	(769)
Equity- method investment activity, net of tax	(22)	(96)	(4)
Net income	$ 596	$ 2,371	$ 3,033
Basic earnings per share	$ 1.28	$ 5.01	$ 6.32
Diluted earnings per share	$ 1.25	$ 4.90	$ 6.15
Weighted – average share used in computation of earnings per share:$			
Basic	467	474	480
Diluted	477	484	493

Starting at the top we see that Amazon has two different revenue streams – products and services – which combine to form total revenue.

There is no gross profit subtotal, as the cost of sales is grouped will all other expenses, which include fulfillment, marketing, technology, content, general and administration (G&A), and other expenses.

After deducting all the above expenses we finally arrive at the first subtotal on the income statement, Operating Income (also known as EBIT or Earnings before Interest and Taxes).

Everything below Operating Income is not related to the ongoing operation of the business – such as non-operating expenses, provision for income taxes (i.e., future taxes) and equity-method investment activity (profits or losses from minority investments), net of tax.

Finally, we arrive at the net income (or net loss) which is then divided by the weighted average shares outstanding to determine the Earnings Per Share (EPS).

Steps to Build an Income Statement in a Financial Model

After preparing the skeleton of an income statement as such, it can then be integrated into a proper financial model to forecast future performance.

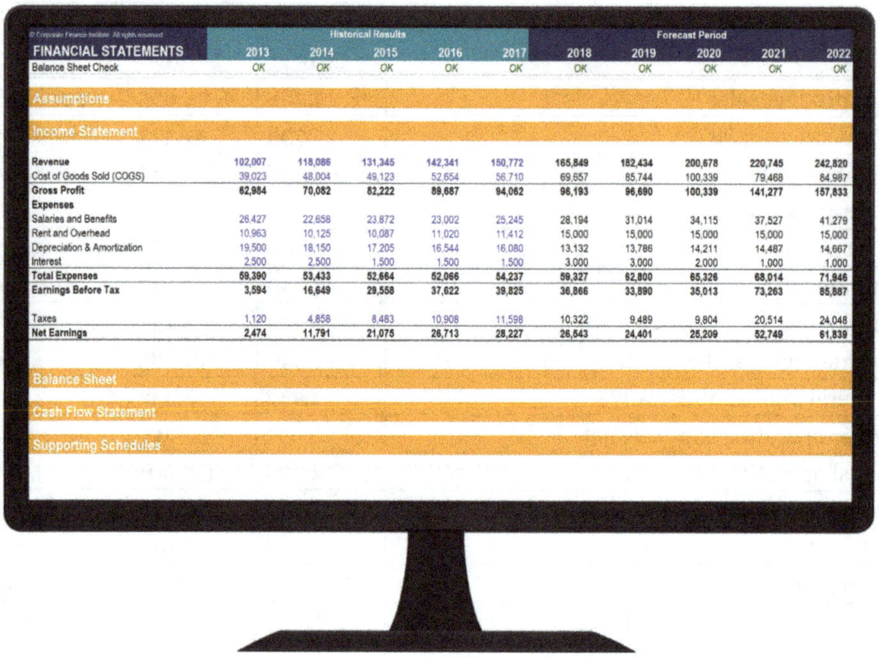

Step 1: First, input historical data for any available time periods into the income statement template in Excel. Format historical data input using a specific format in order to be able to differentiate between hardcoded data and calculated data. As a reminder, a common method of formatting such data is to color any hardcoded input in blue, while coloring calculated data or linking data in black.

Doing so enables the user and reader to know where changes in inputs can be made, and to know which cells contain formulae and, as such, should not be changed or tampered with. Regardless of the formatting method chosen, however, remember to remain consistent usage in order to avoid confusion.

Step 2: Next, analyze the trend in the available historical data to create drivers and assumptions for future forecasting. For example, analyze the trend in sales to forecast sales growth, analyzing the COGS as a percentage of sales to forecast future COGS. Learn more about forecasting methods.

Step 3: Finally, using the drivers and assumptions prepared in the previous step, forecast future values for all the line items within the income statement. Forecast specific line items, and use these to calculate subtotals. For example, for future gross profit, it is better to forecast COGS and revenue and subtract them from each other, rather than to forecast future gross profit directly.

What are Common Drivers for Each Income Statement Item?

Line Item	Driver or Assumption
Sales Revenue	Selected growth percentage, pegged growth percentage based on index (such as GDP)
Cost of Goods Sold	Percentage of sales, Fixed dollar value

Line Item	Driver or Assumption
SG&A	Percentage of sales, fixed amount, trend, fixed dollar value
Depreciation and Amortization	Depreciation Schedule
Interest Expense	Debt Schedule
Income Tax	Percentage of pre-tax income (effective tax rate)

While these drivers are commonly used, they are just general guidelines. There are situations where intuition must be exercised to determine the proper driver or assumption to use. For example, a specific entity may have zero revenue. As such, the percentage of sales driver cannot be used for COGS. Instead, an analyst may have to rely on examining the past trend of COGS to determine assumptions for forecasting COGS into the future.

The core statements used in financial modeling are the same core statements used in accounting. There are three: the Income Statement, the Balance Sheet, and the Cash Flow Statement. In a financial model, each of these statements will impact the values of the other statements.

Recognition Principle

The revenue recognition principle provides guidelines for reporting revenue in the income statement. The principle generally requires that revenue be recognized in the financial statements when: (1) realized or realizable and (2) earned. Revenues are realized when products or services are exchanged or performed for cash or claims to cash. Revenues also are realizable when a company's things of monetary value (assets), such as products and debts owed to the company, are readily convertible into cash. Revenues are considered earned when a business has substantially accomplished what it must do to be entitled to the benefits represented by the revenues. Recognition through sales or the providing (performance) of services provides a uniform and reasonable test of realization. Limited exceptions to the basic revenue principle include recognizing revenue during production (on long-term construction contracts), at the completion of production (for many commodities), and subsequent to the sale at the time of cash collection (on installment sales).

In recognizing expenses, accountants rely on the matching principle because it requires that efforts (expenses) be matched with accomplishments (revenues) whenever it is reasonable and practical to do so. For example, matching (associating) the cost of goods sold with revenues from the interrelated sales that resulted directly and jointly from the same transaction as the expense is reasonable and practical. To recognize costs for which it is difficult to adopt some association with revenues, accountants use a rational and systematic allocation policy that assigns expenses to the periods during which the related assets are expected to provide benefits, such as depreciation, amortization, and insurance. Some costs are charged to the current period as expenses (or losses) merely because no future benefit is anticipated, no connection with revenue is apparent, or no allocation is rational and systematic under the circumstances, i.e., under an immediate recognition principle.

The current operating concept of income includes only those value changes and events that are controllable by management and that are incurred in the current period from ordinary, normal, and recurring operations. Any unusual and nonrecurring items of income or loss would be recognized directly in the statement of retained earnings. Under this concept of income, investors are primarily interested in continuing income from operations.

In the late 1990s, however, the FASB moved closer to adopting all-inclusive or comprehensive income reporting. The all-inclusive concept of income includes the total changes in equity recognized during a specific period, except for dividend distributions and capital transactions. this concept requires companies to include unusual and nonrecurring income or loss items in their income statements for the appropriate accounting period.

Consolidated Income Statements

Accountants prepare consolidated income statements by combining the revenues, gains, expenses, and losses of a parent company's accounts the accounts of its subsidiary operations. A subsidiary is a company with more than 50 percent of its voting stock owned by a parent company. Revenues and expenses that result from transactions between parent and subsidiary companies—intercompany transactions—are not included or are eliminated because they do not affect the assets of the overall company, when viewed as a consolidted operation. Intercompany transactions include sales between parent and subsidiary companies and rent received from or paid by affiliated companies to each other.

Advantages of Income Statements

- Information about revenue: Income statement provides thorough information about normal costs such as COGS and expenses associated with managing operations. It also accounts for additional costs including statutory taxes which is applied to gross revenue to arrive at net profit. Revenue also includes income from indirect sources such as interest income from business investments.

- Providing for Investor Analysis: Income Statement is an important document to provide information to prospective investors looking to buy stake in the business. Income statement makes it easier for calculation of earnings per share using the net profit. The higher the earnings per share, the better the prospect of business is going forward. Income statement is therefore an important checklist for the investors to gain stake in the business.

- Tracking the performance of business: Performance means profit and income statement, it is both gross profit and net profit. Performance growth is bottom line growth which needs to be tracked on regular basis. While analyzing revenue over various accounting periods, overall performance of the business must be reviewed and opined on. This helps the user to spot the trend early as possible and eliminate one-time charges that may affect the data.

- Means for Effective forecasting: Financial modelling requires the effective forecast of future accounting periods. Generally, the forecasts are prepared to sketch the future over 3 and 5 years. Income statements perfectly anticipates problems that may arise in the future.

- Overview of Cash Flows: Although cash flow statement is prepared specially for the movement of cash, the income statement can show eagle eye view of the movement of cash along with accruals and receivables on one accounting statement. This helps in making adjustments, following the cash trail and ultimately saving cash access for the future.

- Operating and Non-operating Income: Income Statement segregates into operating income and non-operating income. This helps the business owner to analyze how much of the revenue is derived from operating i.e. regular business activities and how much income is from non-business activities. Robust operating income with growth thereon is a good sign for healthy businesses. It is also needed to be understood that operating income forms at least 80 % of the total revenue of the business. Non-operating income are very irregular income or one-off income that do not impact the financial viability of the business.

Limitations of Income Statement

Income statement is of vital importance for the users of the financial statements. However, it suffers from the following limitations:

- The accounting process is based on various assumptions and estimates. Therefore, the net income (or loss) measured by preparing an income statement is not absolutely accurate. An example of estimates used in the accounting process is the depreciation which is computed on the basis of estimated useful life of assets such as building, plants and equipment etc.
- The use of judgments and estimates in the accounting process enables management to use such figures that would generate desired net income or net loss figure for the period.
- A manipulation in net income is possible by using a particular inventory valuation method such as FIFO method, LIFO method and average costing method. The company may use such method that generates the desired result.
- While preparing income statement we take into account only those activities whose value can be objectively measured. For example, a sound customer's relation policy can develop a good customer base that can certainly be beneficial for a profitable business operation but its value cannot be objectively measured unless evidenced by an actual business transaction.

Income Tax

Income tax refers to annual taxes levied by the federal government and most state governments on individual and business income. By law, businesses and individuals must file federal and state income tax returns every year to determine whether they owe taxes. Governments use the taxes they collect to fund their activities.

Example:

Income tax is applied to both earned income (wages, salaries and commission) and unearned income (dividends, interest and rents).

The U.S. and many other countries employ a progressive income tax system in which higher income earners pay a higher tax ratecompared to their lower earning counterparts. The intent of progressive systems is to distribute wealth more evenly across a population.

Here's an example of how a progressive tax is structured: Assume you are single and report $80,000 in taxable income for the 2010 tax year (filing in 2011). In accordance with the federal tax rates defined for single filers in 2010, the first $8,350 of your income is taxed at 10%; the next $8,351 through $33,950 of earnings are taxed at 15%; and the remaining $33,951 through $80,000 of your earnings are taxed at 25%.

Importance of Income Tax

Income taxes reduce the amount of earnings that individuals and businesses are allowed to keep. There are a couple of strategies investors can use to retain more of their income. The first is investing in tax-advantaged assets like U.S. government bondsand municipal bonds.

The second is to open a retirement account that is tax-advantaged. An IRA, 401(k), SEP IRA and Roth IRA are all examples of tax-advantaged accounts. Investors can hold any asset they like within these accounts. The tax benefits of a retirement account don't depend on the investments you hold in the account.

The Balance Sheet

The balance sheet is one of the most important financial statements and is useful for doing accounting analysis and modeling. Balance Sheet is the "Snapshot" of a company's financial position at a given moment. Balance Sheet reports the amount of a company's.

- Assets – Current assets/Long-term assets.
- Liabilities – Current Liabilities/Long-term liabilities.
- Stockholders' (or owner's) equity – Common stock / Retained earnings.

Balance Sheet December 31, 2015				
Assets			**Liabilities**	
Current Assets			Current Liabilities	
Cash		32,800	Accounts Payable	49,000
Accounts Receivable		300	Accrued Expenses	450
Prepaid Rent		1,000	Unearned Revenue	1,000
Inventory		39,800	Total Current Liabilities	50,450
			Long-term Liabilities	99,500
Total Current Assets		73,900	**Total Liabilities**	149,950
			Owner's Equity	
Long-term Assets			Owner's Equity	
Leasehold Improvements	100,000		Retained Earnings	11,950
Accumulated Depreciation	(2,000)	98,000	Common Stock	10,000
Total Long-term Assets		98,000	Total Owner's Equity	21,950
Total Assets:		171,900	**Total Liabilities and Owner's Equity**	171,900

Assets = Liabilities + Shareholders' Equity

- Unlike Income Statement, Balance Sheets are much less complicated (however, there are many items you need to include under few heads). And Balance Sheets portray the overall picture of a company's financial affair altogether.
- Balance Sheets can't be formed without first setting up the income statement. Because we need to know the retained earnings from the income statement. Through Income Statement, we can ascertain the net profit. The portion of net profit that is not distributed among the shareholders is called "retained earnings".

Balance Sheet Structure

Assets are arranged on the left-hand side and the liabilities and shareholders' equity would be on the right-hand side. However, in most of the cases, companies put the assets first and then they set up liabilities and at the bottom shareholders' equity. The total assets should be equal to the total liabilities and total shareholders' equity.

Assets = Liabilities + Shareholders' Equity

Balance Sheet Format is as follows :

- Current Assets
- Current Liabilities
- Long Term Assets
- Long Term Liabilities
- Shareholder's Equity.

FastTrack Movers & Packers Inc Balance Sheet, December 31st 2007					
Assets			**Liabilities & Stockholder's Equity**		
Current assets			Current Liabilities		
Cash		$ xxx	Short-term debt		$ xxx
Accounts Receivables	1	$ xxx	Accounts Payable	2	$ xxx
Inventory		$ xxx	Total current liabilities		$ xxx
Total current assets		$ xxx			
			Long term Liabilities		
Long term assets			Long term debt	4	$ xxx
Plant and Equipment	3	$ xxx			
Less:Acc depreciation		($ xxx)	Stockholder's Equity		
Net PPE		$ xxx	Common Stock		$ xxx
			Retained Earnings	5	$ xxx
			Total Stockholder's Equity		$ xxx
Total Assets		**$ xxx**	**Liabilities & Stockholder's Equity**		**$ xxx**

Current Assets

Current assets are expected to be consumed, sold, or converted into cash either in one year or in the operating cycle, whichever is longer. An operating cycle is an average time it takes to convert an investment in inventory back into cash. Current assets are presented in order of liquidity.

Assets are arranged on the basis of how quickly they can be converted into cash (means how liquid they are). That means, in the balance sheet, the first things we will put in are current assets. Under current assets, these are the items you can consider –

- Cash & Cash Equivalents – Cash could also include an amount required to be held for deposit to satisfy the terms of a lending agreement. Cash equivalents are securities (e.g. US Treasury bills) that have term of less than or equal to 90 days.
- Short-term investments – Short Term Marketable Securitiesprimarily includes Bond Investments and Capital Stock Investments. Short-Term Marketable Securities are not as ready as money in your account, but they provided added cushion if some immediate need were to arise.

- Inventories – Inventory consists of merchandise a business owns but has not sold. Classified as current assets because investor assumes that inventory can be sold in the near future, turning it into cash.
- Trade & Other Receivables – Money that is owed to the company by the customers
- Prepayments & Accrued Income – Sometimes a business will have to pay for goods or services before they actually receive the product. Expenses that have been paid in the current fiscal period but that will not be subtracted from revenue until a subsequent fiscal period

Other current assets also include Derivative Assets, Current Income Tax Assets, Assets Held for Sale etc.

Current Assets will look like following:

	X (in US $)	Y (in US $)
Cash	10000	3000
Cash Equivalent	1000	500
Accounts Receivable	1000	5000
Inventories	500	6000
Total Current Assets	12500	14500

Current Liabilities

Current Liabilities are probable future payments of assets or services that a firm is obligated to make as a result of previous operations. These obligations are expected to require the use of existing current assets or the creation of other current liabilities.

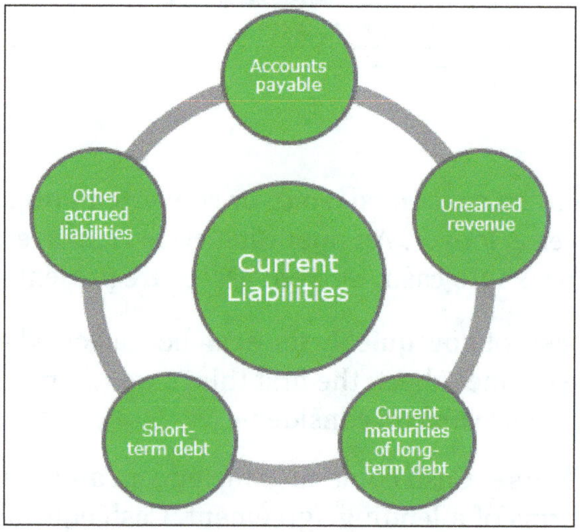

"Current Liabilities" generally include the following :

- Accounts Payable – Amounts owed to suppliers for goods and services that have been purchased on credit. Accounts payable are debts that must be paid off within a given period of time in order to avoid default.

- Short Term Debt – Short Term Debt is also referred to as Notes Payable. Sometimes when the demand is high, a company may raise short-term loans to stock up the inventory (Utilizing leverage).
- Current Maturities of Long-Term Debt – Any portion of long-term debt that is to be repaid within a year of the balance sheet date is reclassified from the noncurrent liability section to the current liability section of the title, current maturities of long-term debt.
- Unearned Revenues – Unearned revenue is created when customers pay for services or products before delivery.
- Other Accrued Liabilities – This could include Money owed to employees as salary and bonus that the company has not yet paid.

Other than that, current liabilities also include accounts payable, sales taxes payable, income taxes payable, interest payable, bank overdrafts, payroll taxes payable, customer deposits in advance, accrued expenses, short-term loans, current maturities of long-term debt etc.

Current Liabilities will look like following:

	X (in US $)	Y (in US $)
Accounts Payable	4000	3000
Current Taxes Payable	5000	6000
Current Long-term Liabilities	11000	9000
Total Current Liabilities	20000	18000

Long Term Assets

Long term assets are typically physical assets that the company own and are employed in the production process of the firm and have a useful life greater than one year. Long term assets are not for sale to the firm's customers.

Long-term assets can be classified into three main categories:

- Tangible Assets: These assets have physical existence. Assets like Real Estate, Buildings, Offices, Machinery, Furniture, Telephone belong to this category. The process of allocating the cost of tangible assets over the useful life is called "depreciation".
- Natural Resources: These assets have an economic value derived from Earth and used up over time. Examples include Oil fields, mines etc.
- Intangible Assets: These assets have no physical existence and they cannot be felt or touched or seen. Examples include trademarks, copyrights, patents, franchise, and goodwill. The cost of intangible assets is allocated to periods over which it provides benefits through a process called amortization.

Long term assets are generally reported at their carrying value or book value. If the asset has lost its revenue generating ability, it may be written down (asset impairment, amount of written down is recorded as loss).

Long Term Liabilities

Long-Term Liabilities are obligations that are not expected to require the use of current assets or not expected to create current liabilities within one year or the normal operating cycle (whichever is longer)

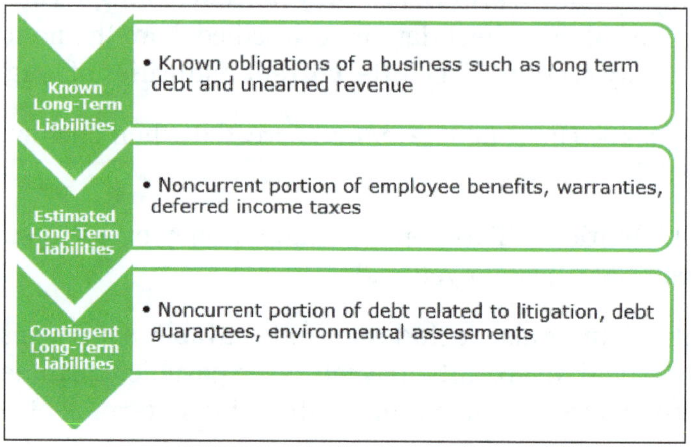

- In most cases, it contains long-term debt. Long-term debt is subject to various covenants or restrictions. Long-term debt can be obtained from many sources and may differ in the structure of interest and principal payments and the claims creditors have on the assets of the firm.
- Bonds are contracted between the borrowers and the lender that obligates the bond issuer to make payments to the bondholder over the life of the bond
- Creditors claims could be subdivided into two types:
  - Senior
  - Subordinate

Shareholder's Equity

Stockholders' Equity is the residual interest of the stockholders in the assets of the corporation. There are two primary sources of Equity – Paid-in Capital and Retained Earnings.

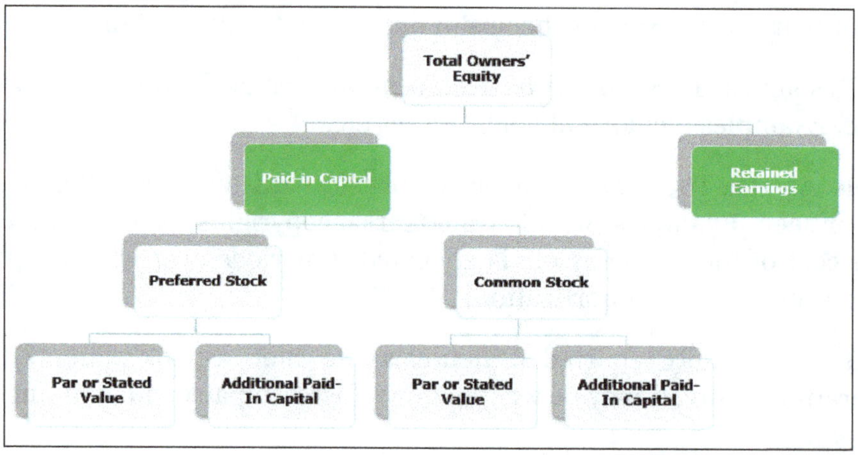

Each share of common stock conveys certain rights to the:

- Attend stockholders' meetings.
- Elect directors and vote on other matters.
- Receive dividends as declared by the board of directors.
- Preemptive right: The preemptive right is a shareholder's right to purchase a proportionate amount of any new stock issued at a later date Shareholder's Accounts need to be maintained for:
    - Par Value (Par value has no economic significance)
    - Additional Paid-in Capital

Preferred stock has certain preferences or features not possessed by common stock.

Method to Read the Balance Sheet

Balance Sheet provides useful information about company's financial affairs. As an investor, you need to know how to read the Balance Sheet to be able to extract the most of it.

These are the steps that can help you read Balance Sheets:

- The first thing is really the first thing. You need to know the balance sheet equation. You need to see whether the total assets and total liabilities & total shareholders' equity are equal. Assets = Liabilities + Equity.
- Then you will look at the current assets. These assets will give ideas about the liquidity of the company and where the company expects to liquidate the assets from. These assets can easily be converted into cash.
- Then you should follow the non-current assets which include fixed assets and intangible assets (like patents etc.) as well. You need to find out the wear and tear (depreciation) and other expenses and whether they have been taken into account or not. Match it up with the income statement and cash flow statement to understand whether there is any loophole or not.
- Then you need to learn about the liabilities of the company. They can be both current and non-current. Current liabilities are items which can be dealt quickly and the keyword for it is "short term". In the case of non-current liabilities, it takes longer for the firm to pay off which includes long-term loan and other payables.
- The last step is to look through the shareholders' equity. Check out the retained earnings and compare it with a net profit. And you will get an idea about how much dividend is being paid (if any).
- It is important for you to know that you shouldn't skip any step mentioned above. Don't look at shareholders' equity until you have completed looking at all other items in the balance sheet. The best way is to keep a pen and paper and take notes while looking through the items and matching them up with the other financial statements.

Balance Sheet Example – Vertical Analysis

For understanding Colgate's Balance sheet trends over the period of time, we can perform Vertical Analysis. Vertical Analysis on the Balance Sheet normalizes the Balance Sheet and expresses each item in the percentage of total assets/liabilities. It helps us to understand how each item of the balance sheet has moved over the years.

- For each year, Balance Sheet line items are divided by its respective year's Top Assets (or Total Liabilities) number.
- For example, for Accounts Receivables, we calculate as Receivables / Total Assets. Likewise for other balance sheet items.

	Dec-07	Dec-08	Dec-09	Dec-10	Dec-11	Dec-12	Dec-13	Dec-14	Dec-15
Assets									
Current Assets									
Cash and cash equivalents	4.2%	5.6%	5.4%	4.4%	6.9%	6.6%	6.9%	8.1%	8.1%
Receivables	16.6%	16.0%	14.6%	14.4%	13.2%	12.5%	11.8%	11.5%	11.9%
Inventories	11.6%	12.0%	10.9%	10.9%	10.4%	10.2%	10.3%	10.3%	9.9%
Other current assets	3.3%	3.7%	3.4%	3.7%	4.1%	4.8%	5.8%	6.2%	6.7%
Total current assets	35.8%	37.2%	34.2%	33.4%	34.6%	34.0%	34.8%	36.1%	36.7%
Property, plant and equipment, net	29.8%	31.3%	31.6%	33.1%	[illegible]	28.7%	29.4%	30.3%	31.7%
Goodwill, net	22.5%	21.6%	20.7%	21.1%	19.6%	18.7%	17.8%	17.1%	17.6%
Other intangible assets, net	8.4%	8.4%	7.4%	7.4%	11.8%	11.2%	10.8%	10.5%	11.3%
Deferred income taxes	0.0%	0.0%	0.0%	0.8%	0.9%	0.7%	0.6%	0.6%	0.6%
Other assets	3.6%	1.6%	6.2%	4.2%	4.3%	6.8%	6.7%	5.3%	2.2%
Total assets	100.0%	100.0%	100.0%	100.0%	100.0%	100.0%	100.0%	100.0%	100.0%

- Cash and Cash equivalents have increased from 4.2% in 2007 and are currently standing at 8.1% of the total assets.
- Receivables have decreased from 16.6% in 2007 to 11.9% in 2015.
- Inventories have decreased too from 11.6% to 9.9% overall.
- What is included in "other current assets"? It shows a steady increase from 3.3% to 6.7% of the total assets over the last 9 years.

Liabilities and Shareholders' Equity	Dec-07	Dec-08	Dec-09	Dec-10	Dec-11	Dec-12	Dec-13	Dec-14	Dec-15
Current Liabilities									
Notes and loans payable	1.5%	1.1%	0.3%	0.4%	0.3%	0.4%	0.1%	0.1%	0.0%
Current portion of long-term debt	1.4%	0.9%	2.9%	5.0%	2.7%	1.9%	6.4%	3.6%	2.5%
Accounts payable	10.6%	10.6%	10.5%	10.4%	9.8%	9.6%	9.7%	9.1%	9.3%
Accrued income taxes	2.6%	2.7%	3.5%	2.4%	3.1%	1.9%	1.7%	2.2%	2.3%
Other accruals	15.2%	14.2%	15.1%	15.1%	13.4%	[illegible]	14.3%	14.2%	15.4%
Total current liabilities	31.3%	29.6%	32.3%	33.4%	29.2%	27.9%	32.2%	29.3%	29.6%
Long-term debt	31.9%	35.9%	25.3%	25.2%	[illegible]	36.8%	34.2%	41.9%	52.4%
Deferred income taxes	2.6%	0.8%	0.7%	1.0%	2.0%	[illegible]	3.2%	1.9%	1.9%
Other liabilities	10.6%	13.2%	12.3%	[illegible]	[illegible]	[illegible]	12.1%	16.5%	16.4%
Total liabilities	76.3%	79.5%	70.7%	[illegible]	80.0%	82.2%	81.7%	89.7%	100.4%
Commitments and contingent liabilities									
Shareholders' Equity									
Preference stock	2.0%	1.8%	1.5%	[illegible]	0.0%	0.0%	0.0%	0.0%	0.0%
Common stock	7.2%	7.3%	6.6%	6.6%	5.8%	10.9%	10.6%	10.9%	12.3%
Additional paid-in capital	15.0%	16.1%	15.8%	10.1%	10.5%	6.1%	7.2%	9.2%	12.0%
Retained earnings	105.1%	117.8%	118.2%	128.3%	123.0%	126.6%	129.4%	139.9%	157.7%
Accumulated other comprehensive income (los:	-16.5%	-24.8%	-18.8%	-18.9%	[illegible]	-19.6%	-17.7%	-26.1%	-33.0%
Unearned compensation	-2.2%	-1.9%	-1.2%	-0.9%	[illegible]	-0.3%	-0.2%	-0.1%	-0.1%
Treasury stock, at cost	-88.1%	-97.2%	-94.1%	-101.2%	[illegible]	-107.4%	-112.7%	-125.3%	-151.4%
Total Colgate-Palmolive Company shareholders' equity	22.6%	19.3%	28.0%	23.9%	18.7%	16.3%	16.6%	8.5%	-2.5%
Noncontrolling interests	1.1%	1.2%	1.3%	1.3%	1.3%	1.5%	1.7%	1.8%	2.1%
Total shareholders' equity	23.7%	20.5%	29.3%	25.2%	20.0%	17.8%	18.3%	10.3%	-0.4%
Total liabilities and shareholders' equity	100.0%	100.0%	100.0%	100.0%	100.0%	100.0%	100.0%	100.0%	100.0%

- On the liabilities side, there can be many observations we can highlight. Accounts payable decreased continuously over the past 9 years and currently stands at 9.3% of the total assets.
- There has been a significant jump in the Long-Term Debt to 52,4% in 2015. For this, we need to investigate its SEC Filings further.
- Non-controlling interests have also increased over the period of 9 years and is now at 2.1%.

Cash Flow

A cash flow statement provides information about the changes in cash and cash equivalents of a business by classifying cash flows into operating, investing and financing activities. It is a key report to be prepared for each accounting period for which financial statements are presented by an enterprise.

Monitoring the cash situation of any business is the key. The income statement would reflect the profits but does not give any indication of the cash components. The important information of what the business has been doing with the cash is provided by the cash flow statement. Like the other financial statements, the cash flow statement is also usually drawn up annually, but can be drawn up more often. It is noteworthy that cash flow statement covers the flows of cash over a period of time (unlike the balance sheet that provides a snapshot of the business at a particular date). Also, the cash flow statement can be drawn up in a budget form and later compared to actual figures.

Objectives of Preparing Cash Flow Statement

- Cash flow statement shows inflow and outflow of cash and cash equivalents from various activities of a company during a specific period under the main heads i.e., operating activities, investing activities and financing activities.
- Information through the Cash Flow statement is useful in assessing the ability of any enterprise to generate cash and cash equivalents and the needs of the enterprise to utilize those cash flows.
- Taking economic decisions requires an evaluation of the ability of an enterprise to generate cash and cash equivalents, which is provided by the cash flow statement.

Cash and cash equivalents generally consist of the following:

- Cash in hand
- Cash at bank
- Short term investments that are highly liquid
- Bank overdrafts comprise an integral element of the organization's treasury management.

Classification of Activities

Cash flow activities are to be classified into three categories:This is done to show separately the cash flows generated / used by these activities, thereby helping to assess the impact of these activities on the financial position and cash and cash equivalents of an enterprise.

- Operating activities
- Investing activities
- Financing activities.

Cash from Operating Activities

Operating activities are the activities that comprise of the primary / main activities of an enterprise during an accounting period. For example, for a garment manufacturing company, operating activities include procurement of raw material, sale of garments, incurrence of manufacturing expenses, etc. These are the principal revenue generating activities of the enterprise.

Profit before tax as presented in the income statement could be used as a starting point to calculate the cash flows from operating activities.

Cash Inflows from Operating Activities

- Cash receipts from sale of goods and rendering services.
- Cash receipts from fees, royalties, commissions and other revenues.

Cash Outflows from Operating Activities

- Cash payments to suppliers for goods and services.
- Cash payments of income taxes unless they can be specifically identified with financing and investing activities.

Following adjustments are required to be made to the profit before tax to arrive at the cash flow from operations:

- Elimination of non cash expenses (e.g. depreciation, amortization, impairment losses, bad debts written off, etc).
- Removal of expenses to be classified elsewhere in the cash flow statement (e.g. interest expense should be classified under financing activities).
- Removal of income to be presented elsewhere in the cash flow statement (e.g. dividend income and interest income should be classified under investing activities unless in case of for example an investment bank).
- Elimination of non cash income (e.g. gain on revaluation of investments).

The amount of cash from operations indicates the internal solvency level of the company. It is a key indicator of the extent to which the operations of the enterprise have generated sufficient cash flows to maintain its operating potential.

Cash from Investing Activities

Cash flow from investing activities includes the movement in cash flows owing to the purchase and sale of assets. It relates to purchase and sale of long-term assets or fixed assets such as machinery, furniture, land and building, etc.

Cash Outflows from Investing Activities

- Cash payments to acquire fixed assets including intangibles and capitalized R&D.
- Cash advances and loans made to third party (other than advances and loans made by a financial enterprise wherein it is operating activities).
- Cash payments to acquire shares, warrants or debt instruments of other enterprises other than the instruments those held for trading purposes.

Cash Inflows from Investing Activities

- Cash receipt from disposal of fixed assets including intangibles.
- Cash receipt from the repayment of advances or loans made to third parties (except in case of financial enterprise).
- Dividend received from investments in other enterprises.
- Cash receipt from disposal of shares, warrants or debt instruments of other enterprises except those held for trading purposes.

Cash from Financing Activities

It includes financing activities related to long-term funds or capital of an enterprise. Financing activities are activities that result in changes in the size and composition of the owners' capital and borrowings of the enterprise. e.g., cash proceeds from issue of equity shares, debentures, raising long-term loans, repayment of bank loans, etc.

Cash Inflows from Financing Activities

- Cash proceeds from issuing shares (equity / preference).
- Cash proceeds from issuing debentures, loans, bonds and other short/ long-term borrowings.

Cash Outflows from financing activities:

- Cash repayments of amounts borrowed.
- Interest paid on debentures and long-term loans and advances.
- Dividends paid on equity and preference capital.

Main Heads of Cash Flow Statement

Cash Flow Statement (Main heads only)

- Cash flows from operating activities xxx
- Cash flows from investing activities xxx
- Cash flows from financing activities xxx

Net increase (decrease) in cash and cash xxx equivalents (A + B + C) + Cash and cash equivalents at the beginning xxx = Cash and cash equivalents at the end xxxx

Methods of Preparing the Cash Flow Statements

Operating activities are the main source of revenues and expenditures, thereby cash flow from the same needs to be ascertained. The cash flow can be reported through two ways:

Direct method that discloses the major classes of gross cash receipts and cash payments and Indirect method that has the net profit or loss adjusted for effects of (1) transactions of a non-cash nature, (2) any deferrals or accruals of past/future operating cash receipts and (3) items of income or expenses associated with investing or financing cash flows.

Direct Method

In the direct method, the major heads of cash inflows and outflows (such as cash received from trade receivables, employee benefits, expenses paid, etc.) are to be considered.

As the different line items are recorded on accrual basis in statement of profit and loss, certain adjustments are to be made to convert them into cash basis such as the following:

- Cash receipts from customers: Revenue from operations + Trade receivables in the beginning – Trade receivables in the end.
- Cash payments to suppliers: Purchases + Trade Payables in the beginning – Trade Payables in the end.
- Purchases: Cost of Revenue from Operations – Opening Inventory + Closing Inventory.
- Cash expenses: Expenses on accrual basis + Prepaid expenses in the beginning and Outstanding expenses in the end – Prepaid expenses in the end and Outstanding expenses in the beginning.

Indirect Method

Indirect method of ascertaining cash flow from operating activities begins with the amount of net profit/loss. This is so because statement of profit and loss incorporates the effects of all operating activities of an enterprise. However, Statement of Profit and Loss is prepared on accrual basis (and not on cash basis). Moreover, it also includes certain non-operating items such as interest paid, profit/loss on sale of fixed assets, etc.) and non-cash items (such as depreciation, goodwill to be written-off, etc. Therefore, it becomes necessary to adjust the amount of net profit/loss as shown by Statement of Profit and Loss for arriving at cash flows from operating activities.

Example: Following is a cash flow statement prepared using indirect method:

Company A Cash Flow Statement For the Year Ended March 31,2015		
Cash Flow From Operating Activity		
Operating Income (EBIT)	489,000	
Deprecation Income ((EBIT)	112,400	
Loss of Sale of Equipment	7,300	
Gain on Sale of land	-51,000	
Increase in Account Receivable	-84,664	
Decrease in Prepaid Expense	8,000	
Decrease in Account Payable	-97,370	
Decrease in Accrued Expenses	-113,860	
Net Cash Flow From Operating Activities		269,806
Cash Flows From Investing Activities		
Sales of Equipment	89,000	
Sale of Lord	247,000	
Purchase of Equipment	-100,000	
Net Cash Flow From Investing Activities		136,000
Cash flows from financing activities		
Payments of dividends	-90,000	
Payments of bond payable	-200,000	
Net Cash Flow From Financing Activities		-290,000
Net Change in Cash		115,806
Beginning Cash Balance		319,730
Ending Cash Balance		435,536

Purpose and Importance of Cash Flow Statements

- Statement of cash flows provides important insights about the liquidity and solvency of a company which are vital for survival and growth of any organization.
- It enables analysts to use the information about historic cash flows for projections of future cash flows of an entity on which to base their economic decisions.
- By summarizing key changes in financial position during a period, cash flow statement serves to highlight priorities of management.
- Comparison of cash flows of different entities helps reveal the relative quality of their earnings since cash flow information is more objective as opposed to the financial performance reflected in income statement.

Advantages of Cash Flow Statement

- Cash Flow Statements help in knowing the liquidity / actual cash position of the company which funds flow and P&L are unable to specify.

- As the liquidity position is known, any shortfalls can be arranged for or excess can be used for the growth of the business.
- Any discrepancy in the financial reporting can be gauged through the cash flow statement by comparing the cash position of both.
- Cash is the basis of all financial operations. Therefore, a projected cash flow statement will enable the management to plan and control the financial operations properly.
- Cash Flow analysis together with the ratio analysis helps measure the profitability and financial position of business.
- Cash flow statement helps in internal financial management as it is useful in formulation of financial plans.

Disadvantages of Cash Flow Statement

- Through the cash flow statement alone, it is not possible to arrive at actual P&L of the company as it shows only the cash position. It has limited usage and in isolation it is of no use and requires BL, P&L for its projections. Cash flow statement does not disclose net income from operations. Therefore, it cannot be a substitute for income statement.
- The cash balance as shown by the cash flow statement may not represent the real liquidity position of the business because it can be easily influenced by postponing the purchases and other payments.
- Cash flow statement cannot replace the funds flow statement. Each of the two has a separate function to perform.

Single Entry System

A single entry system records each accounting transaction with a single entry to the accounting records, rather than the vastly more widespread double entry system. The single entry system is centered on the results of a business that are reported in the income statement. The core information tracked in a single entry system is cash disbursements and cash receipts. Asset and liability records are usually not tracked in a single entry system; these items must be tracked separately. The primary form of record keeping in a single entry system is the cash book, which is essentially an expanded form of a check register, with columns in which to record the particular sources and uses of cash, and room at the top and bottom of each page in which to show beginning and ending balances. An example of a cash book is.

Nbr	Date	Description	Revenue	Expense	Inventory	Payroll
		Balance forward	$41,000	$23,000	$5,700	$8,500
1000	6/15	Utilities		400		
1001	6/18	Merchandise			12,300	
1002	6/20	Wages				4,500

	6/21	Bank deposit	13,100			
1003	6/22	Supplies		1,200		
		Ending Balance	$54,100	$24,600	$18,000	$13,000

The most significant problems associated with a single entry system include:

- Assets: Assets are not tracked, so it is easier for them to be lost or stolen.
- Audited financial statements: It is impossible to obtain an audit opinion on the financial results of a business using a single entry system; the information must be converted to a double entry format for an audit to even be a possibility.
- Errors: It is much easier to make clerical errors in a single entry system, as opposed to the double entry system, where separate entries to different accounts must match.
- Liabilities: Liabilities are not tracked, so you need a separate system for determining when they are due for payment, and in what amounts.
- Reporting: There is much less information available upon which to construct the financial position of a business, so management may not be fully aware of the performance of the business.

Single entry systems are strictly use for manual accounting systems, since all computerized systems utilize the double entry system instead.

Salient Features of Single Entry System

- This system is followed by a sole proprietorship firm or a partnership firm. The companies cannot follow this system.
- Under this system, only one Cash Book is maintained which mixes up both the private and business transactions.
- Usually personal accounts are recorded only, i.e., Real and Nominal accounts are ignored.
- Lack of uniformity is noticed if accounts are kept under Single Entry basis.
- Profit or loss, under this system, can be ascertained but not the financial position as a whole.
- Arithmetical accuracy of the account is not possible since Trial Balance cannot be prepared.
- Practically, this system is the admixture of Single Entry, Double Entry and no entry.

Advantages of Single Entry System

- Since this system is very simple, anyone can maintain it without any adequate knowledge of accounting.
- Limited accounts are to be opened under this system since the transactions relating to personal accounts are recognised only and not the Real and Nominal accounts.
- Since the number of books is limited, expenses related to the keeping of records are also very nominal.

- In the case of accounting for an event, i.e., household, social and festival etc., it is very helpful.

Disadvantages of Single Entry System

- Arithmetical accuracy of the books of account is not possible since the Trial Balance cannot be prepared under this system.
- It is also not possible to ascertain the correct amount of profit or loss of the firm—i.e., results from operation—since the nominal accounts are missing under this system.
- Similarly, Balance Sheet cannot be prepared since the real accounts are not recognised. Therefore, the real financial position cannot be known at the end of the accounting period.
- As arithmetical accuracy is not possible, possibility of committing fraud or manipulation is greater in comparison with Double Entry System.
- Any statistical information relating to the business or the comparison between the two firms or the interim accounts etc.—which help the management to take decision or to formulate policy in future—is not possible under this system.

Double Entry System

Double Entry is a fundamental concept which, states that every financial transaction has equal and opposite effects in at least two different accounts. It is used to satisfy the accounting equation:

Assets = Liabilities + Equity

With a double entry system, credits are offset by debits in a general ledger or T-account.

In the double-entry system, transactions are recorded in terms of debits and credits. Since a debit in one account offsets a credit in another, the sum of all debits must equal the sum of all credits. The double-entry system of bookkeeping or accounting makes it easier to prepare accurate financial statements and detect errors.

Types of Accounts

Bookkeeping and accounting are ways of measuring, recording, and communicating a firm's financial information. A business transaction is an economic event that is recorded for accounting/bookkeeping purposes. In general terms, it is a business interaction between economic entities, such as customers and businesses or vendors and businesses.

Under the systematic process of accounting, these interactions are generally classified into accounts. There are seven different types of accounts that all business transactions can be classified:

- Assets
- Liabilities

- Equities
- Revenue
- Expenses
- Gains
- Losses.

Book keeping and accounting track changes in each account as a company continues operations.

Debits and Credits

Debits and credits are essential to the double entry system. In accounting, a debit refers to an entry on the left side of an account ledger, and credit refers to an entry on the right side of an account ledger. To be in balance, the total of debits and credits for a transaction must be equal. Debits do not always equate to increases and credits do not always equate to decreases.

A debit may increase one account while decreasing another. For example, a debit increases asset accounts but decreases liability and equity accounts, which supports the general accounting equation of Assets = Liabilities + Equity. On the income statement, debits increase the balances in expense and loss accounts, while credits decrease their balances. Debits decrease revenue and gains account balances, while credits increase their balances.

Double-entry Accounting System

Double-entry bookkeeping was developed in the mercantile period of Europe to help rationalize commercial transactions and make trade more efficient. It also helped merchants and bankers understand their costs and profits. Some thinkers have argued that double-entry accounting was a key calculative technology responsible for the birth of capitalism.

The accounting equation forms the foundation of the double-entry accounting and is a concise representation of a concept that expands into the complex, expanded and multi-item display of the balance sheet. The balance sheet is based on the double-entry accounting system where total assets of a company are equal to the total of liabilities and shareholder equity.

Essentially, the representation equates all uses of capital (assets) to all sources of capital (where debt capital leads to liabilities and equity capital leads to shareholders' equity). For a company keeping accurate accounts, every single business transaction will be represented in at least of its two accounts.

For instance, if a business takes a loan from a financial entity like a bank, the borrowed money will raise the company's assets and the loan liability will also rise by an equivalent amount. If a business buys raw material by paying cash, it will lead to an increase in the inventory (asset) while reducing cash capital (another asset). Because there are two or more accounts affected by every transaction carried out by a company, the accounting system is referred to as double-entry accounting.

This practice ensures that the accounting equation always remains balanced – that is, the left side value of the equation will always match with the right side value.

Example of Double Entry

A bakery purchases a fleet of refrigerated delivery trucks on credit; the total credit purchase was $250,000. The new set of trucks will be used in business operations and will not be sold for at least 10 years—their estimated useful life.

To account for the credit purchase, entries must be made in their respective accounting ledgers. Because the business has accumulated more assets, a debit to the asset account for the cost of the purchase ($250,000) will be made. To account for the credit purchase, a credit entry of $250,000 will be made to notes payable. The debit entry increases the asset balance and the credit entry increases the notes payable liability balance by the same amount.

Double entries can also occur within the same class. If the bakery's purchase was made with cash, a credit would be made to cash and a debit to asset, still resulting in a balance.

Advantages of the Double Entry system of Accounting

The advantages of the double entry bookkeeping may be summed up as under:

- Under this system, each transaction is recorded with its twofold aspect, so the total of one side must be equal to the total of other side. This helps in proving the accuracy of records.
- Maximum information under this system can be obtained by the owner of the business and other interested parties.
- Under this system, each transaction of revenue and expenses are recorded so correct information regarding income or losses can be had.
- The financial position of the business on any day can be had.
- There are lesser chances of errors, if it is committed, it can be located easily.
- It reflects the comprehensive record of business.
- Arithmetical accuracy of business can be ascertained.
- The profit earned or loss beard for any particular period can be calculated.
- This system can be adopted by any type of organization.
- All the amounts which are receivable or payable can be ascertained.
- The transaction relating to external or internal nature can be easily dealt.
- As the previous year's financial statements are available, their comparative analysis with current year's financial statements become easy.
- By using double entry bookkeeping the value of cash in hand can be ascertained at any time.
- It helps in making managerial decisions.

Disadvantages of Double Entry Bookkeeping

- Under double entry bookkeeping inflation cannot be handled as money is an inflexible unit of measurement.
- If any event which cannot be expressed in terms of money, will not be recorded.
- Sometimes it becomes very different to locate error if the wrong amount is entered in the record.
- This system is dependent on the personal judgment of accountant which can be inconsistent and biased.
- To maintain double entry bookkeeping is a very time consuming and hectic job, therefore, it is not suitable for small businesses where the owner is himself looking after all the affairs of business.

Financial Statement Analysis

Financial statement analysis involves gaining an understanding of an organization's financial situation by reviewing its financial reports. The results can be used to make investment and lending decisions. This review involves identifying the following items for a company's financial statements over a series of reporting periods:

- Trends: Create trend lines for key items in the financial statements over multiple time periods, to see how the company is performing. Typical trend lines are for revenue, the gross margin, net profits, cash, accounts receivable, and debt.
- Proportion analysis: An array of ratios are available for discerning the relationship between the size of various accounts in the financial statements. For example, one can calculate a company's quick ratio to estimate its ability to pay its immediate liabilities, or its debt to equity ratio to see if it has taken on too much debt. These analyses are frequently between the revenues and expenses listed on the income statement and the assets, liabilities, and equity accounts listed on the balance sheet.

Financial statement analysis is an exceptionally powerful tool for a variety of users of financial statements, each having different objectives in learning about the financial circumstances of the entity.

Users of Financial Statement Analysis

There are a number of users of financial statement analysis. They are:

- Creditors: Anyone who has lent funds to a company is interested in its ability to pay back the debt, and so will focus on various cash flow measures.
- Investors: Both current and prospective investors examine financial statements to learn about a company's ability to continue issuing dividends, or to generate cash flow, or to continue growing at its historical rate (depending upon their investment philosophies).

- Management: The company controller prepares an ongoing analysis of the company's financial results, particularly in relation to a number of operational metrics that are not seen by outside entities (such as the cost per delivery, cost per distribution channel, profit by product, and so forth).
- Regulatory authorities: If a company is publicly held, its financial statements are examined by the Securities and Exchange Commission (if the company files in the United States) to see if its statements conform to the various accounting standards and the rules of the SEC.

Methods of Financial Statement Analysis

There are two key methods for analyzing financial statements. The first method is the use of horizontal and vertical analysis. Horizontal analysis is the comparison of financial information over a series of reporting periods, while vertical analysis is the proportional analysis of a financial statement, where each line item on a financial statement is listed as a percentage of another item. Typically, this means that every line item on an income statement is stated as a percentage of gross sales, while every line item on a balance sheet is stated as a percentage of total assets. Thus, horizontal analysis is the review of the results of multiple time periods, while vertical analysis is the review of the proportion of accounts to each other within a single period.

The second method for analyzing financial statements is the use of many kinds of ratios. Ratios are used to calculate the relative size of one number in relation to another. After a ratio is calculated, you can then compare it to the same ratio calculated for a prior period, or that is based on an industry average, to see if the company is performing in accordance with expectations. In a typical financial statement analysis, most ratios will be within expectations, while a small number will flag potential problems that will attract the attention of the reviewer. There are several general categories of ratios, each designed to examine a different aspect of a company's performance. The general groups of ratios are:

1. Liquidity ratios: This is the most fundamentally important set of ratios, because they measure the ability of a company to remain in business:
    - Cash coverage ratio: Shows the amount of cash available to pay interest.
    - Current ratio: Measures the amount of liquidity available to pay for current liabilities.
    - Quick ratio: The same as the current ratio, but does not include inventory.
    - Liquidity index: Measures the amount of time required to convert assets into cash.
2. Activity ratios: These ratios are a strong indicator of the quality of management, since they reveal how well management is utilizing company resources. Click the following links for a thorough review of each ratio:
    - Accounts payable turnover ratio: Measures the speed with which a company pays its suppliers.
    - Accounts receivable turnover ratio: Measures a company's ability to collect accounts receivable.
    - Fixed asset turnover ratio: Measures a company's ability to generate sales from a certain base of fixed assets.

- Inventory turnover ratio: Measures the amount of inventory needed to support a given level of sales.
- Sales to working capital ratio: Shows the amount of working capital required to support a given amount of sales.
- Working capital turnover ratio: Measures a company's ability to generate sales from a certain base of working capital.

3. Leverage ratio: These ratios reveal the extent to which a company is relying upon debt to fund its operations, and its ability to pay back the debt. Click the following links for a thorough review of each ratio:
   - Debt to equity ratio: Shows the extent to which management is willing to fund operations with debt, rather than equity.
   - Debt service coverage ratio: Reveals the ability of a company to pay its debt obligations.
   - Fixed charge coverage: Shows the ability of a company to pay for its fixed costs.
4. Profitability ratios: These ratios measure how well a company performs in generating a profit. Click the following links for a thorough review of each ratio:
   - Breakeven point: Reveals the sales level at which a company breaks even.
   - Contribution margin ratio: Shows the profits left after variable costs are subtracted from sales.
   - Gross profit ratio: Shows revenues minus the cost of goods sold, as a proportion of sales.
   - Margin of safety: Calculates the amount by which sales must drop before a company reaches its break even point.
   - Net profit ratio: Calculates the amount of profit after taxes and all expenses have been deducted from net sales.
   - Return on equity: Shows company profit as a percentage of equity.
   - Return on net assets: Shows company profits as a percentage of fixed assets and working capital.
   - Return on operating assets: Shows company profit as percentage of assets utilized.

Problems with Financial Statement Analysis

While financial statement analysis is an excellent tool, there are several issues to be aware of that can interfere with the interpretation of the analysis results. These issues are:

- Comparability between periods: The company preparing the financial statements may have changed the accounts in which it stores financial information, so that results may differ from period to period. For example, an expense may appear in the cost of goods sold in one period, and in administrative expenses in another period.

- Comparability between companies: An analyst frequently compares the financial ratios of different companies in order to see how they match up against each other. However, each company may aggregate financial information differently, so that the results of their ratios are not really comparable. This can lead an analyst to draw incorrect conclusions about the results of a company in comparison to its competitors.
- Operational information: Financial analysis only reviews a company's financial information, not its operational information, so you cannot see a variety of key indicators of future performance, such as the size of the order backlog, or changes in warranty claims. Thus, financial analysis only presents part of the total picture.

Horizontal Analysis

Horizontal analysis of financial statements is the comparison of historical financial information over a series of reporting periods, or of the ratios derived from this information. It is used to see if any numbers are unusually high or low in comparison to the information for bracketing periods, which may then trigger a detailed investigation of the reason for the difference. It can also be used to project the amounts of various line items into the future. The analysis is most commonly a simple grouping of information that is sorted by period, but the numbers in each succeeding period can also be expressed as a percentage of the amount in the baseline year, with the baseline amount being listed as 100%.

A common problem with horizontal analysis is that the aggregation of information in the financial statements may have changed over time, due to on-going changes in the chart of accounts, so that revenues, expenses, assets, or liabilities may shift between different accounts and therefore appear to cause variances when comparing account balances from one period to the next.

When conducting a horizontal analysis, it is useful to conduct the analysis for all of the financial statements at the same time, so that you can see the complete impact of operational results on a company's financial condition over the review period. For example, in the two examples below, the income statement analysis shows a company having an excellent second year, but the related balance sheet analysis shows that it is having trouble funding growth, given the decline in cash, increase in accounts payable, and increase in debt.

Horizontal Analysis of the Income Statement

Horizontal analysis of the income statement is usually in a two-year format, such as the one shown below, with a variance also shown that states the difference between the two years for each line item. An alternative format is to simply add as many years as will fit on the page, without showing a variance, so that you can see general changes by account over multiple years. A third format is to include a vertical analysis of each year in the report, so that each year shows expenses as a percentage of the total revenue in that year.

	20X1	20X2	Variance
Sales	$1,000,000	$1,500,000	$500,000
Cost of goods sold	400,000	600,000	(200,000)
Gross margin	600,000	900,000	300,000

Salaries and wages	250,000	375,000	(125,000)
Office rent	50,000	80,000	(30,000)
Supplies	10,000	20,000	(10,000)
Utilities	20,000	30,000	(10,000)
Other expenses	90,000	110,000	(20,000)
Total expenses	420,000	615,000	(195,000)
Net profit	$180,000	$285,000	$105,000

Horizontal Analysis of the Balance Sheet

Horizontal analysis of the balance sheet is also usually in a two-year format, such as the one shown below, with a variance showing the difference between the two years for each line item. An alternative format is to add as many years as will fit on the page, without showing a variance, so that you can see general changes by account over multiple years. A less-used format is to include a vertical analysis of each year in the report, so that each year shows each line item as a percentage of the total assets in that year.

	20X1	20X2	Variance
Cash	$100,000	80,000	$(20,000)
Accounts receivable	350,000	525,000	175,000
Inventory	150,000	275,000	125,000
Total current assets	600,000	880,000	280,000
Fixed assets	400,000	800,000	400,000
Total assets	$1,000,000	$1,680,000	$680,000
Accounts payable	$180,000	$300,000	$120,000
Accrued liabilities	70,000	120,000	50,000
Total current liabilities	250,000	420,000	170,000
Notes payable	300,000	525,000	225,000
Total liabilities	550,000	945,000	395,000
Capital stock	200,000	200,000	0
Retained earnings	250,000	535,000	285,000
Total equity	450,000	735,000	285,000
Total liabilities and equity	$1,000,000	$1,680,000	$680,000

Horizontal analysis can be misused to report skewed findings. This can happen when the analyst modifies the number of comparison periods used to make the results appear unusually good or bad. For example, the current period's profits may appear excellent when only compared with those of the previous month, but are actually quite poor when compared to the results for the same month in the preceding year. Consistent use of comparison periods can mitigate this problem.

Horizontal analysis can be performed in one of the following two different methods i.e. absolute comparison or percentage comparison:

- Absolute Comparison: One way of performing horizontal analysis is comparing the absolute currency amounts of some items over the period of time. For example, cash in hand at the end of an accounting period can be compared to other accounting periods. This method is helpful in identifying the items which are changing the most.

- Percentage Comparison: In the second method of horizontal analysis, percentage differences in certain items are compared over a period of time. The absolute currency amounts are converted into the percentages for the purpose of comparison. For example, a change in cash from $5,000 to $5,500 will be reported as 10% increase in cash. It can also be reported as 110%, which means that the cash is 110% of the cash at the end of previous accounting period. This method is useful when comparing performance of two companies of different scale and size.

Here we have the YoY growth rates of Colgate's Income statement from 2008 until 2015. We calculate the growth rate of each of the line items with respect to the previous year.

For example, to find growth rate of Net Sales of 2015, the formula is (Net Sales 2015 – Net Sales 2014) / Net Sales 2014.

Horizontal Analysis	Dec-08	Dec-09	Dec-10	Dec-11	Dec-12	Dec-13	Dec-14	Dec-15
Net sales	11.2%	0.0%	1.5%	7.5%	2.1%	2.0%	-0.8%	-7.2%
Cost of sales	10.9%	-5.7%	0.6%	12.3%	0.1%	0.9%	-0.7%	-7.4%
Gross profit	11.3%	4.4%	2.2%	4.2%	3.6%	[illegible]	-0.9%	-7.0%
Selling, general and administrative expenses	9.0%	-2.6%	2.5%	6.4%	3.0%	4.9%	-3.9%	-8.7%
Other (income) expense, net	90.7%	7.8%	171.2%	-103.0%	-1355.6%	273.5%	35.1%	-89.1%
Operating profit	14.0%	16.6%	-3.5%	10.1%	1.2%	[illegible]	0.0%	-21.6%
Interest expense, net	-38.9%	-19.8%	-23.4%	-11.9%	[illegible]	-160.0%	-366.7%	8.3%
Income before income taxes	17.2%	17.7%	-3.1%	10.5%	2.2%	[illegible]	-0.9%	-21.8%
Provision for income taxes	27.5%	17.9%	-2.1%	10.6%	0.6%	-7.1%	3.4%	1.8%
Net income including noncontrolling interests	12.9%	17.7%	-3.5%	10.4%	3.0%	-8.4%	[illegible]	-33.8%
Less: Net income attributable to noncontrolling interests	19.4%	32.5%	3.8%	11.8%	29.3%	6.3%	-5.9%	3.1%
Net income attributable to Colgate-Palmolive Company	12.7%	17.1%	-3.8%	10.3%	1.7%	-9.3%	-2.7%	-36.5%

Here are the following observations from Colgate's Horizontal Analysis:

- The last two years Colgate has seen a dip in Net Sales figures. In 2015, Colgate saw a de-growth of -7.2% in 2015.

- Cost of Sales, however, has decreased (positive from company's point of view). Why is this so?

- Net Income decreased in the last three years, with as much as 36.5% decline in 2015.

Interpretation

- From income statement and balance sheet, a company may portray pretty good hold on their financial affairs. But as an investor, it's your responsibility to check each item and understand why there is a difference. Your minute attention to details may help you discover something about the company which the company wanted to hide from all the potential investors.

- Companies can inflate profit or show undervalued statement by changing few things here and there. But if you pay attention to details you would be able to discover what's actually going on within the company.
- With such analysis you would be able to understand how this company may do in the upcoming years, what they are trying to accomplish over the years and what's their recent purchase, sales, revenue, net income, fixed assets, current assets, capital structure and every minute data mentioned in the balance sheet and income statement.
- Unlike other ratios, this technique gives investors an overall picture of where a company stands in terms of financial matters, what they are trying to do with the funds and how profitable the company can be in near future.

Horizontal Analysis in Forecasting and Financial Modeling

Horizontal Analysis is very useful for Financial Modeling and Forecasting. The approach used here is fairly simple:

- Perform the horizontal analysis on the historical data.
- Based on the YoY or QoQ growth rates, you can make an assumption about future growth rates.

Let us now look at Colgate 10K 2013 report. We note that in the income statement, Colgate has not provided segmental information, however, as an additional information.

	2013	2012	2011
Net Sales			
Oral, Personal and Home Care			
North America	$ 3,072	$ 2,971	$ 2,878
Latin America	5,012	5,032	4,895
Europe/South Pacific	3,396	3,417	3,508
Asia	2,472	2,264	2,074
Africa/Eurasia	1,257	1,241	1,207
Total Oral, Personal and Home Care	15,209	14,925	14,562
Pet Nutrition	2,211	2,160	2,172
Total Net Sales	$ 17,420	$ 17,085	$ 16,732

The future sales of Colgate on the basis of this available data. We will use the sales growth approach across segments to derive the forecasts. Please see the below picture. We have calculated the year-over-year growth rate for each segment.

Segmental Information	Dec-11	Dec-12	Dec-13	Dec-14	Dec-15	Dec-16	Dec-17	Dec-18
Oral, Personal and Home Care								
North America	$ 2,878	$ 2,971	$ 3,072					
% growth (yoy)		3.2%	3.4%					
Latin America	4,895	5,032	5,012					
% growth (yoy)		2.8%	-0.4%					
Europe/South Pacific	3,508	3,417	3,396					
% growth (yoy)		-2.6%	-0.6%					
Asia	2,074	2,264	2,472					
% growth (yoy)		9.2%	9.2%					
Africa/Eurasia	1,207	1,241	1,257					
% growth (yoy)		2.8%	1.3%					
Total Oral, Personal and Home Care	14,562	14,925	15,209					
		2.5%	1.9%					
Pet Nutrition	2,172	2,160	2,211					
% growth (yoy)		-0.6%	2.4%					
Total Net sales	$ 16,734	$ 17,085	$ 17,420	$ -	$ -	$ -	$ -	$ -

Based on these sales growth, we can project the future sales of each segment

Now we can assume a sales growth percentage based on the historical trends and project the revenues under each segment. Total Net sales are the sum total of Oral, Personal & Home Care and Pet Nutrition Segment.

Segmental Information	Dec-11	Dec-12	Dec-13	Dec-14	Dec-15	Dec-16	Dec-17	Dec-18
Oral, Personal and Home Care								
North America	$ 2,878	$ 2,971	$ 3,072	=I69*(1+J70)		3,456	3,594	3,738
% growth (yoy)		3.2%	3.4%	4.0%	4.0%	4.0%	4.0%	4.0%
Latin America	4,895	5,032	5,012	5,062	5,113	5,164	5,216	5,268
% growth (yoy)		2.8%	[illegible]	1.0%	1.0%	1.0%	1.0%	1.0%
Europe/South Pacific	3,508	[illegible]	3,396	3,430	3,464	3,499	3,534	3,569
% growth (yoy)		[illegible]	-0.6%	1.0%	1.0%	1.0%	1.0%	1.0%
Asia	[illegible]	[illegible]	2,472	2,719	2,991	3,290	3,619	3,981
% growth (yoy)		[illegible]	9.2%	10.0%	10.0%	10.0%	10.0%	10.0%
Africa/Eurasia	[illegible]	[illegible]	1,257	1,276	1,295	1,314	1,334	1,354
% growth (yoy)		[illegible]	1.3%	1.5%	1.5%	1.5%	1.5%	1.5%
Total Oral, Personal and Home Care	[illegible]	[illegible]	15,209	15,513	15,824	16,140	16,463	16,792
		2.5%	1.9%	2.0%	2.0%	2.0%	2.0%	2.0%
Pet Nutrition	2,172	2,160	2,211	2,266	2,323	2,381	2,441	2,502
% growth (yoy)		-0.6%	2.4%	2.5%	2.5%	2.5%	2.5%	2.5%
Total Net sales	$ 16,734	$ 17,085	$ 17,420	$ 17,780	$ 18,146	$ 18,521	$ 18,903	$ 19,294

Forecasting Sales using the assumed growth rates of each segment

Vertical Analysis

Vertical analysis is the proportional analysis of a financial statement, where each line item on a financial statement is listed as a percentage of another item. This means that every line item on an income statement is stated as a percentage of gross sales, while every line item on a balance sheet is stated as a percentage of total assets.

The most common use of vertical analysis is within a financial statement for a single reporting period, so that one can see the relative proportions of account balances. Vertical analysis is also useful for trend analysis, to see relative changes in accounts over time, such as on a comparative basis over a five-year period. For example, if the cost of goods sold has a history of being 40% of sales in each of the past four years, then a new percentage of 48% would be a cause for alarm.

Vertical Analysis of the Income Statement

The most common use of vertical analysis in an income statement is to show the various expense line items as a percentage of sales, though it can also be used to show the percentage of different revenue line items that make up total sales. An example of vertical analysis for an income statement is shown in the far right column of the following condensed income statement:

	$ Totals	Percent
Sales	$1,000,000	100%
Cost of goods sold	400,000	40%
Gross margin	600,000	60%
Salaries and wages	250,000	25%
Office rent	50,000	5%

Supplies	10,000	1%
Utilities	20,000	2%
Other expenses	90,000	9%
Total expenses	420,000	42%
Net profit	180,000	18%

The information provided by this income statement format is useful not only for spotting spikes in expenses, but also for determining which expenses are so small that they may not be worthy of much management attention.

Vertical Analysis of the Balance Sheet

The central issue when creating a vertical analysis of a balance sheet is what to use as the denominator in the percentage calculation. The usual denominator is the asset total, but one can also use the total of all liabilities when calculating all liability line item percentages, and the total of all equity accounts when calculating all equity line item percentages. An example of vertical analysis for a balance sheet is shown in the far right column of the following condensed balance sheet:

	$ Totals	Percent
Cash	$100,000	10%
Accounts receivable	350,000	35%
Inventory	150,000	15%
Total current assets	600,000	60%
Fixed assets	400,000	40%
Total assets	$1,000,000	100%
Accounts payable	$180,000	18%
Accrued liabilities	70,000	7%
Total current liabilities	250,000	25%
Notes payable	300,000	30%
Total liabilities	550,000	55%
Capital stock	200,000	20%
Retained earnings	250,000	25%
Total equity	450,000	45%
Total liabilities and equity	$1,000,000	100%

The information provided by this balance sheet format is useful for noting changes in a company's investment in working capital and fixed assets over time, which may indicate an altered business model that requires a different amount of ongoing funding.

Advantages of the Vertical Analysis

- It is one of the easiest methods of financial analysis.

- Vertical analysis of financial statement provides a comparable percentage which can be used to compare with the previous years.
- Different organization statements can be compared as the comparison is made in percentage.
- Vertical analysis is also very useful to compare the financial statements with the previous year's statement and analyze the profit or loss of the period.
- Where it helps to understand the percentage/share of the individual items.
- Where it helps to understand the structural composition of the various components like cost, expenses, assets, and liabilities.

Disadvantages of the Vertical Analysis

- The vertical analysis of financial statement does not help to take a firm decision as there is no standard percentage or ratio regarding the change in the components of the income statement or the balance sheet.
- The accounting concepts and conventions are not followed vigilantly in the vertical analysis.
- Liquidity of the organization cannot be measured exactly by using the analysis.
- Quality analysis is not done by using vertical analysis of financial statements. As there is no consistency in the ratio of the elements.

Ratio Analysis

Ratio analysis refers to the comparisons between different pieces of financial information in the financial statements of a business. They are mainly used by external analysts to determine various aspects of a business such as its profitability, liquidity, and solvency.

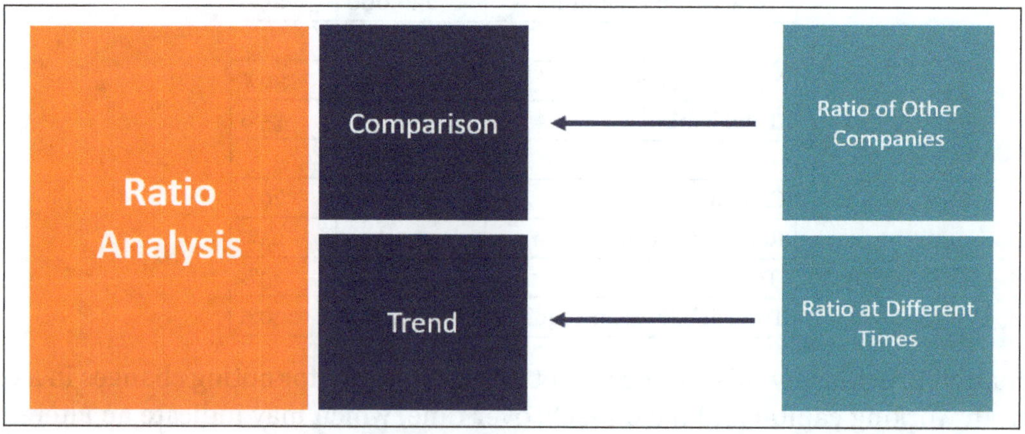

Analysts rely on the current and past financial statements to obtain the correct data to evaluate the financial performance of a company. They also use the data to determine if a company's financial health is on an upward or downward trend and draw a comparison against other competing firms.

Uses of Ratio Analysis

Comparisons

One of the uses of ratio analysis is to compare the company's financial performance to similar firms in the industry to understand the company's position in the market. Obtaining data from known competitors and comparing it to the company's ratios can help the management identify market gaps and elaborate on its competitive advantages, strengths, and weaknesses. The management can then use the information to formulate decisions that improve the company's position in the market.

Trend Line

Companies can also use ratios to see if there is a trend in financial performance. Established companies collect data from the financial statements over a large number of reporting periods. The trend obtained can be used to predict the direction of future financial performance, and also identify any expected financial turbulence that would not be possible to predict using ratios for a single reporting period.

Operational Efficiency

The management of a company can also use financial analysis to determine the degree of efficiency in the management of assets and liabilities. At any time, the management expects the assets to be put to optimal use, but that does not happen all the time. Inefficient use of assets such as motor vehicles, land, and building results in unnecessary expenses that ought to be eliminated. Financial ratios can also determine if the financial resources are over- or under-utilized.

Categories of Financial Ratios

There are numerous financial ratios that are used for ratio analysis, and they are grouped into the following categories:

Liquidity Ratios

Liquidity ratios measure a company's ability to meet its debt obligations as they come using its current assets. When a company is experiencing financial difficulties and is unable to pay its debts, it can convert its assets into cash and use the money to settle any pending debts with ease.

Some common liquidity ratios include quick ratio, cash ratio, and current ratio. Liquidity ratios are used by banks, creditors, and suppliers to determine if a client has the ability to honor their financial obligations as they come.

Solvency Ratios

Solvency ratios measure a company's long-term financial viability, and if they can stay solvent in the long term by paying debt and accumulated interests. The ratio compares the debt levels of a company to its assets, equity, and annual earnings.

Important solvency ratios include debt to capital ratio, debt ratio, interest coverage ratio, equity multiplier, etc. Solvency ratios are mainly used by governments, banks, employees, and institutional investors.

Profitability Ratios

Profitability ratios measure a business' ability to earn profits that are relative to their associated expenses. Recording a higher profitability ratio relative to a similar ratio in the previous financial reporting period shows that the business is healthy. The profitability ratio can also be compared to a similar firm's relative value to determine how profitable the business is.

Some examples of important profitability ratios include return on equity, return on assets, profit margin, gross margin, and return on capital employed.

Efficiency Ratios

Efficiency ratios measure how well the business is using its assets and liabilities to generate sales and earn profits. It calculates the use of inventory, machinery utilization, turnover of liabilities, as well as the usage of equity. The ratios are important because, when there is an improvement in the efficiency ratios, the business stands to generate more revenues and profits.

Some of the important efficiency ratios include asset turnover ratio, inventory turnover, payables turnover, working capital turnover, fixed asset turnover, receivables turnover, etc.

Coverage Ratios

Coverage ratios measure a business' ability to service its debts and other obligations related to the debt. Analysts can use the coverage ratios across several reporting periods to draw a trend that predicts the company's financial position in the future. A higher coverage ratio means that a business can service its debts and associated obligations with ease.

Key coverage ratios include debt coverage, interest coverage, fixed charge coverage, EBIDTA coverage, etc.

Market Prospect Ratios

Market prospect ratios help investors to predict how much they will earn from specific investments. The earnings can be in the form of higher stock value or future dividends. Investors can use current earnings and dividends to determine how much the stock prices will be in the future, and the dividends they should expect to earn.

Key market prospect ratios include dividend yield, earnings per share, price-to-earnings ratio, and dividend payout ratio.

Objectives of Ratio Analysis

Interpreting the financial statements and other financial data is essential for all stakeholders of an entity. Ratio Analysis hence becomes a vital tool for financial analysis and financial management. Let us take a look at some objectives that ratio analysis fulfils.

Measure of Profitability

Profit is the ultimate aim of every organization.Context is required to measure profitability, which is provided by ratio analysis. Gross Profit Ratios, Net Profit Ratio, Expense ratio etc provide a measure of the profitability of a firm. The management can use such ratios to find out problem areas and improve upon them.

Evaluation of Operational Efficiency

Certain ratios highlight the degree of efficiency of a company in the management of its assets and other resources. It is important that assets and financial resources be allocated and used efficiently to avoid unnecessary expenses. Turnover Ratios and Efficiency Ratios will point out any mismanagement of assets.

Ensure Suitable Liquidity

Every firm has to ensure that some of its assets are liquid, in case it requires cash immediately. So the liquidity of a firm is measured by ratios such as Current ratio and Quick Ratio. These help a firm maintain the required level of short-term solvency.

Overall Financial Strength

There are some ratios that help determine the firm's long-term solvency. They help determine if there is a strain on the assets of a firm or if the firm is over-leveraged. The management will need to quickly rectify the situation to avoid liquidation in the future. Examples of such ratios are Debt-Equity Ratio, Leverage ratios etc.

Comparison

The organizations' ratios must be compared to the industry standards to get a better understanding of its financial health and fiscal position. The management can take corrective action if the standards of the market are not met by the company. The ratios can also be compared to the previous years' ratio's to see the progress of the company. This is known as trend analysis.

Advantages of Ratio Analysis

When employed correctly, ratio analysis throws light on many problems of the firm and also highlights some positives. Ratios are essentially whistle-blowers, they draw the managements attention towards issues needing attention. Let us take a look at some advantages of ratio analysis:

- Ratio analysis will help validate or disprove the financing, investment and operating decisions of the firm. They summarize the financial statement into comparative figures, thus helping the management to compare and evaluate the financial position of the firm and the results of their decisions.
- It simplifies complex accounting statements and financial data into simple ratios of operating efficiency, financial efficiency, solvency, long-term positions etc.
- Ratio analysis helps identify problem areas and bring the attention of the management to such areas. Some of the information is lost in the complex accounting statements, and ratios will help pinpoint such problems.

- Allows the company to conduct comparisons with other firms, industry standards, intra-firm comparisons etc. This will help the organization better understand its fiscal position in the economy.

Limitations of Ratio Analysis

While ratios are very important tools of financial analysis, they'd have some limitations, such as:

- The firm can make some year-end changes to their financial statements, to improve their ratios. Then the ratios end up being nothing but window dressing.
- Ratios ignore the price level changes due to inflation. Many ratios are calculated using historical costs, and they overlook the changes in price level between the periods. This does not reflect the correct financial situation.
- Accounting ratios completely ignore the qualitative aspects of the firm. They only take into consideration the monetary aspects (quantitative).
- There are no standard definitions of the ratios. So firms may be using different formulas for the ratios. One such example is Current Ratio, where some firms take into consideration all current liabilities but others ignore bank overdrafts from current liabilities while calculating current ratio.
- And finally, accounting ratios do not resolve any financial problems of the company. They are a means to the end, not the actual solution.

References

- Financial-statements-meaning-nature-and-importance-accounting, meaning-financial-statements, financial-statements, accounting: yourarticlelibrary.com, Retrieved 2 April, 2019
- Income-statement, financial-statements: myaccountingcourse.com, Retrieved 12 March, 2019
- Income-statement, accounting: corporatefinanceinstitute.com, Retrieved 22 July, 2019
- Income-Statement: referenceforbusiness.com, Retrieved 7 May, 2019
- Income-statement: accountingformanagement.org, Retrieved 27 August, 2019
- Income-tax: investinganswers.com, Retrieved 3 January, 2019
- Balance-sheet: wallstreetmojo.com, Retrieved 13 May, 2019
- Cash-flow-statement-in-detail: edupristine.com, Retrieved 27 March, 2019
- What-is-a-single-entry-system: accountingtools.com, Retrieved 23 February, 2019
- Single-entry-system-meaning-features-and-advantages, single-entry-accounting, accounting: yourarticlelibrary.com, Retrieved 8 June, 2019
- Horizontal-analysis: accountingtools.com, Retrieved 28 April, 2019
- Horizontal-analysis-of-financial-statements: readyratios.com, Retrieved 2 August, 2019
- Horizontal-analysis: wallstreetmojo.com, Retrieved 23 April, 2019
- Meaning-objectives-advantages-and-limitations-of-ratio-analysis, accounting-ratios, accountancy: toppr.com, Retrieved 10 January, 2019

Permissions

All chapters in this book are published with permission under the Creative Commons Attribution Share Alike License or equivalent. Every chapter published in this book has been scrutinized by our experts. Their significance has been extensively debated. The topics covered herein carry significant information for a comprehensive understanding. They may even be implemented as practical applications or may be referred to as a beginning point for further studies.

We would like to thank the editorial team for lending their expertise to make the book truly unique. They have played a crucial role in the development of this book. Without their invaluable contributions this book wouldn't have been possible. They have made vital efforts to compile up to date information on the varied aspects of this subject to make this book a valuable addition to the collection of many professionals and students.

This book was conceptualized with the vision of imparting up-to-date and integrated information in this field. To ensure the same, a matchless editorial board was set up. Every individual on the board went through rigorous rounds of assessment to prove their worth. After which they invested a large part of their time researching and compiling the most relevant data for our readers.

The editorial board has been involved in producing this book since its inception. They have spent rigorous hours researching and exploring the diverse topics which have resulted in the successful publishing of this book. They have passed on their knowledge of decades through this book. To expedite this challenging task, the publisher supported the team at every step. A small team of assistant editors was also appointed to further simplify the editing procedure and attain best results for the readers.

Apart from the editorial board, the designing team has also invested a significant amount of their time in understanding the subject and creating the most relevant covers. They scrutinized every image to scout for the most suitable representation of the subject and create an appropriate cover for the book.

The publishing team has been an ardent support to the editorial, designing and production team. Their endless efforts to recruit the best for this project, has resulted in the accomplishment of this book. They are a veteran in the field of academics and their pool of knowledge is as vast as their experience in printing. Their expertise and guidance has proved useful at every step. Their uncompromising quality standards have made this book an exceptional effort. Their encouragement from time to time has been an inspiration for everyone.

The publisher and the editorial board hope that this book will prove to be a valuable piece of knowledge for students, practitioners and scholars across the globe.

Index

M

N

O

P

R

S

T

U

V

W

www.ingramcontent.com/pod-product-compliance
Lightning Source LLC
LaVergne TN
LVHW080649210926
848485LV00003B/351
* 9 7 8 1 6 4 1 7 2 6 1 9 1 *